THE PICTORIAL ATLAS OF THE UNIVERSE

THE PICTORIAL
ATLAS
OF THE
UNIVERSE

by
Kevin Krisciunas
and
Bill Yenne

MALLARD PRESS

Page one: The Pleiades, or 'Seven Sisters,' (M 45) in the constellation Taurus. This open star cluster contains 400 stars in a spacial volume that has a 25 light year radius, and is 410 light years from Earth. The seven most prominent stars in the cluster give the constellation its name—the brightest of these being third magnitude Alcyone. (Photo by Bill Iburg)

Pages 2–3: The Aurora Borealis, or 'northern lights,' as photographed from Red Bluff, California with a 21mm lens at f/2.8, on 12 April 1981 at 8:07pm PST, during a 30 second exposure. Auroras occur 50–62 miles above the Earth's surface, and are products of the ionization of the atmosphere in that region. (Photo by Bill Iburg)

These pages: The beautiful open star cluster M 35, in the vicinity of Gemini and Taurus. Also visible here—but barely distinguishable from M 35—is the larger cluster's companion, NGC 2158. M 35 is a cluster of 100 stars, and is a comparatively close 2200 light years from Earth; NGC 2158 contains 40 stars, and is 16,000 light years away, near the edge of our galaxy. (Photo by Bill Iburg)

ACKNOWLEDGMENTS

Kevin Krisciunas thanks Elizabeth Bridger and Tom Geballe for their suggestions for improving the clarity of the text. Bill Yenne would like to extend his appreciative thanks to Dr Mary Kay Hemenway, of the Astronomy Department at the University of Texas, and Bing F Quock, Assistant Chairman of the Morrison Planetarium in San Francisco, for reviewing the solar system section to ensure the utmost scientific accuracy.

Finally, we'd like to thank the staff of the Planetary Data Facility of the US Geological Survey, specifically Ray Badson, Pat Bridges, Mary Strobell and Jody Swan, for the great deal of help they supplied with cartography and nomenclature.

Unless otherwise noted, all photos and artwork are courtesy of the National Aeronautics & Space Administration (NASA), and all the *topographical* maps are courtesy of the Planetary Data Facility of the US Geologic Survey (USGS). The photos and artwork on pages 36-37 *(bottom)*, 41*(top)*, 58 *(both)*, 80-81, 86-87 *(bottom)*, 98 *(bottom)*, 102-103 *(bottom)*, and 114-115 *(bottom)* are © Bill Yenne. The photos on pages 56 and 56-57 *(bottom)* are courtesy of the US Department of Interior. The map on pages 62-63 is from the US Defense Mapping Agency.

Designed by Bill Yenne; Captioned by Marie Cahill, Timothy Jacobs, Kevin Krisciunas and Bill Yenne.

TABLE OF CONTENTS

INTRODUCTION

A BRIEF HISTORY OF THE UNIVERSE

by Kevin Krisciunas

If one wishes to study the universe—everything we can know and see, everything that exists—then one must enter the realms of physics and metaphysics, or, more specifically, astronomy and theology. Both deal with questions of the origin of the universe, but with some differences. Astronomy seeks to answer 'When?,' 'How?,' and 'What?' by means of observational methods and the interpretation of data in terms of mathematics and the laws of physics as we understand them. Theology seeks to answer 'Why?' (ie, 'What is our purpose in the universe?')

No human areas of reasoning are infallible, and discussions of the universe as a whole are filled with uncertainty. Yet we cannot dismiss carefully obtained data as inconvenient. Bishop James Ussher (1581-1656) derived a chronology of the Old Testament that placed the creation in the year 4004 BC, and subsequent scholars went so far as to specify that it happened at 9 AM on the morning of 21 September of that year. Radioactive dating methods place the Earth's age at 4.6 billion years, yet modern creationists somehow manage to dismiss this. Galileo Galilei, who stood trial before the Roman Inquisition in 1633 for advocating that the Earth revolved around the Sun, once stated that the Bible teaches us how to go to heaven, not how the heavens go. I add 'that one day is with the Lord as a thousand years, and a thousand years as one day' (2 Peter 3:8). The question is not what an all-powerful God could have done. It is our job to find out what He did do. Consequently, we must rely on ever further refined measurements of the observable universe to say how it is structured and what it is made of.

Understanding the astronomical universe involves such diverse things as the study of subatomic particles and superclusters of galaxies. While galaxies are held together by gravity, electrons are bound to atomic nuclei by electromagnetic forces, and atomic nuclei are held together by nuclear forces. These forces are very different in strength—gravity is the weakest at close range, but is the only force whose effects are felt over vast distances.

Most objects in the universe are observed by the detection of their light at some wavelength, usually related to the temperature of the object, but sometimes dependent on atomic and molecular processes. The Sun is a normal star whose outer atmosphere, the photosphere, is at a temperature of 6000 degrees above absolute zero (degrees Kelvin, or degrees K). A hotter white star has a corresponding temperature of 10,000 degrees K. A still hotter blue star is at 25,000 degrees K, while cooler orange and red stars have photospheres as cool as 2500 degrees K. Hot stars are best observed at ultraviolet wavelengths, the Sun is best observed at optical wavelengths, and the distribution of red giant stars in a galaxy is best studied at infrared wavelengths. Cold clouds of gas, as cold as 10 degrees K (or −441 degrees F, −263 degrees C), are best studied at far infrared and submillimeter wavelengths.

Other kinds of radiation are detectable by specialized telescopes. Clusters of galaxies, hot intergalactic gas, stellar explosions, and accretion disks around black holes produce X-rays, which we must observe from orbiting satellites. Radio telescopes on the ground can detect many frequencies of radio waves which are due to generally distributed gas (such as atomic hydrogen) in our galaxy and in other galaxies.

Electrons spiralling along magnetic field lines give off radiation called synchrotron emission, which is detectable at radio wavelengths. Vibrating molecules produce radiation at near- and mid-infrared wavelengths, and rotating molecules give us far infrared and submillimeter emission. These 'fingerprints' tell one not only what atoms and mole-

At right: **A section of the Milky Way that contains the Lagoon Nebula (M 8) and the Trifid Nebula (M 20), near Scutum and the Teapot. M 8 is the larger—both visually and actually—and is 4800 light years from Earth. With an integrated magnitude of nine, M 20 is approximately 2000 light years from Earth. (Photo by Lee Coombs)**

cules are present in the interstellar clouds, but one can use the data to derive the temperatures, densities, and motions of the gas.

Thus, to observe the objects in the universe one needs an array of instruments, some perched on high mountaintops, some orbiting our planet in space. To answer questions such as 'What is a star?' or 'What is a galaxy?' one must combine various observations and try to construct mathematical and physical models that match the observations. Twenty thousand astronomers worldwide are working on these and other questions.

We presently feel we understand the evolution of single stars rather well, the present composition of the galaxy, and various methods of determining distances in our portion of the universe. Many other areas of research are less refined because of difficulties obtaining and interpreting the data, or because these areas are theoretical, with no corresponding observational basis whatsoever!

A few fruitful areas of research are: the investigation of processes taking place in interacting binary stars (two stars that may be close enough to touch each other or distort each other's shape, and which are imbedded in streaming gases); the search for planets around other stars; unravelling star formation processes in giant gas clouds; determining the expansion rate of the universe; and determining the origin and eventual fate of the universe. This last-mentioned example may hinge largely on results from particle physics theory and experiment.

Many theoretical, or essentially philosophical, conceptions of the origin and history of the universe have been elaborated over the centuries. Observational cosmology, which is inevitably tied to General Relativity, began in this century.

In 1917 Einstein derived an equation relating the contents of space to its geometry, based on General Relavitity. He considered that the universe was neither contracting nor expanding, as he had no reason to suspect otherwise at that time. He found that the universe was not infinite in extent and was 'non-Euclidean,' in the sense that the sum of three angles of a triangle added up to more than 180 degrees (space was 'positively curved'). In order to describe the universe as static (neither

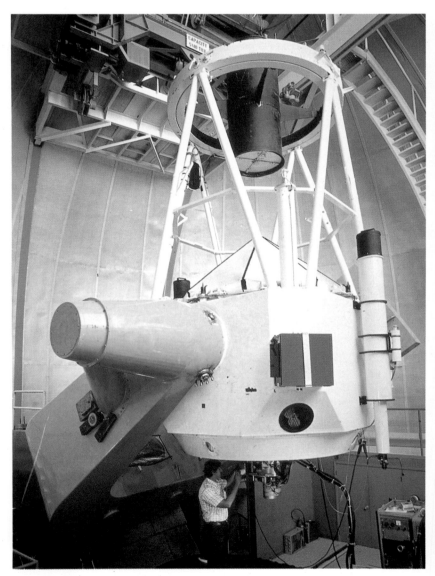

Above: **The 84-inch (2.1-meter) telescope at Kitt Peak Observatory: a big-mirrored reflector with good light gathering capacity for sharp deep-space imaging. (Photo courtesy of the Kitt Peak Observatory)** *At right:* **The Great Galaxy in Andromeda (M 31), our galactic neighbor at 2.2 million light years. (Photo by Bill Iburg)**

expanding or shrinking) Einstein's equation had to contain a 'cosmological constant,' which had the effect of producing a repulsive force at very great distances; later Einstein regarded the decision to include the cosmological constant as the biggest mistake of his scientific career.

During 1916 and 1917 the Dutch astronomer Willem de Sitter wrote three papers on General Relativity, in which he obtained a different solution to Einstein's fundamental equations. (This was due to differing assumptions about the 'boundary conditions' of the equations.) De Sitter assumed that the cosmological constant was equal to zero, and the result was that one would observe the spectral lines of more and more distant galaxies to be shifted more and more toward longer wavelengths (the so-called red shifts, as the red end of the optical portion of the spectrum has longer wavelengths than the blue end).

As early as 1914, the American astronomer VM Slipher had shown that some galaxies had implied velocities of recession much greater than the speeds of stars in our galaxy (up to 1100 kilometers per second), and by 1917 Slipher had obtained the radial velocities of 25 spiral galaxies. All but a couple of galaxies had positive velocity shifts—the galaxies, on the whole, were moving away from each other. However, the measurements of Slipher were unknown to Einstein and de Sitter in Europe, owing to the disruption of international scientific communications brought about by World War I.

In the 1920s astronomers were able to determine that our galaxy was on the order of 100,000 light years (about 30,000 parsecs) or more in diameter. It was shown that some of the nearby 'spiral nebulae' could be resolved into individual stars, and from the apparent brightness of certain types of stars, the distances to these nearby galaxies could be determined.

One of the key players in this activity was Edwin Hubble, who at one time practiced law. (Hence, he was trained to base conclusions on a preponderance of substantiated evidence.) In 1929 Hubble published a classic paper in which he demonstrated that the recessional velocities of the galaxies were proportional to their distances. He obtained a rate of expansion of 500 kilometers per second per Megaparsec (km/sec/Mpc). Thus, on the whole, if galaxies were one Mpc away (about 3.26 million light years), they were, on the average, receding at 300 miles per second (about 500 km/sec). Hubble's 1929 paper contained data on galaxies as distant as two Megaparsecs away, but in 1931 he was able to extend his sample to include some galaxies 30 Mpc away.

Due to such factors as the improved calibration of the innate brightness of the stars used in distance determinations of galaxies and the extension to very faint and distant galaxies, the 'Hubble constant' (indicated by H_0) has been revised over the past 60 years. Modern estimates range from $H_0 = 50$ to $H_0 = 100$ km/sec/Mpc.

As the universe is expanding, that means it will be larger tomorrow, still larger next year, and much larger a billion years from now. Similarly, it was smaller yesterday, and much smaller a million or a billion years ago. If the density of matter in the universe is sufficient to halt the general expansion owing to the combined gravitational attraction of all matter on all other matter, then the universe will eventually reach a maximum size, after which it will begin to shrink. Then, many billions of years in the future, it will get squeezed together, destroying everything we know and love, in one tremendous Big Crunch. However, we have only been able to account for about 10 percent of the critical density, so for now it looks more likely that the universe will expand forever.

The rate of expansion (the value of the Hubble constant, H_0) is related to the present age of the universe. If $H_0 = 50$ km/sec/Mpc, the universe is 19.6 billion years old. If $H_0 = 100$ km/sec/Mpc, the universe is 9.8 billion years old. (These values relate to a 'near empty' universe and must be reduced to 13.1 and 6.5 billion years old, respectively, if there is just enough matter in the universe to halt the general expansion. This is related to the curvature of space caused by matter.) The problem with the shorter time scale associated with $H_0 = 100$ is that we believe we can identify stars in our galaxy that are in excess of 13 billion years old. Unless our theories of stellar evolution are very wrong, the longer time scale and smaller value of H_0 are to be preferred.

It is generally accepted by modern astronomers that the universe began in a fiery Big Bang. Reckoning the present expansion of the universe backwards in time, we are led to the suggestion that at one time

At left: **The Horse's Head Nebula (NGC 2024), in Orion, contains an emission and an absorption nebula: the former is the translucent red cloud which is ionized by, and tinges our view of, the stars within and behind it; the latter is the 'horse's head' and dark band, which obscure the stars within and behind them. (Photo by Lee Coombs)**

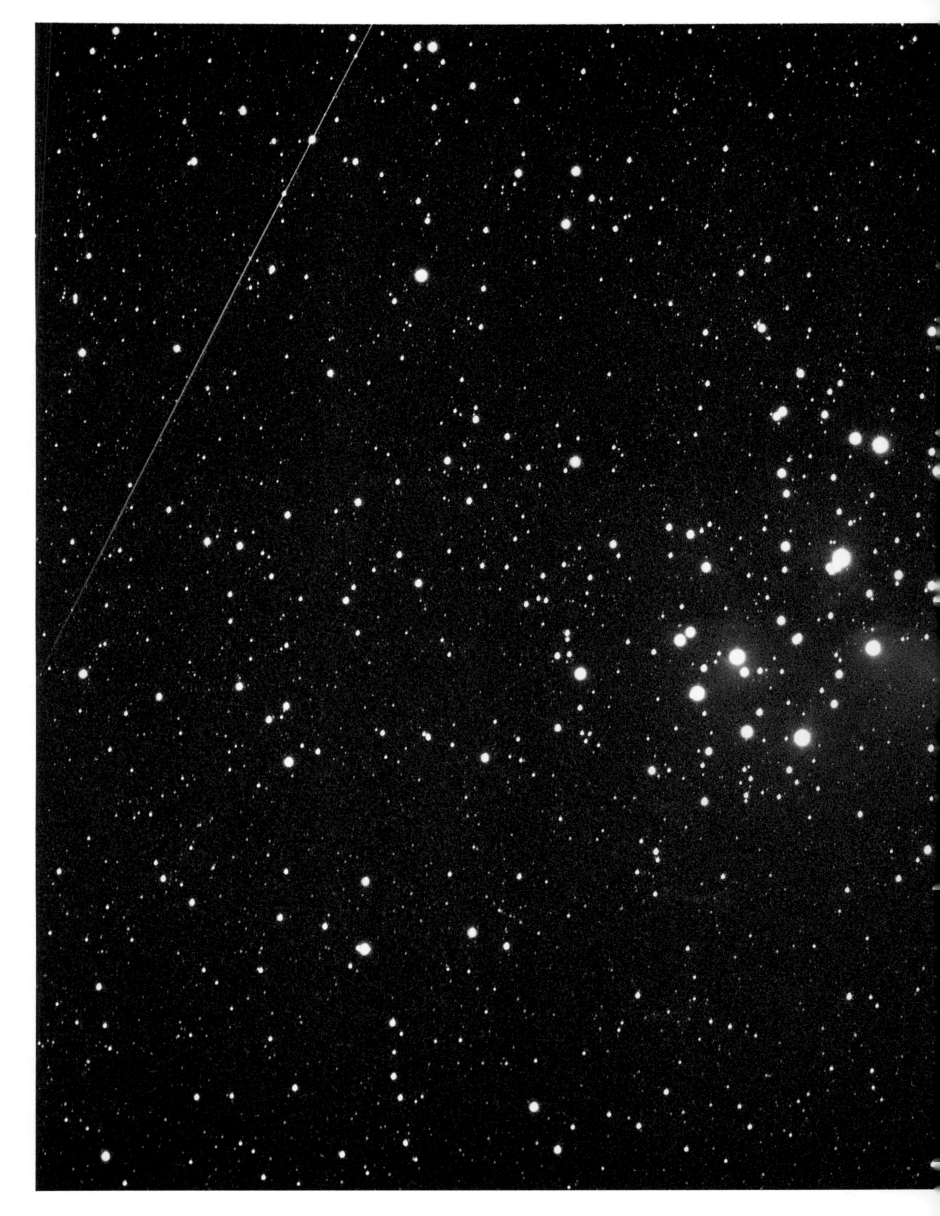

long ago the universe was very, very dense. The limit of this line of reasoning would be a universe of infinite density in a space of zero volume (admittedly, a conclusion that we cannot believe intuitively). Let us stop just short of that and presume that there was a state of immense density and extremely high temperature when the universe was very small. Then there was the explosion we call the Big Bang, which took place 10 to 20 billion years ago, depending on the value of the present rate of expansion of the universe and whether or not that rate has been increasing or decreasing. One may laugh at the suggestion by Bishop Ussher and his successors that the universe began at a particular known instant on a particular day in a particular year, but we do agree that there was some instant when it did, in fact, take place.

We are not sure exactly what happened during the first minute fraction of a second after the Big Bang, but particle physicists have mapped out a tentative sequence of events. What is really needed for a more complete explanation is a quantum theory of gravity, a theory which has yet to be worked out, but which would unite the two great accomplishments of twentieth century physics—quantum mechanics (which describes the motions of particles like protons and electrons) and General Relativity (which describes the relationships between masses and the curvature of space).

Suffice it to say that the physics of the first 10^{-43} seconds after the Big Bang is indeterminate. This is called the Planck Era. According to American astrophysicist David Schramm:

'To assert there was a singularity [a region of zero size and infinite density] 10^{-43} seconds prior to this time may be totally wrong. There could be an infinite stretch of time prior to this point. The 10^{-43} figure comes from extrapolation from longer times back to infinite temperatures and zero time. We can't, in fact, really do this extrapolation, because all of our physics breaks down in this region. Actually, the whole concept of time breaks down at this point. Even the term "prior" is a cheat, since it implies timelike knowledge.'

After the end of the Planck Era, however long that took, came an era described by the 'inflationary scenario.' Within 10^{-35} seconds the universe expanded by a factor of 10^{10^8}, or 10 raised to the power 100 million (a one followed by 100 million zeroes). This sounds like a lot, but if the universe had almost zero size at the time of the Big Bang, such great expansion did not necessarily leave it large by today's standards. In fact, after the inflationary period the universe was only one part in 10^{27} of its present size, and its temperature was 10^{27} degrees.

To account for the present structure of the universe—made up as it is of galaxies, clusters and superclusters of galaxies, and exhibiting a sort of bubbly structure on the very largest scales—there must have been fluctuations in the original energy field when the universe was very small and very hot. The originators of the inflationary scenario believe that details of their theory can account for the existence of galaxies.

We must account for not only the gross structure of the universe, but also for the types of particles there are now, and the forces governing the processes which happen. The three prime building blocks of the universe are protons, electrons, and neutrons. Except for hydrogen atoms, which have nuclei of individual protons, all atomic nuclei are built up of protons and neutrons, held together by the strong nuclear force. Atoms consist of nuclei, each surrounded by a 'cloud' of one or more electrons. A hydrogen atom has only one electron. For a heavier atom, if the number of electrons equals the number of protons in the nucleus, the atom is electrically neutral. If the atom has had one or more electrons stripped away, it is said to be 'ionized." (Giant clouds of gas like the Orion Nebula are ionized by the ultraviolet light from hot stars imbedded in the gas.)

About 10^{-30} seconds after the Big Bang the first particles were formed, such as quarks (*see Glossary*), along with some antimatter. Why there is now so much more regular matter than antimatter is not clearly understood. But various 'Grand Unification Theories' address this problem and suggest that the laws of physics are not the same for matter and antimatter.

Regarding this epoch after the Big Bang, present theories can distinguish the existence of the strong nuclear force. But one must wait until the universe is about 10^{-8} seconds old (one hundred millionth of a second after the Big Bang) before one can distinguish the electromagnetic force (which binds electrons to protons) and the weak nuclear force

At left: **The Pleiades (M 45) in Taurus, imaged with an eight-inch Schmidt in a seven minute exposure. This open cluster contains hundreds of hot young stars—the brightest of which, and their magnitudes, are: Alcyone (2.9), Atlas (3.6), Electra (3.7), Maia (3.9), Merope (4.2) and Taygete (4.3). (Photo by Bill Iburg)**

(which is responsible for the radioactive decay of unstable atomic nuclei).

One hundred thousandth of a second after the Big Bang the universe had a temperature of 10^{13} degrees. Protons and antiprotons were created from high energy light waves. They did not last long—as they are corresponding types of matter and antimatter, they annihilated each other. There was *almost* an equilibrium state between the high energy photons, the protons, and the antiprotons. Because the universe was expanding and cooling, the protons and antiprotons lasted longer and longer. When the universe had expanded by another factor of 1800 it had cooled enough for electrons and their anti-particles (positrons) to form.

We said at the outset that all human intellectual endeavors have weak spots, and various things we've said in the previous few paragraphs will go out of fashion or will be proven wrong. Past this point, our under-

standing of the physics is on much firmer ground. Starting about one one-hundredth of a second after the Big Bang the universe entered an epoch when protons and neutrons were fused into a relatively small number of varieties of atomic nuclei. Initially, the number of protons was equal to the number of neutrons. But it turns out that free neutrons are not stable particles. If one had a cloud of neutrons, after 10.1 minutes half of them would have decayed into protons, electrons, and particles called antineutrinos.

Now the speed of the particles in a gas is a measure of the temperature of the gas, and vice versa. As the universe cooled, the speed of the

Below: A computer generated sky map by O Lahav, of galaxies with blue apparent magnitudes brighter than 14.5. The dark vertical band represents the 'zone of avoidance' caused by dust in our galaxy's plane. The Virgo (V), Centaurus (C), Hydra (H), and Antlia (A) clusters are indicated. (Reproduced by permission of Sandra Faber and O Lahav.)

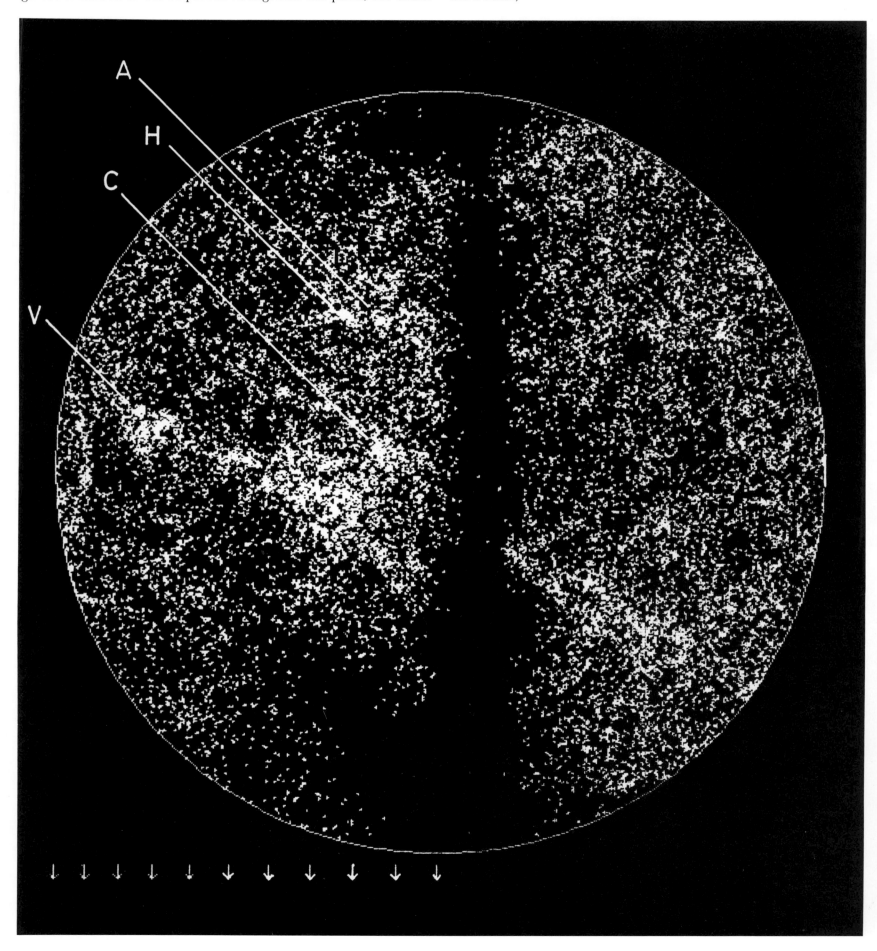

protons and neutrons decreased to the point that if a proton collided with a neutron, the two could stick together. This is the nucleus of a heavy hydrogen (deuterium) atom. Some deuterium nuclei were struck by other neutrons, forming tritium, another type ('isotope') of hydrogen which, it turns out, is not stable and decays on a time scale of 12 years into helium-3 nuclei (each containing two protons and a neutron). Another important process that took place at this epoch was the collision of deuterium nuclei with each other. When such a collision took place, a stable atom of helium was formed. Further collisions caused the creation of a small amount of nuclei of the third element, lithium. Several minutes after the Big Bang, the era of element production was over. Since any of the primeval deuterium that ended up in the cores of present-day stars would be destroyed, the present abundance of deuterium (in interstellar space and in the atmospheres of stars) gives us an upper limit to the rate of nuclear reactions that happened 10 or 20 billion years ago during the Big Bang, as well as information concerning the density of the universe during the era of element production.

The early history of the universe is described in terms of the production of a very small number of elements—hydrogen, helium, and lithium. At the age of 10 minutes the universe was made of these building blocks (in a gaseous state), many high energy photons (light waves) and particles such as neutrinos.

The reader may wonder how we can be sure that there was a Big Bang, based solely on the fact that the universe is presently expanding. That fact alone is not sufficient, and it led Fred Hoyle, Tom Gold, and Herman Bondi to postulate the Steady State Theory in 1948. Their theory called for the continuous creation of matter, at a rate of only one

Below: **The Rosette Nebula (NGC 2237–39) in Monoceros, with the galactic cluster NGC 2244 shining through its center. The Rosette—2600 light years from Earth—is a condensing hydrogen cloud, and is thus a generator of stars. (Photo by Lee Coombs)**

particle per cubic kilometer per year to keep the density of the universe constant. If we are willing to accept the notion that all the universe blew out in a primeval fireball, why not the mild creation of a proton and electron here and there?

In 1946, two years prior to the postulation of the Steady State Theory, the Russian-born physicist George Gamow realized that if the universe started with a Big Bang, not only could one account for the synthesis of light elements, but there would be a low level glow still in evidence—a remnant of the Big Bang observable as background radiation, now corresponding to a low temperature (about five degrees K). In 1965 two Bell Telephone Company physicists, Arno Penzias and Robert Wilson, discovered a source of energy detectable wherever they pointed a sensitive microwave antenna (operating at a wavelength of 7.3 centimeters). No matter where they looked in the universe, the sky was not completely dark. The temperature of this radiation was 3.5 ± 1.0 degrees K, just about what Gamow predicted in the 1940s. More modern measurements of the cosmic background radiation show that it corresponds to a 'black body' at 2.75 degrees. This discovery by Penzias and Wilson spelled the effective death of the Steady State Theory.

Not much more happened in the universe until several million years after the Big Bang. By then the universe had cooled to less than 10,000 degrees K. Instead of a sea of positively charged nuclei and negatively charged electrons whizzing around, the electromagnetic force allowed the electrons to become bound to the nuclei, forming neutral atoms. This took place in order according to the attractive power of the nuclei. First, each lithium nucleus (with a charge of $+3$) captured one electron. Then the doubly ionized lithium ions ($+2$) and helium nuclei (also $+2$) captured more single electrons, forming singly ionized lithium and helium (both $+1$). Next the helium ions captured their second electrons, forming neutral helium. Free protons each then captured an electron, forming neutral hydrogen atoms. Deuterium became neutral at this juncture also. Finally, singly ionized lithium ions captured elec-

trons, forming neutral lithium. (Effectively, no tritium was left at this point, since its half-life is 12 years.)

Two of the key questions of modern astronomy are: 1) When did galaxies form after the Big Bang?, and 2) How exactly do stars form in clouds of gas? The answers to both of these depend on the temperatures and densities of the masses of gas involved.

At the age of 10 million years, when the universe had a temperature of 4000 degrees K and a size of about 1/1500 its present size, the hydrogen atoms were still ionized. That is to say, electrons absorbed enough energy to become unbound from parent protons, but these electrons were soon captured by other protons (only for a short while). If we had a spectrum of the universe at that point, it would look very much like the spectrum of a present-day diffuse nebula in our galaxy, with the familiar emission lines of hydrogen.

Other than the general expansion, an additional process helped to cool the universe. When the universe was cold enough to form molecular hydrogen, collisions of these molecules with atoms and other molecules caused the molecules to vibrate and rotate. This, in turn, gave rise to the emission of certain frequencies of infrared light. The colliding particles were left with smaller velocities and the number of infrared photons in the universe increased.

The time scales are very uncertain, but it seems likely that a few hundred million years after the Big Bang the universe was able to fragment into billions of knots of warm gas, the precursors of the galaxies seen today. The universe as a whole was still expanding, but portions of it were collapsing into flattened disk-like structures or football-shaped lumps under the influence of gravity. Today these are spiral and elliptical galaxies, respectively.

Below: **A vintage winter view of the Lick Observatory, long one of the world's distinguished observatories.** *Below right:* **NGC 253 in Sculptor, a Type Sc spiral galaxy (see also text, Part Four of this volume). It was imaged with a Konica SR 400 and a 14-inch Celestron, using a 40-minute exposure time. (Photo by Bill Iburg)**

Since the information we receive from distant galaxies travels at the speed of light, which is not infinite, the more distant a galaxy is, the longer it takes its light to reach us. Thus, when we are looking at more and more distant galaxies, we are looking further and further back into time. The Hubble Space Telescope will be the next great tool for probing the origin of galaxies.

The formation of the first generation of stars took place about 13.5 billion years ago, based on estimates of the ages of stars in globular clusters in our own galaxy. We should be able to observe this initial stage of star formation in galaxies with red shifts of 3.5 (receding from us at about 90 percent of the speed of light). Only very recently have we been able to observe galaxies at this epoch. To do so has required advanced imaging devices and spectrometers attached to some of the world's largest telescopes, such as the United Kingdom Infrared Telescope and the Canada-France-Hawaii Telescope, both situated at Mauna Kea on the island of Hawaii.

Various theoretical work and observations of cold molecular clouds have shown, given the densities of the gases in stellar nurseries, that the temperatures must be on the order of 10 to 30 degrees K for gravitational collapse to win out over the thermal agitation of the gas. The cosmic background radiation (stipulating the coldest temperature an object can achieve) was 30 degrees when the universe was about ten percent of its present age. At a third of its present age the temperature of the universe was 10 degrees or warmer everywhere. In some regards, stars are a new phenomenon, as it took billions of years for them to form after the Big Bang.

Now a star is nothing more than a nuclear fusion reactor. In its core a star fuses lighter atomic nuclei into heavier ones. A small percentage of each such transaction becomes energy according to Einstein's equation $E = mc^2$. The proportionality constant c^2 is very large—a little transformed mass becomes a great deal of energy. In fact, one gram of protons converted into *nearly* one gram of helium nuclei liberates enough energy to power a 100 watt light bulb for 200 years. Each second the Sun produces 10^{38} more helium nuclei, more than 600 million metric tons. Even at this rate the Sun can continue processing hydrogen into helium for another five billion years.

In order to be hot enough to fuse hydrogen into helium in its core (our minimum definition of a star), a star must have at least eight percent of the mass of the Sun. The most massive stars are about 40 times the Sun's mass. It is somewhat disappointing to consider what the 'average' star amounts to. Many puny, faint ones form for each bright one. In our galaxy approximately one in every thousand stars has a mass greater than eight solar masses. By far the largest number are only two-tenths of a solar mass. They are red dwarf stars and shine with luminosities 250 times less than that of the Sun. Though such a star, compared to the Sun, has only 20 percent of the fuel that it can transform into helium, because it shines 250 times more dimly, it will last for 50 times the lifetime of the Sun, or 500 billion years. On the other end of the scale, very hot, massive stars of 20 solar masses use up their core fuel in only six million years—very short on cosmic time scales.

Our Sun is not a first generation star, since it was born five to 15 billion years after the Big Bang. Massive stars which formed during the first epoch of star formation burned themselves out long ago, and each in a spectacular fashion as a supernova—an exploding star more massive than eight solar masses, which has a luminosity 100 million times that of the Sun. Not only did each massive star transform hydrogen into helium, but many heavier atoms were formed in nuclear reactions: carbon, nitrogen, oxygen, silicon—in fact all the atoms up to and including iron. During a supernova explosion the temperatures are sufficiently high that even heavier atoms are produced, and these ingredients are dispersed to the interstellar medium by the explosion. Thus, the original stars consisted almost entirely of hydrogen and helium, but subsequent generations of stars contain carbon, iron, even gold and uranium. So when you hear the commodity prices on rare

metals or have a new filling in a tooth, remember that such material may have been unearthed in a deep mineshaft, but it originally came from a massive, exploding star.

What about the stars that did not explode as supernovae? It turns out that once the core of a star has finished processing its core hydrogen, the star swells up to become a red giant (like Arcturus) or a red supergiant (like Betelgeuse). If the core of the star has less than 1.4 solar masses, it then becomes a white dwarf star. Prior to this it expels a planetary nebula—a spherical and expanding shell of gas which glows by the radiation of the hot stellar core (a white dwarf) which is left behind. (One should note that a planetary nebula is called such because in a small telescope it looks somewhat like the disk of a planet.)

The Sun and stars less massive than the Sun are not required to expel their outer atmospheres as red giants in order to become white dwarfs. Six billion years from now the Sun will be about the size of the present-day Earth, and it will have a temperature of about 20,000 degrees K. The planet Mercury will have been burned to a cinder by the Sun during the red giant phase, and the conditions on Venus and the Earth will have been radically changed. Because the Sun will be 100 times more luminous in the red giant phase than it is now, life forms that now dominate our planet (including humans) will not survive. When the Sun becomes a white dwarf it will be 10,000 times less luminous than it is now. If the Earth survives the Sun's red giant phase, it may be heated more efficiently by its own volcanoes than by incident sunlight.

We have already discussed the death of stars because that is something that has been observed directly for centuries. Ancient Chinese annals describe what we know were supernova explosions. The outburst that led to the existence of the Crab Nebula was observed throughout the world (except, curiously, in Europe) in the year 1054. The supernova visible in the Large Magellanic Cloud, whose light reached us on 24 February 1987 is still being studied by hundreds of researchers.

Observations at optical wavelengths of star clusters have produced a great deal of information on the evolution of stars. By analogy, it is not necessary to observe the complete life cycle of an individual redwood tree to understand the stages of its development. One finds the seeds and determines what makes the seeds grow; one also counts trees of different sizes and studies trees that die or are cut down. The correlation of observable data on stars—their luminosities, spectral characteristics, temperatures, compositions, changes in brightness, and their masses (from observations of orbiting binary stars)—coupled with modern physics relating to nuclear fusion processes allows one to formulate a rather complete picture of the evolution of stars, at least once they have become individual stars. (The evolution of close binary stars is more complex, because the stars interfere with each other's development.)

But what of stellar births in the first place? This is a rather new area of observational astronomy, because the key processes take place in cold interstellar gas and in regions of the galaxy which are obscured by very opaque dust. Only with the development of millimeter wave, submillimeter, and infrared astronomy have we begun to understand how stars form, and with them planets and life on Earth. Optical astronomy based on astrophysical methods got its start in the mid-nineteenth century, but the non-optical branches of astronomy just mentioned are only 20 years old and are undergoing rapid development.

So far astronomers have not discovered a bona fide protostar—a condensation which is experiencing the infall of material. Chronologically, astronomers first studied young star clusters and stellar associations. Next they discovered hot young stars imbedded in dust clouds where the stars undoubtedly formed, and more recently stars were found which may be in the process of contraction on their way to becoming regular hydrogen fusion reactors. Some of these stars appear to be infrared objects too cool to be considered bare stars as yet, but they are nevertheless warm enough to be blowing away their surrounding gas by light pressure. Thus the research has progressed to earlier and earlier stages of the star formation process. We are now studying cooler and cooler objects (compared to optical astronomy).

As mentioned above, stars form in cold molecular clouds where the temperature is on the order of 20 degrees K. A typical cloud of hydrogen gas about one parsec in diameter at this temperature has sufficient self-gravitational attraction to collapse and form a star of about 10 solar masses. However, minute differences of velocity or density in the col-

At right: The Helix Nebula (NGC 7293) in Aquarius—at 400 light years from Earth, it is the nearest planetary nebula. NGC 7293 is a two-part gas bubble. The 'ring' is composed of nitrogen and hydrogen, while the center is ionized oxygen. (Photo by Bill Iburg)

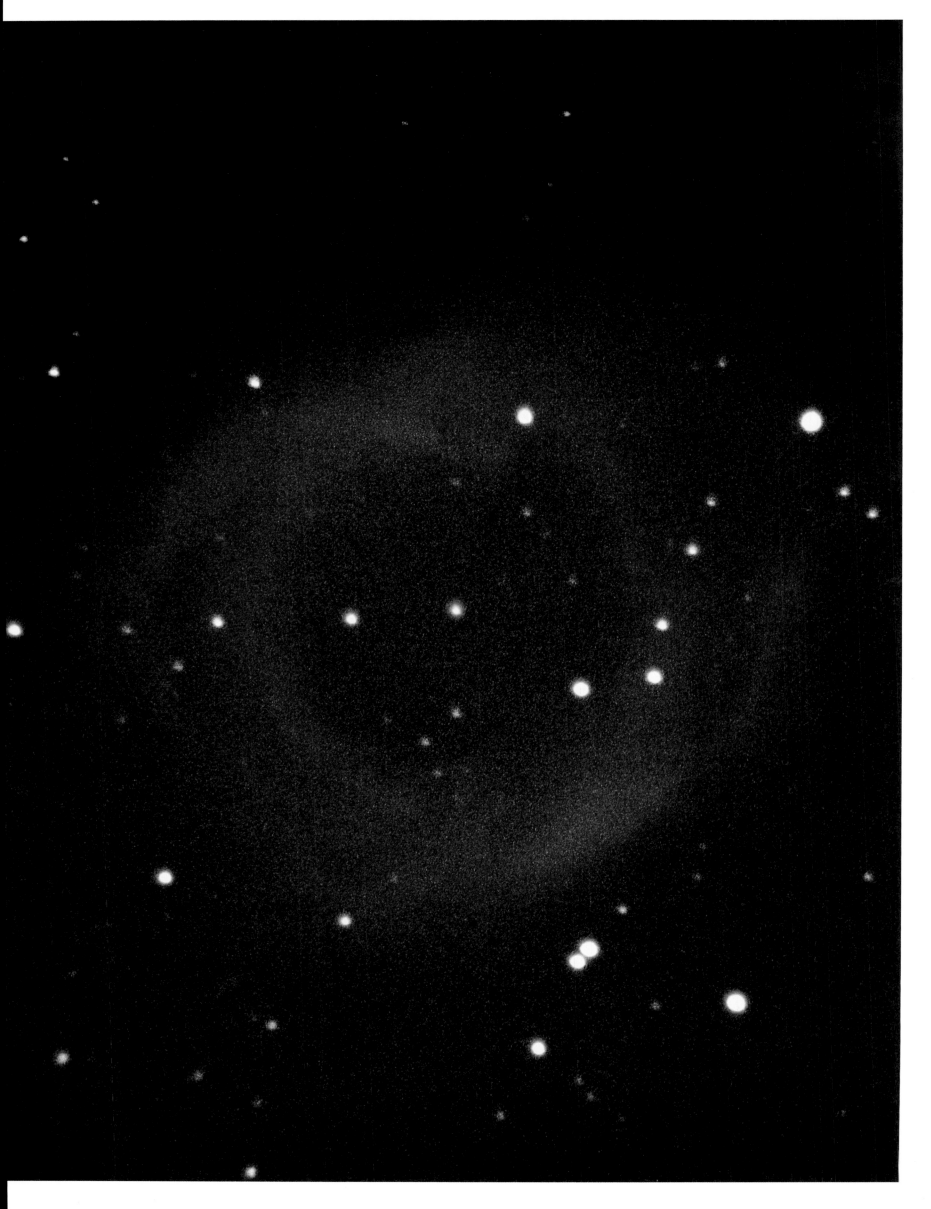

lapsing cloud can easily cause it to fragment into smaller pieces. Indeed, since the most frequently formed stars have about 0.2 solar masses, they formed from self-gravitating clouds only one-sixtieth of a parsec in size (or 40 times the diameter of the orbit of Pluto). Since a galaxy contains a billion or hundreds of billions of solar masses of material, and a giant molecular cloud contains 10,000 solar masses of material, while each star contains 40 solar masses or less, there had to have been extensive fragmentation of fewer, larger clouds into many, many smaller and smaller clouds in order for stars to have formed.

A likely scenario for star formation is as follows. Many low mass stars begin forming throughout a giant molecular cloud. Some high mass stars form as well. The time scale for each collapse is about a million years. When the high mass (ie, hot) stars have formed, they heat up the surrounding gas and give off strong winds. These winds compress the gas just outside the region where the first high mass stars have formed. The compression of the gas triggers a second wave of star formation several million years after the initial burst of star birth. Not long after this the most massive stars of the original batch die as supernovae. The heating effect of the hot stars and the speed of the gas blown out by a supernova explosion can dissipate the remaining cold gas in the molecular cloud. Only four percent or so of the original gas becomes stars during that incarnation of the cloud. The gas is dispersed into the interstellar realms, where it must cool again in order to collapse piece-

meal into a combination of low mass and high mass stars. Where the former molecular cloud was one finds an association of hot blue stars and a population of cooler yellow, orange and red stars.

Most of the stars that form in this way are only loosely bound to each other. They move through the galaxy as groups of a hundred or so stars, but these 'stellar associations' are slowly torn apart by the collective effect of encounters with other star clusters and molecular clouds. Some stars (about 10 percent) form in groups tight enough to be bound by gravity into a stable system. These we see as open star clusters, also known as galactic clusters (as they are found in the plane of our galaxy). For example, five of the seven stars in the Big Dipper belong to a loose cluster of about twenty stars, and this cluster is part of the larger Ursa Major-Sirius moving group.

There are reasons for believing that star formation in our galaxy happens in fits and spurts, and that two populations of stars are born. More massive, warmer molecular clouds (with temperatures of 20 degrees K and 1000 to 100,000 solar masses) form a population of stars having masses no less than two to three times the Sun's mass. Colder (10 degrees K), less massive clouds (10 to 1000 solar masses) give rise to

Below: **NGC 281—a 7.5 magnitude cluster in Cassiopeia—imaged with a 14-inch f/6.5 Celestron and a Konica SR 400. (Photo by Bill Iburg)** *At right:* **The North America Nebula (NGC 7000), near Cygnus: a star-creating cloud of diffuse hydrogen and opaque dust 45 light years in diameter and approximately 1600 light years distant.**

stars as small as 0.08 solar masses. Certain peculiar galaxies have such luminosities that they may be made up almost entirely of the more massive population of stars.

In order to account for the abundances of certain elements on the Earth, there must have been a sufficient number of high mass stars in the early history of the Sun's vicinity of the galaxy. Given that the Earth's crust is made primarily of oxides of silicon, magnesium, iron, aluminum and calcium, such elements had to have existed in the primordial solar nebula, and these elements must have originated from the exhalation of planetary nebulae or the debris of supernovae.

Just as the development of theories of the origin of the universe began in the realm of philosophy and proceeded to modern astrophysical and computational methods, so did theories of the origin of the solar system evolve. The most important early exposé on cosmogony was written by the German philosopher Immanuel Kant. Before he went on to write such tomes as *The Critique of Pure Reason*, Kant was interested in natural philosophy, what we call science today. His first major work was called *The General Natural History and Theory of the Heavens*. Written in 1755, it was not distributed until a dozen years later, owing to the bankruptcy of the publisher. When Kant considers the collapse of a cloud of gas, in accord with Newtonian mechanics, he gives us this not so archaic-sounding description:

'The first effect of this general fall is the formation of a body at this centre of attraction which, so to speak, grows from an infinitely small nucleus by rapid strides; and in the proportion in which this mass increases, it also draws with greater force the surrounding particles to unite with it. When the mass of this central body has grown so great that the velocity with which it draws the particles to itself from great distances, is bent sideways by the feeble degrees of repulsion with which they impede each other, and when it issues in lateral movements which are capable by means of the centrifugal force of encompassing the central body in an orbit, then there are produced whirls or vortices of particles, each of which by itself describes a curved line by the composition of the attracting force and the force of revolution that has been bent sideways. These kinds of orbits all intersect each other, for which their great dispersion in this space gives place...'

In 1796 the French mathematician Laplace published a very similar description of how the solar system formed. Thus was born the Nebular Hypothesis.

Other theories of the formation of the planets involve some catastrophic process. In 1749 the French encyclopedist Buffon suggested that the Sun was hit by a large comet, which pulled out a piece of the Sun; this material later condensed into the planets. Later on it was proposed that another star almost collided with the Sun, pulling out the material. There are several problems with the catastrophic scenarios. A comet does not have enough mass to damage the Sun. (In fact, the Sun regularly destroys comets that stray too close.) The near collision of stars in our portion of the galaxy is very rare. (The distance between the Sun and the nearest star is 30 million times the diameter of the Sun.) And evidence of the abundances of elements suggest that the Earth formed from very cold material. Also, gas pulled out of the Sun would more likely disperse than collapse into planets.

Our present understanding is that the primeval Sun was surrounded by a flattened mass of dusty material. Within this many lumps called planetesimals (or planetoids) formed. The bigger ones swept up more material and collided with other planetesimals. Like building a snowman from many snowballs, these building blocks accumulated into planets. If the orbit of a planetesimal were elliptical, then it could have swept out larger regions of the primeval solar nebula. But the coagulation process would have tended to make the orbits more circular with time. Material not swept up could have formed asteroids or the moons of the larger planets. Some of the original dust can be seen as the zodiacal light—a diffuse glow seen after sunset in the west and before sunrise in the east and most easily observed at tropical latitudes, which is due to the reflection of sunlight off of the dust still distributed in the plane of the solar system. The entire process of planetary formation took about 100 million years.

The evolution of the bodies that make up the solar system has depended strongly on how closely these bodies come to each other. The

At right: **The Omega Nebula (M 17) in Sagittarius, a cloud of interstellar hydrogen that is 5870 light years distant, has 800 times the Sun's mass and is 37 by 46 light years in size, with an integrated magnitude of seven. (Photo by Lee Coombs)**

Moon, Mars, and Mercury show much evidence of bombardment by smaller objects. The Earth too is under a barrage of meteorites and occasional small asteroids, but most of the rocky debris that enters the Earth's atmosphere burns up before hitting the ground. Also, because of erosion, craters that are formed by larger impacting bodies are not always identified.

Mars exhibits the type of erosion that is attributed to the flow of liquids, one would presume water. At one time there was enough water on Mars to cover the planet over to a depth of 150 feet (46 meters), but that water has evaporated and even escaped from the Martian atmosphere, or is frozen solid into the rocks and polar caps.

Venus has a thick, mostly carbon dioxide atmosphere that lets in sunlight but does not allow the atmosphere to cool off. The surface temperature reaches nearly 900 degrees F (740 degrees K). The clouds are mostly made of sulfuric acid. Venus has evolved a most hostile environment!

The Earth's interior is heated to a molten state by radioactive decay. Earthquakes, lava flows, and continental drift rearrange the crust of our planet. The Earth's atmosphere is a dynamic entity, which apparently even has the self-regulating capability to counteract trends such as widespread forest fires or man-made pollutants. Some people advocate the Gaia Hypothesis, that the Earth is the largest living organism in the solar system.

The Earth is not the only body in the solar system to experience vulcanism. Mars has the gigantic extinct volcano Olympus Mons. The innermost large moon of Jupiter, Io, still has live volcanoes. Venus too may have live volcanoes.

A cloud of perhaps 1.2 to two quadrillion comets surrounds our solar system. They occasionally fall in towards the Sun on highly elliptical orbits. If the motion of such a comet is perturbed by, say, Jupiter, the comet can plunge headlong into the Sun, or the orbit can be modified to a much less elliptical shape with a much shorter period of revolution. That is how periodic comets such as Comet Halley became part of the planetary realm of the solar system.

It has been suggested that the bombardment of the Earth by comets brought the right mix of chemicals or seed bacteria to the Earth. We do not know if life originated on this planet or was brought here. Comets are also proposed as the cause of the demise of the dinosaurs. There seem to be periods when many species become extinct, every 30 million years or so.

The collision of a cometary nucleus a few miles in diameter with the Earth has the explosive power of a 100 million megaton nuclear warhead. If the Earth were hit by a such a comet there would be an earthquake of Richter 13 and thousand foot high tidal waves. Furthermore, dust amounting to ten times the mass of the comet could be spewed into the upper atmosphere. This dust could block out enough sunlight to trigger an ice age. If it were cold enough for long enough (like a nuclear winter scenario), the dominant life forms on the planet could die out.

Right now the most important factor in the evolution of our own planet is the behavior of the human species. If we continue to pollute the waters, cut down the rain forests, pump extra carbon dioxide into the atmosphere (by burning fossil fuels), and deplete the ozone layer at the present rate, the planet will not have a chance to adjust. We are beginning to see the Greenhouse Effect, exactly what makes Venus unliveable. Global thinking is required, and also long range planning.

Before we turn to the pictorial sections of this book we must speak of the ultimate fate of the objects in the universe. Barring the destructive bombardment of the Earth by comets or asteroids, many people feel that the fate of the Earth is in mankind's hands, at least for the next five billion years, until the Sun swells up to be a red giant star. The Sun will then shrink to become a white dwarf star and cool slowly over many billions of years until it reaches the temperature of the cosmic background radiation. More massive stars than the Sun will produce planetary nebulae and other white dwarf stars. The most massive stars will become supernovae. One thing not mentioned yet is that a supernova does not completely blow to pieces when it goes off. Most often a rapidly rotating neutron star of three solar masses or less is left behind. These are also known as pulsars. They are compact remnants only about 20 kilometers in diameter with densities of 1.7 billion tons per cubic inch. If a supernova leaves behind a remnant with more than three solar

Star systems in the making. *At right:* **The Lagoon Nebula (M 8) in Sagittarius. More than 4800 light years distant, it contains the bright star cluster NGC 6530, one of the youngest clusters known. (Photo courtesy of Kitt Peak National Observatory)**

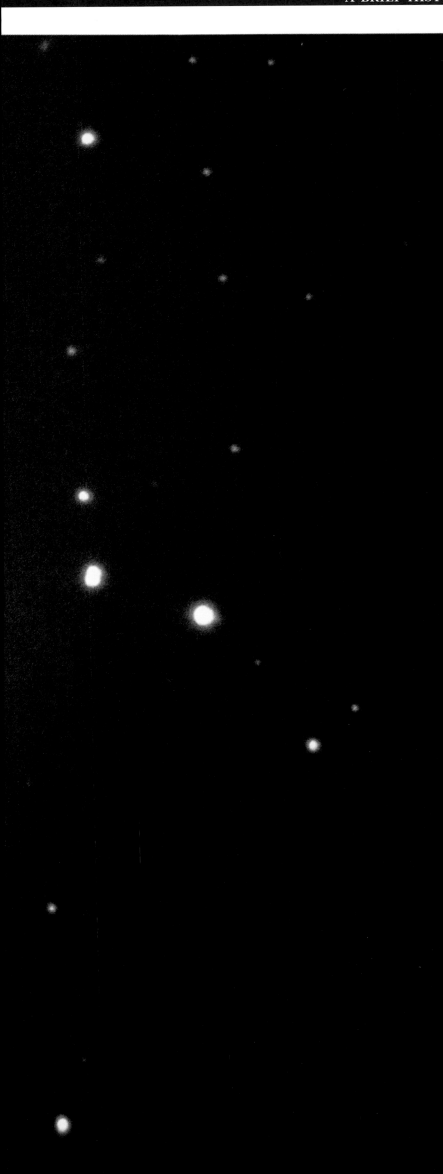

masses, it collapses to become a black hole, an object so dense that even light cannot escape.

Eventually, if the universe expands forever, all the gas in the universe will be bound up in stellar remnants or will be sparsely distributed between the galaxies.

The evidence at this point is that the universe will expand forever. The galaxies will eventually consist of cool, low mass stars, cooling white dwarfs, neutron stars, black holes, and a smattering of planets, asteroids and dust. About five trillion years after the Big Bang all the stars will have died out. Black holes (wherever they exist) could become more and more massive by swallowing up stellar remnants. The seed of such a black hole (of a few hundred solar masses) may already exist in the center of our galaxy. Globular cluster cores and the nuclei of other galaxies give us evidence for the existence of black holes there.

The time scales then become truly enormous. Though near collisions between stars are rare, they do happen. And after 10^{27} years (ie, 10^{17} *times* the age of the present universe) about 99 percent of the stellar remnants in each galaxy could be ejected by encounters into intergalactic space, leaving behind massive black holes of a billion times the Sun's mass.

Some theories predict that protons are not perenially stable particles, but rather evaporate after 10^{30} years, becoming high energy photons.

Stephen Hawking has shown that black holes are not totally black—that if one takes into consideration quantum phenomena, a black hole can lose energy and slowly evaporate. 10^{27} years after the Big Bang black holes will be warmer than the cosmic background radiation, at which point they will radiate more energy than they absorb. The three solar mass black holes will evaporate on a time scale of 10^{64} years, and the billion solar mass black holes will evaporate on a time scale of 10^{90} years.

The reader will have noticed that astronomers are particularly fond of numbers that are the nearest power of ten. Because of the wide range of masses, time scales, temperatures and velocities, it is difficult to be accurate. If the distance to an individual object is uncertain to ± 20 percent, that is considered an accurate measurement. In linear terms the error may amount to a million light years, but it is the relative error that is really important. Indeed, if an astronomer were to describe the life of a person, the time scale would read like this: gestation period—one year, birth to maturity—10 years, life expectancy—100 years. That is accurate to about 50 percent, and the relative order is correct.

While some aspects of astronomy involve extremely accurate measurements (star positions are measured to better than 0.01 arc seconds), for the most part astronomy is a qualitative science, at least to one trained in modern astrophysical methods. The scientist is more interested in relationships and processes. On a personal level, exactly how much money you made the previous year (the quantitative measure) is not as important as the qualitative measures: Did you spend more than you earned? Did you get a raise? Did you stay ahead of inflation?

We shall now take a tour of the universe, beginning with the solar system, and then extending our realm of consideration to the local portion of the galaxy, the galaxy as a whole, the nearby galaxies, and, finally, the rest of the observable universe.

For Further Reading

Cohen, Martin, *In Darkness Born: The Story of Star Formation* (Cambridge: Cambridge University Press), 1988.

Feynman, Richard P, *QED: The Strange Theory of Light and Matter* (Princeton, NJ: Princeton University Press), 1985

Hawking, Stephen W, *A Brief History of Time: From the Big Bang to Black Holes* (Toronto: Bantam), 1988.

Islam, Jamal N, *The Ultimate Fate of the Universe* (Cambridge: Cambridge University Press), 1983.

Linde, Andrei, 'Particle Physics and Inflationary Cosmology,' *Physics Today*, September 1987, pp 61-68.

Parker, Barry, *Creation: The Story of the Origin and Evolution of the Universe* (New York: Plenum), 1988.

Schramm, David N, 'The Early Universe and High-Energy Physics,' *Physics Today*, April 1983, pp 27-33.

Silk, Joseph, *The Big Bang*, revised edition (New York: WH Freeman), 1989.

Weinberg, Steven, *The First Three Minutes: A Modern View of the Universe* (New York: Basic Books), 1976.

At left: **M 81, a spiral galaxy in Ursa Major: like our own Milky Way galaxy, it could contain countless solar systems. With its neighbor galaxy M 82 (see page 164), M 81 forms the nucleus of a small galactic group that may be the closest of *any* to our own Local Group (see Part Four), notwithstanding that the Virgo Cluster is the closest of the *large* groups (see page 174). (Photo by Bill Iburg) *Pages 30–31:* The Eagle Nebula (M 16) in Serpens. (Photo courtesy of Kitt Peak National Observatory)**

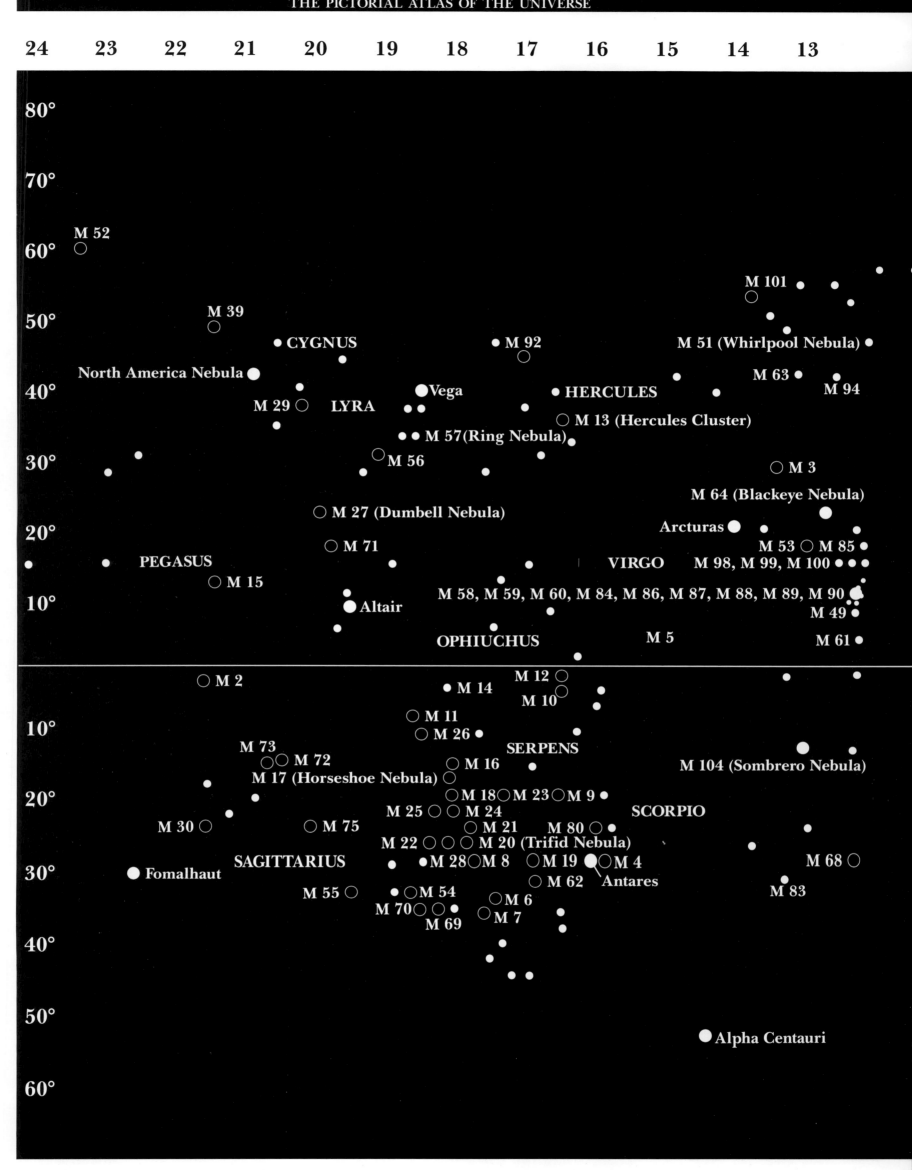

24 **23** **22** **21** **20** **19** **18** **17** **16** **15** **14** **13**

80°

70°

60° M 52

M 101

50° M 39

CYGNUS M 92 M 51 (Whirlpool Nebula)

North America Nebula M 63

40° M 94

M 29 LYRA Vega HERCULES

M 13 (Hercules Cluster)

M 57(Ring Nebula)

30° M 56 M 3

M 64 (Blackeye Nebula)

M 27 (Dumbell Nebula)

20° Arcturas M 53 M 85

M 71 M 98, M 99, M 100

PEGASUS VIRGO

M 15 M 58, M 59, M 60, M 84, M 86, M 87, M 88, M 89, M 90

10° Altair M 49

OPHIUCHUS M 5 M 61

M 2 M 12

M 14 M 10

10° M 11

M 26 SERPENS

M 73 M 104 (Sombrero Nebula)

M 72

M 17 (Horseshoe Nebula) M 16

20° M 18 M 23 M 9

M 25 M 24 SCORPIO

M 30 M 75 M 21 M 80

M 22 M 20 (Trifid Nebula) M 68

30° SAGITTARIUS M 28 M 8 M 19 M 4 M 83

Fomalhaut M 62 Antares

M 55 M 54

M 70 M 6

M 69 M 7

40°

50°

Alpha Centauri

60°

Simplified Mercator projected star chart showing Messier Objects and major stars.

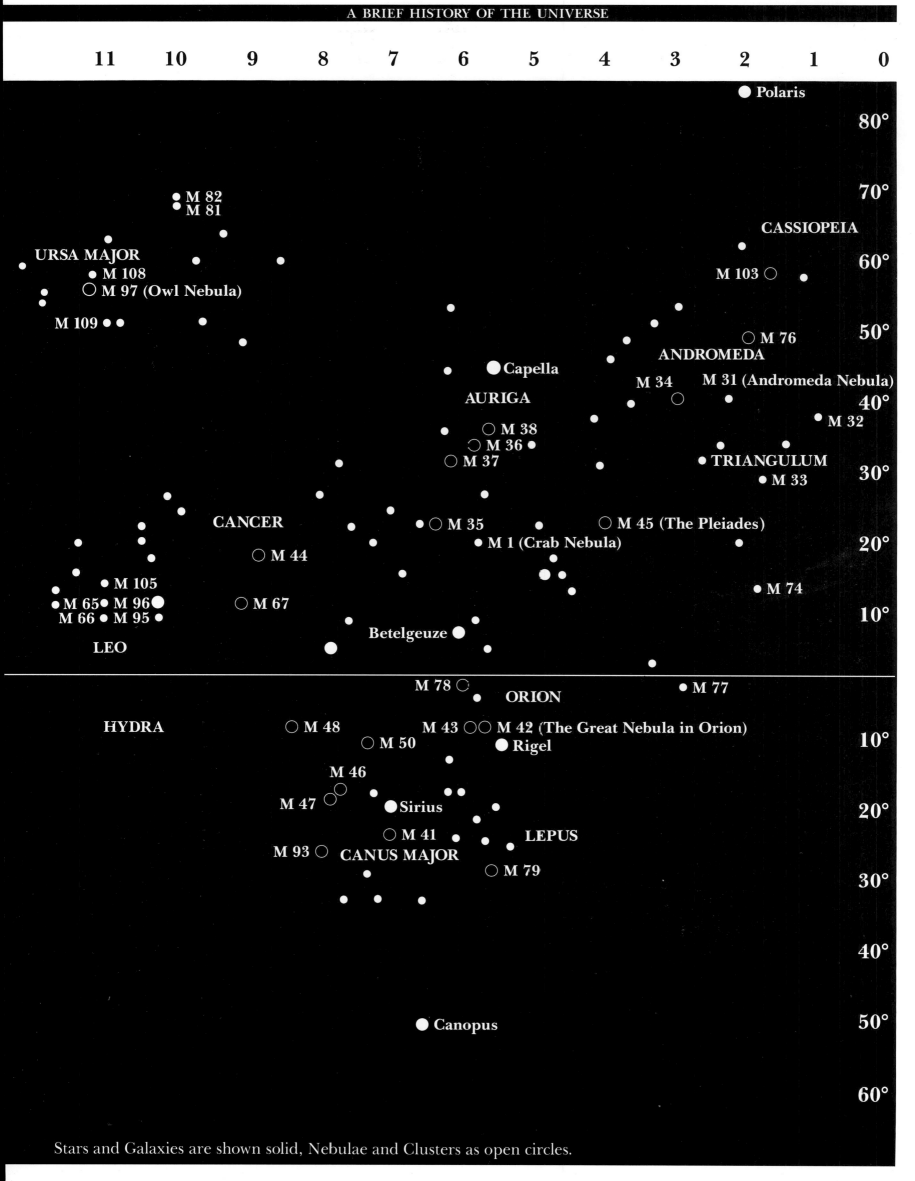

Stars and Galaxies are shown solid, Nebulae and Clusters as open circles.

The brightest stars are Sirius (Mag − 1.43), Canopus (Mag − 0.73), Alpha Centauri (Mag − .27), Arcturas (Mag − 0.06), Vega (Mag 0.04), Capella (Mag 0.09) and Rigel (θ:15).

PART ONE

OUR SOLAR SYSTEM

by Bill Yenne

The mapping of the Solar System beyond the Earth and its Moon has come a long way since the first Pioneer and Mariner spacecraft began exploring the terrestrial planets in the early 1970s. Solar System cartography, however, is still in much the same place as that of the Earth in the early sixteenth century. One is reminded that the maps of that era are marked with great empty, unknown spaces identified only as *terra incognita*. It should be remembered, however, that it was an immense step, both in the history of cartography and in the history of mankind itself, for mapmakers to be able to conceptualize that there *was* existing *terra* which *was incognita*! Mankind had at last reached the point where it could conceive of the spherical reality of the globe, and this, in turn, inspired the broadened imaginations and horizons of the brave explorers who struck out to investigate *terra incognita* first hand.

The flights of the Soviet Venera and American Viking spacecraft have provided a great deal of information about Earth's nearest neighbors in the Solar System, and the American Voyager 1 and Voyager 2 spacecraft have provided vastly more information about the great planets of the outer Solar System than was known before 1979, or could ever have been uncovered by Earth-based observers.

The voyages of these spacecraft are the equivalent, on a Solar System scale, to the sea-borne voyages of global discovery that began with Columbus in 1492. There still exists a great deal of *terra incognita* in the Solar System. This Atlas provides a compendium of what *is* known and what *has* been mapped, as well as a possible point of departure to imagining what further treasures await discovery in the 'backyard' of our own star.

The Universe is so vast that its size is virtually incomprehensible. Even that small portion of it that is visible from Earth is so broad that light waves traveling at the rate of 186,281.7 miles every second will take several billion years to make their way across it. Distances are so great

within the Universe that they are measured in light years, or the distance that light travels in one year—5.88 trillion miles.

The Universe as we know and understand it is filled with untold millions of *galaxies*, which are systematic clusters of *stars* grouped into formations that appear as spirals or discs— technically referred to as *ovoids*. There are, in turn, millions of stars within each of the galaxies spinning and spiraling around the respective galactic centerpoints. There are also elliptical galaxies, however, in which stars do not revolve like planets around the Sun, but rather display a motion similar to random kinetic motion.

One such galaxy, known as the Milky Way Galaxy, is home to the star which we call the Sun, and which is the centerpoint of our Solar System. The Milky Way Galaxy is 100,000 light years in diameter, and despite its appearance as a nearly solid mass of starlight, the distances between the individual stars within it are immense. The star nearest our Sun, for example, is Alpha Proxima, part of the Alpha Centauri group, which is four light years, or nearly 24 trillion miles, away!

The Sun and the entire Solar System are themselves revolving around the center of the Milky Way Galaxy. It seems hard to believe that this delicately balanced Solar System is, in its entirety, hurtling through space at a speed of 630,000 mph.

Our Sun and its Solar System are a relatively tiny part of the Milky Way Galaxy—which is, in turn, a relatively minute part of the known Universe.

By definition, the Solar System is the Sun and the objects which revolve in orbit around it. The Sun itself accounts for 99 percent of the mass of the Solar System, and most of the balance is made up by the nine

Right: An artist's rendition of the historic Voyager 2 and Saturn encounter in 1981, during this spacecraft'a remarkable 12-year journey through our Solar System. Plunging below the ring plane, Voyager 1 explored Saturn's southern hemisphere, while Voyager 2 explored the northern hemisphere before it moved on to Uranus.

known planets and their moons (which are in orbit around their planets as those planets are in orbit around the Sun). Prior to the 1989 arrival near Neptune of the American observation spacecraft Voyager 2, there were 54 moons positively identified within the Solar System, with more than half of them in orbit around Jupiter and Saturn, the two largest planets. Other objects within the Solar System include asteroids, or minor planets, which number more than 3000 and exist primarily in a belt between the orbits of Mars and Jupiter. Also present are meteoroids—small fragments of rock which exist throughout the Solar System, but which are too small to be seen until they plunge into the Earth's atmosphere, leaving their distinctive fiery trails. More spectacular are comets, which are icy objects that appear to take on great fiery tails when their extremely elliptical orbits bring them close to the Sun.

The Solar System originated 4.6 billion years ago, when protostellar (nebular) material, a hot, swirling cloud of mostly pure hydrogen gas (the simplest of elements) gradually collapsed—succumbing to gravity—and cooled. Gravitational contraction heated this protostar and, in turn, a nuclear fusion reaction was sparked amid the hottest and densest gas that condensed by centrifugal force at the center, and the Sun was born. The planets were formed from the remaining disc of material still swirling around the Sun, although theories about exactly how this happened disagree. The four largest planets were, and remain, composed largely of hydrogen as well as helium. As such, they and the Sun are relics of the cloud of protostellar nebular material that existed 4.6 billion years ago. The silicate rock, metals, oxygen, nitrogen, carbon and other materials found in the other planets and moons are probably relics of the impurities that existed in the original cloud. Heavy elements are believed to originate in other, more massive stars. They are, in turn, distributed through space when these stars explode as supernovae.

The Solar System displays several fundamental regularities in its

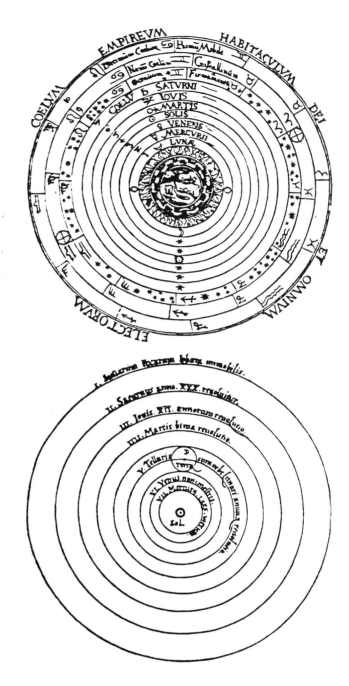

Upper left: **Our Solar System—outward from the Sun—a typical, highly elliptical comet path; Mercury; Venus; Earth; Mars; Jupiter; Saturn; Uranus; Neptune; and the outermost planet Pluto, (its unusual orbit represented in yellow) shown here at the point at which its eccentricity actually brings it within the Neptunian orbit.**

Above: **In the Ptolemaic universe (at top) the Earth was surrounded by a system of concentric spheres to which the planets and stars were fixed. The Copernican system placed the Sun at the center of the universe.**

Left: **Fact or fantasy in the twenty-first century? The first human travelers to walk on the surface of Mars, Earthmen set out to explore their Solar System after nearly a year-long journey from their home planet. A crew of two is exploring Noctis Labyrinthus in the Valles Marineris system of enormous canyons. It is just after sunrise, and on the canyon floor four miles below, early morning clouds can be seen. The frost on the surface will melt very quickly as the Sun climbs higher in the Martian sky.**

structure. This seems to indicate that the mechanisms which formed the Solar System were not random, but rather were the actions of orderly (if not fully understood) physical processes. The planets are not randomly arranged, but rather have regular concentric, near-circular (except for Pluto) orbits. They all revolve in the same direction, and all of the major bodies revolve around the Sun in a relatively flat plane. Using the Earth's orbital plane as the zero degree plane, the orbital planes of all of the other planets tilt no more than 3.39 degrees, except for those of Mercury (7.0 degrees) and Pluto (17.2 degrees).

Theoretically, the Solar System extends outward from the Sun to the point (or circular series of points) beyond which the Sun's gravity has no effect. Because theoretical points are hard to measure precisely (and gravity extends indefinitely), we could use the orbital diameter of Pluto, the outermost planet, as the diameter of the Solar System. However, because Pluto's eccentric orbit briefly brings it closer to the Sun than Neptune's more circular orbit, the diameter of what is familiarly known as our Solar System should probably be pegged to the aphelion of Pluto (4.57 billion miles) plus the aphelion of Neptune (2.81 billion miles).

Thus, the diameter of the Solar System is roughly 7.38 billion miles, .00126 light years, or just short of eleven light *hours*. This formula (or the orbital diameter of Pluto, above) falls short, however, of *truly* defining the limits of the Solar System. At a distance of from 5580 billion to 17,440 billion miles from the Sun, there is a spherical cloud containing 2×10^{12} comets, with a total mass seven to eight times that of the Earth. A more massive inner cloud, 100 times the mass of the outer cloud, stretches from Neptune's orbit to a distance of 930 billion miles. Taking these distances into account would indicate a Solar System diameter on the order of 2.5 light years.

Distances *within* the Solar System, while infinitesimal on the galactic scale, are quite large, so astronomers measure intra-Solar System distances in Astronomical Units (AU), which are equivalent to the distance between the Earth and the Sun—93 million miles, or 8.3 light *minutes*.

If a solar system such as ours could form out of a cloud of protostellar nebular material here, it *is* certainly reasonable to assume that planets have formed around others of the billions of stars that exist in the Milky Way Galaxy and beyond. Since our Solar System is governed by—and was probably formed by—orderly physical processes, it is more probable to assume that other Solar Systems do exist, than to assume that they do *not*. Disks of material similar to the disk that was theorized to have formed our Solar System have, in fact, already been observed around other stars, such as Beta Pictoris, Fomalhaut and Vega. In December 1984, Dr Donald McCarthy and Dr Frank Low of the University of Arizona and Dr Ronald Probst of the US National Optical Astronomy Observatories at Tucson detected a nonstellar object in orbit around the star Van Biesbroeck 8. It was heavier and more massive than Jupiter and had a surface temperature equivalent to molten lava. Officially classified as a *brown dwarf* star, the object has not been seen since its original discovery. If relocated, however, it could ultimately be confirmed as the first planet to be identified beyond our Solar System.

Our own Solar System can generally be organized into six parts or zones. Moving outward from the Sun they are:

1. The terrestrial, or solid surfaced, planets (Mercury, Venus, Earth and Mars), with their total of only three moons which span the first 1.6 AU from the Sun.

2. The Asteroid Belt, which spans the 3.8 AU distance from the orbit of Mars to the orbit of Jupiter. Most, but not all, known asteroids are to be found within this belt.

3. Beginning 5.4 AU from the Sun, and spanning a distance of 24.8 AU, the third and widest zone includes the four largest planets (Jupiter, Saturn, Uranus and Neptune), along with their 50 moons. These planets are identified as 'gas giants' because of their composition and because they are much larger than any other body in any other zone.

4. The final zone of the familiar Solar System contains the planet Pluto and its single moon, which orbit in an elliptical path that ranges between 29.5 AU to 49.2 AU in distance from the Sun.

5. The inner of two clouds of comets that extends from 30 AU to 10,000 AU.

6. The second of two clouds of comets that extends from 60,000 AU to 80,000 AU.

Each of the two major groups of planets contains *four* major bodies that are as similar to one another as they are dissimilar to the planets in

The diagrams *below* show the known objects that are within 40 Astronomical Units (3.7 billion miles) of the Sun. Among known objects only Pluto at aphelion is farther from the Sun. The top (and largest) section of the diagram shows the relative distances of the Solar System's moons from their respective planets on a *15 million mile scale*. Most of them, however, are nearer than a million miles.

The center diagram shows the planets themselves on a *40 Astronomical Unit scale*, while the bottom diagram shows a selection of Asteroids on the same scale. The shaded area on the bottom two diagrams is the Asteroid Belt.

The Asteroids are indicated by lines rather than dots because they have highly elliptical orbits and hence a big difference between their respective aphelions and perihelions. In the case of 1 Ceres, this difference is roughly one-half AU, but 2060 Chiron swings wildly in an orbit that varies by 10 AU, or nearly a billion miles!

Right: The Voyager 2 rendezvous with Saturn on 25 August 1981. After exploring its rings and moons, Voyager headed for Uranus and Neptune. Traveling at a speed of 25,000mph, Voyager 2 reached Neptune (*far right*) in September 1989.

Scaled Schematic Map of our Solar System

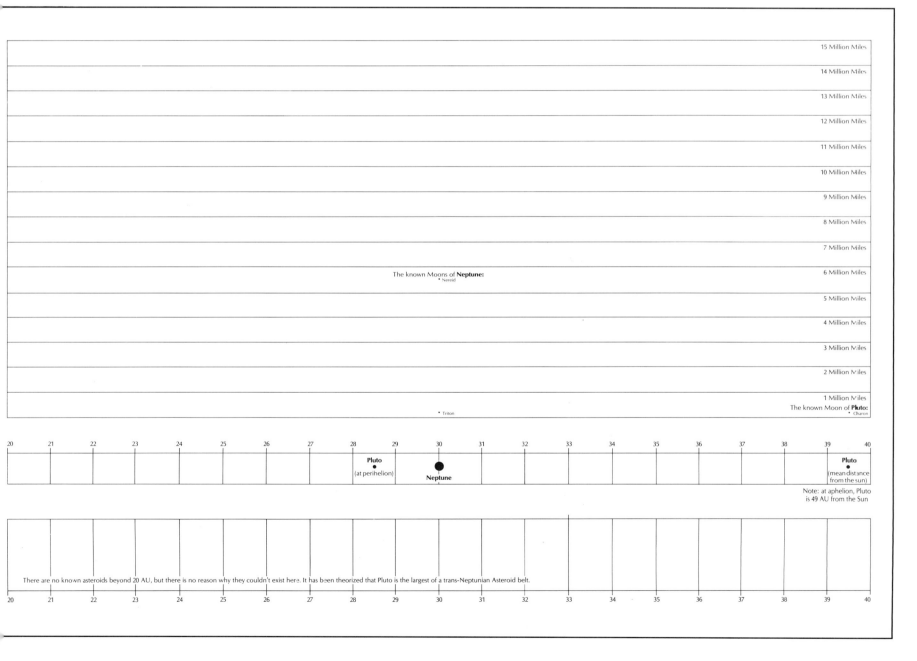

The known Moons of **Neptune:**
* Nereid

15 Million Miles

14 Million Miles

13 Million Miles

12 Million Miles

11 Million Miles

10 Million Miles

9 Million Miles

8 Million Miles

7 Million Miles

6 Million Miles

5 Million Miles

4 Million Miles

3 Million Miles

2 Million Miles

1 Million Miles

The known Moon of **Pluto:**
* Charon

* Triton

20	21	22	23	24	25	26	27	28	29	30	31	32	33	34	35	36	37	38	39	40

Pluto
(at perihelion)

Neptune

Pluto
(mean distance
from the sun)

Note: at aphelion, Pluto
is 49 AU from the Sun

There are no known asteroids beyond 20 AU, but there is no reason why they couldn't exist here. It has been theorized that Pluto is the largest of a trans-Neptunian Asteroid belt.

20	21	22	23	24	25	26	27	28	29	30	31	32	33	34	35	36	37	38	39	40

the other group. The terrestrial planets range in diameter between three and eight thousand miles, while the gas giants have a size range almost exactly ten times greater. The terrestrial planets all have solid silicate rock crusts with interiors that are (or once *were*) molten, while the gas giants are balls of hydrogen and helium and bear a closer resemblance to the composition of the Sun than they do to the composition of the terrestrial planets. (The four terrestrial planets have just three moons between them, while the four gas giants have at least 50 among *them*.)

The compositions of the moons of the outer planets are, however, intriguingly similar to that of the terrestrial planets themselves. Almost all of them are composed of water ice and silicate rock. Because of their hydrogen/helium composition, the gas giants are known to be closely related to the Sun and so their moon systems could be looked upon *almost* as solar systems within a solar system. Jupiter, however, did not become a star because it was not massive enough to have sustained fusion reactions.

The bodies in the Solar System can be classified in another important way. Out of the more than 3000 planets, moons and asteroids in the Solar System, only *eight* are known to have atmospheres consisting of more than barely detectable traces of gases near their surfaces. These include the four gas giants, of course, which could be described as being almost all atmosphere. The others are the terrestrial planets Venus, Earth and Mars, as well as Saturn's moon Titan. Of these four, Venus and Titan have atmospheres that are so thick that their solid surfaces are completely obscured by clouds.

The objects in the Solar System can also be classified by their surface type. Again, of course, the gas giants with their gaseous 'surfaces' are in a class by themselves. Another class would be those with silicate rock surfaces that have been marked primarily by meteorite impact craters. This class would include Mercury, the Earth's Moon, the Martian moons and all the asteroids. A third class, the so-called 'dirty snowballs,' are composed mostly of silicate rock and water ice marked by meteorite impact craters and some inherent geologic activity. This class would include nearly all the moons of the outer Solar System's four gas giants.

Five of the major bodies in the Solar System have surfaces that could truly be classified as unique. Erosion by liquid water has played a significant role in forming the surface features of two planets—Earth and Mars—but while it still plays that part on Earth, liquid water has mysteriously vanished from the surface of Mars. Huge oceans of liquid water and bits of water ice cover 70 percent of the Earth, while a similar percentage of Titan's surface is probably covered with frigid seas of liquid methane filled with methane icebergs. Every solid surfaced body in the Solar System has been, and still is, susceptible to marring by the impact craters of meteorites, but Venus, Titan and the Earth have atmospheres that are so dense that only in rare instances would a meteorite be large enough to not burn up in those atmospheres. Only a handful of bodies in the Solar System have ever had active volcanos, and only two, the Earth and Jupiter's Io, are confirmed to still have them. The most volcanically active object in the Solar System, Io, is home to almost continuous eruptions by sulfurous volcanos, from which liquid sulfur 'lava' constantly resurfaces the planet. This has, in turn, resulted in there being no identifiable meteorite impact on craters on Io.

The Solar System is an amazing place, full of intriguing similarities and inexplicable peculiarities. It is amazing both in its orderliness and its diversity. It interests us and confuses us, for as much as we are able to learn, our new knowledge serves only to inspire new questions.

The sixth through fourteenth largest objects in the Solar System. This montage *(right)* **of photographs taken by NASA spacecraft displays terrestrial, or solid surfaced, planets and larger moons of the solar system at the same scale. The inner planets are shown, as well as Jupiter's large moons Io, Europa, Ganymede and Callisto, and Saturn's large moon Titan. The Sun and the four gaseous giants—Jupiter, Saturn, Uranus and Neptune—are larger.** *Below:* **Voyager 2 witnessing a sunrise over the horizon of Jupiter.**

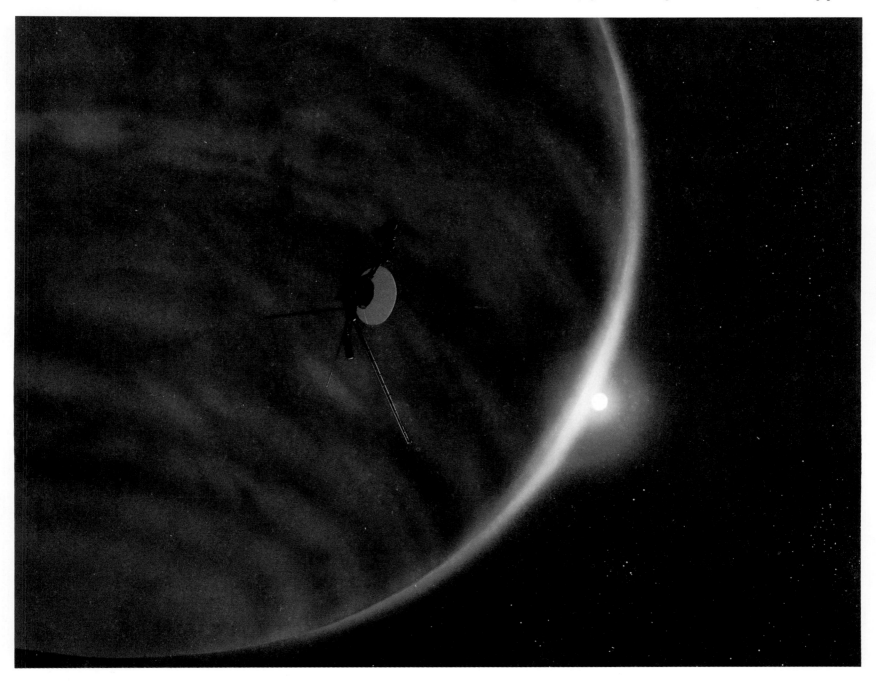

THE SUN

The central body of our Solar System, the Sun is an average-sized star of the *yellow dwarf* variety that formed roughly 4.6 billion years ago at the center of the enormous swirling gas cloud that became the Solar System. The concentration of pressure at the center of this swirling cloud of (mostly) hydrogen triggered a nuclear fusion reaction; thus the star we know as the Sun was born. In this fusion reaction, typical of all stars, four nuclei of hydrogen atoms (the simplest of the elements) fused to form a single helium (the second simplest element, having two protons) nucleus. The resulting reaction released a tremendous amount of energy.

It is theorized that in about five billion years, as its hydrogen becomes depleted, the Sun will expand from its present status of a *yellow dwarf* star to become a *red giant*, swelling to 30 times its present size. According to this generally accepted theory, the Sun will then collapse back to a *white dwarf* type star (smaller than its present size), and gradually become a burnt ember, which would then be ironically referred to as a *black dwarf*.

Though it is not considered to be a particularly large star, the Sun is by far the largest body within the Solar System, containing 99 percent of the matter of the system, thus providing the gravitational force that literally *defines* the Solar System and controls the orbital paths of the other bodies within it. The Sun is also the source of most of the heat in the Solar System, and thus it provides the warmth that makes life possible on at least one of the bodies in the Solar System. The temperature at the core of the Sun is estimated at roughly 20 million degrees Centigrade, the surface temperature averaging 11,000 degrees Fahren-

heit, or approximately 6000 degrees Kelvin. The energy radiated from the Sun is called solar radiation, which (as measured in wavelengths from the longest to the shortest) can be simplified as including: (a) radio waves, (b) microwaves, (c) infrared radiation (perceived on Earth as heat), (d) the visible light spectrum, (e) ultraviolet radiation, (f) x-rays and (g) gamma rays. So powerful is solar radiation that its ultraviolet wavelengths can burn (or tan) human skin on Earth and direct light from the visible spectrum can do permanent damage to the human eye.

Like the other major bodies in the Solar System, the Sun rotates on its axis. However, its equatorial region rotates once every 27.275 days, while its polar regions have a slower rotational period of 34 days.

The Sun, being a gaseous sphere, has no solid surface, nor could any molecular solid exist at such incredible temperatures. The Sun does, however, have a nearly opaque surface—a sea of gaseous firestorms known as the *photosphere*.

The firestorms that comprise the photosphere are roughly 600 miles in diameter and appear as granules in the vastness of the scale of the Sun. Their apparent opacity is due to the presence of negative hydrogen ions. During the approximate eight minute lifespan of the granule, hot gas rises out of the center, pushing cooler gases aside and into the narrow darker and cooler spaces between the granules. Amid the typical granules, there are 'supergranules,' with diameters up to 18,000 miles and lifespans of up to 24 hours.

Other 'surface features' on the photosphere are *solar flares* and *sunspots*. Solar flares are violent surface eruptions that explode from the photosphere with the energy of ten million hydrogen bombs, sending forth a stream of solar radiation that can disrupt radio signals on the Earth.

Solar flares were first observed in 1859 by the English astronomer

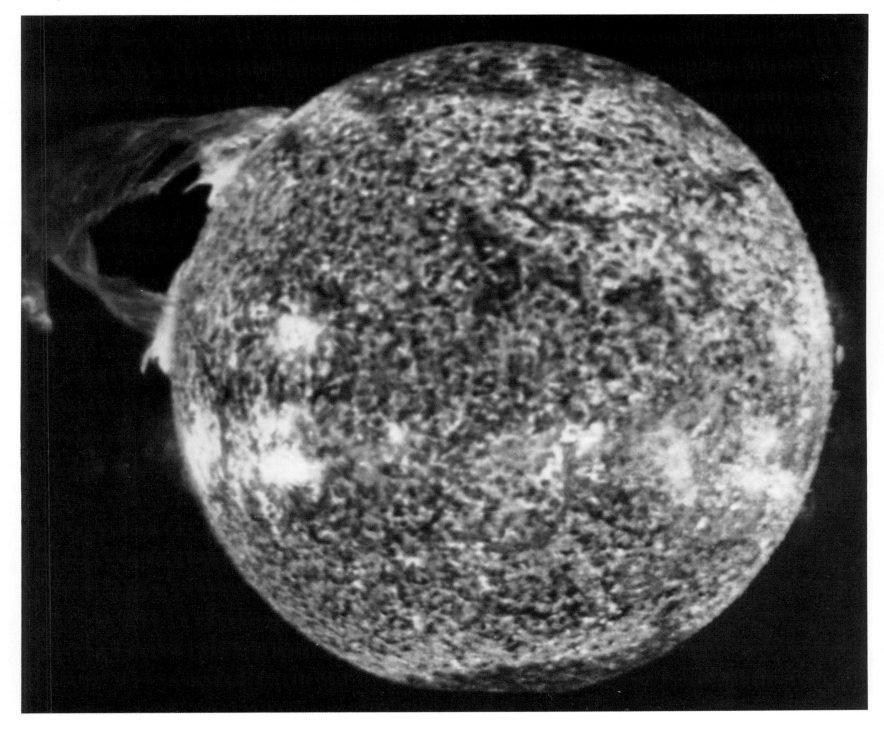

Facing page: Photographed on 19 December 1973, this is one of the most spectacular solar flares ever recorded, spanning more than 367,000 miles across the Sun's surface. The solar poles are distinguishable in this photo by their comparatively uniform dark coloration. Note also the pervasive dark granules, or firestorms. *Below:* The relative intensity of solar regions is color coded in this Orbiting Solar Observatory television display. White represents the greatest intensity, followed in descending order by yellow, red and blue. The dark regions at the poles, extending down across the Sun, are coronal holes. *Above:* The Sun as a thing of beauty when viewed from Earth.

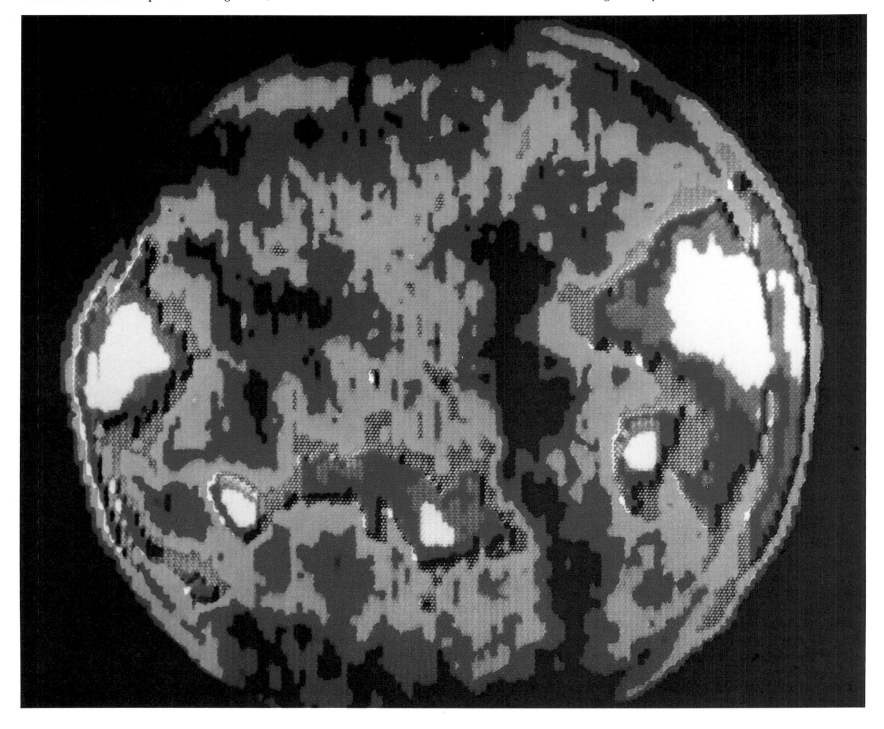

Richard Carrington. They have also been observed to a greater or lesser degree on other stars. The frequency of solar flares can range from several in a single Earth day during periods when the Sun is active, to fewer than one per Earth week during the periods that astronomers describe as 'quiet.' The energy for individual flares may take several hours or even days to build up, but the actual flare, when the energy is released, happens in a matter of minutes. The resulting shockwaves travel outward across the photosphere and up into the chromosphere and corona for hundreds of thousands of miles at speeds on the order of three million mph.

It is not known what triggers solar flares, but magnetic energy almost certainly plays a major role. The study of solar flares is important because of the effect on Earth of the radiation and particles released during solar flares, not to mention the potential negative effect on spacecraft and astronauts beyond the Earth's atmosphere. The charged particles released in the flares are attracted by the Earth's magnetic field and spiral in at the north and south magnetic poles, causing the Aurora Borealis in Earth's atmosphere.

Sunspots are dark regions on the surface of the photosphere which are cooler than the surrounding areas. Like the solar flares, sunspots occur with less frequency during the Sun's quiet periods. During such periods there maybe *no* observable sunspots, while during active periods there may be more than a hundred on the photosphere at one time.

Sunspots were first observed by the Chinese 2000 years ago, and in the seventeenth century, the great Italian astronomer Galileo Galilei (1564-1642) conducted a systematic study of them. His observations of the motion of sunspots across the solar surface led to his discovery of the rotation of the Sun. The frequency of sunspot activity has been recorded as occurring in an 11 year cycle that seems to have an effect on the weather on Earth. The period from 1645 to 1715 was, for example, an era of a very quiet Sun and for *seven years* during this time *no* sunspots were observed. These years also corresponded with the height of the cold spell in the Earth's northern hemisphere that is referred to as the 'little ice age.'

Sunspots vary in size and shape and may be as large as 40,000 miles across. They are composed of a 'penumbra' with a darker 'umbra' in the center (which constitutes about a quarter of the sunspot's area). Sunspots increase to their full size in about a week to 10 days, but in turn take nearly two weeks to decay. Sunspots usually occur in groups, and a large group may have a life span of several weeks.

It is not known what causes sunspots, but the standard theory has it that a powerful magnetic field temporarily restricts the flow of the hottest gasses to that particular part of the photosphere; sunspots seem to appear at places where magnetic field lines have become twisted and rise above the photosphere.

Above the photosphere there is a thinner, more visually transparent layer known as the *chromosphere* (literally 'color sphere'). This layer is roughly 6000 miles thick. The most common feature within the chromosphere are the *spicules*, long thin fingers of luminous gas which appear like a vast field of blades of fiery grass growing up into the chromosphere from the photosphere. They are observed to rise to the upper reaches of the chromosphere (about 6000 miles above the photosphere), and then drop back in the space of about 10 minutes.

Fibrils are horizontal wisps of gas that drift through the chromosphere. They are about the same size as the spicules, but have about twice the duration.

Prominences are gigantic luminous plumes of gas that appear like tongues of flame. They leap from the photosphere into, and beyond, the chromosphere, sometimes reaching altitudes of 100,000 miles. Aside from the less frequent solar flares, prominences are the most spectacular of solar phenomena.

Beyond the chromosphere is the *corona*, a vast field of hydrogen particles that extends for millions of miles into space. The corona is so sparse that it is not visible against the glare of the Sun—except during a total solar eclipse when the Moon passes between the Earth and the Sun, blotting out the photosphere. During periods of quiet Sun, the corona is more or less confined to the solar equatorial regions, with *coronal holes* being present in the polar regions. During periods of more activity, the corona is evenly distributed around the Sun, including the polar regions, but appears most prominent near the regions of the most sunspot activity.

The corona is mysteriously hotter than the photosphere, despite the second law of thermodynamics which holds that heat cannot be con-

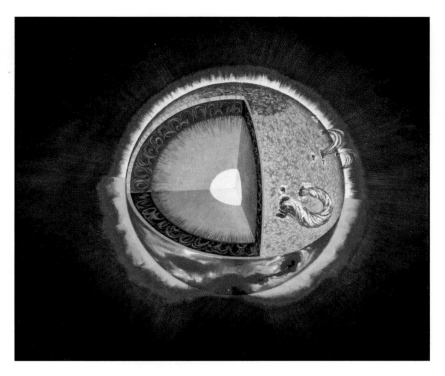

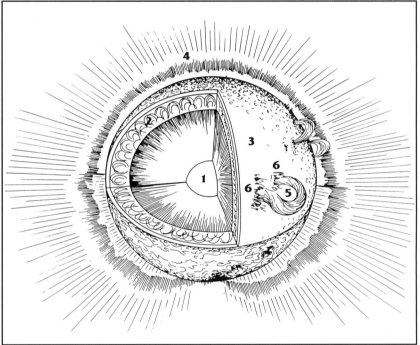

Above is a diagram of the illustration of the Sun *(at top)*, showing (1) the core; (2) the convection zone; (3) the photosphere; (4) the chromosphere; (5) a solar prominence; and (6) sunspots. *Right:* A huge solar eruption can be seen in this spectroheliogram. *Below right:* In this striking computer enhanced view of the solar corona, the colors represent densities of the corona from blue (most dense) to yellow (least dense).

ducted from the cooler to the warmer. The mystery involves the process by which the corona is heated. The dynamics of solar magnetic fields and acoustic energy are suggested as possible answers. Despite its high temperature, the corona's very low density means that it radiates relatively little energy.

Triggered by large prominences or by solar flares, *coronal transients* are blast waves, giant loops of corona material released at speeds of more than a million mph, into the Solar System. Coronal transients are carried by the solar wind to distances beyond the Earth's orbit.

Coronal transients have been observed as having ten times the energy as the flares which trigger them.

Blowing outward from the Sun and its corona is a constant stream of hot, ionized, subatomic particulate plasma known as the *solar wind*. A constant phenomena, the solar wind gusts from 450,000 mph to two million mph, and blows into the distant reaches of the Solar System.

The solar wind spirals out from the Sun, rotating with the Sun until it reaches a distance of approximately 100 million miles (roughly one AU). From that point it travels outward with less interference from the Sun's magnetic field.

Approximately 3000 tons of subatomic particles are blown outward from the Sun in the solar wind every hour. To give some idea of the scale of the Sun, it would, at this rate, take 200,000 billion years for the Sun's entire mass to be dissipated by the solar wind.

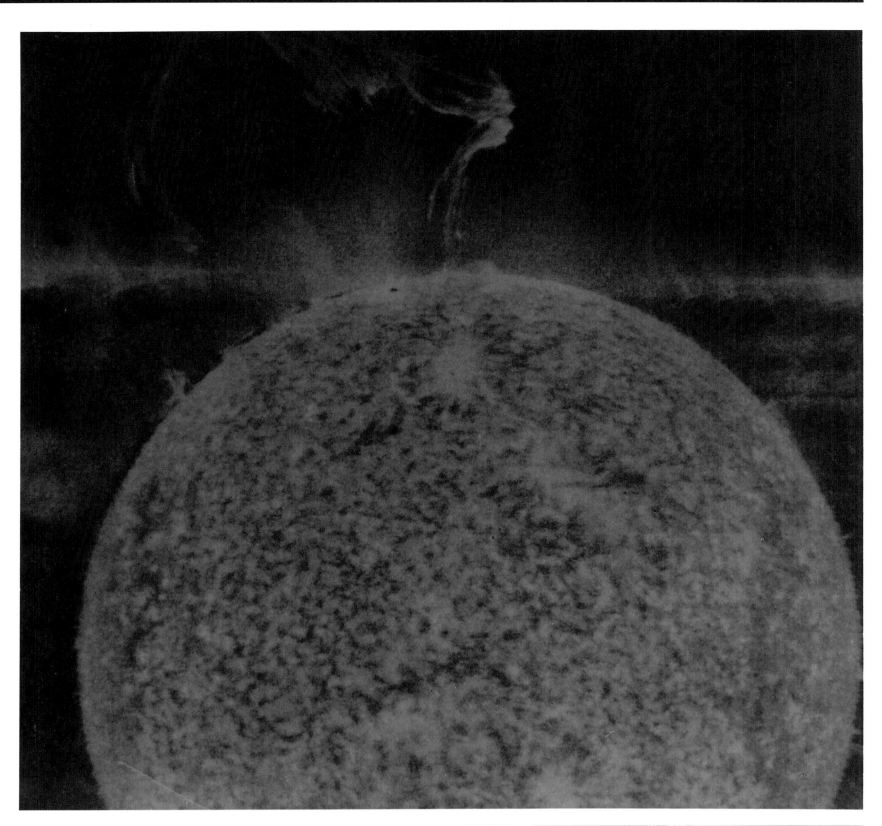

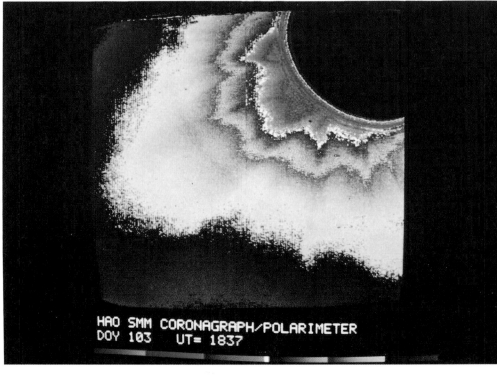

HAO SMM CORONAGRAPH/POLARIMETER
DOY 103   UT= 1837

THE SUN
Diameter: 870,331.25 miles (1,392,530 km)
Mass: 4.3959×10^{30} lb (1.9891×10^{30} kg)
Rotational period
    of equator: 26.8 Earth days
    at latitude 30°: 28.2 Earth days
    at latitude 60°: 30.8 Earth days
    at latitude 75°: 31.8 Earth days
Surface temperature: 10,430° F
Interior temperature: 26,999,500° F
Major photospheric components: Hydrogen (73.46%)
                                    Helium (24.85%)
                                    Oxygen (.77%)
                                    Carbon (.29%)
                                    Iron (.16%)
                                    Neon (.12%)
                                    Nitrogen (.09%)
                                    Silicon (.07%)
                                    Magnesium (.05%)
                                    Sulphur (.04%)

MERCURY

Mercury is the closest planet to the Sun and the second smallest of the nine planets. It has been observed from Earth since prehistoric times, but because of its size it is fainter than Venus, Mars, Jupiter and Saturn—the other planets visible to the naked eye.

Because of its proximity to the Sun, it is always observed within 27 degrees of the Sun in the east before sunrise or in the west after sunset. It has a sidereal period of just three months, the shortest of any planet. As such, it has the appearance from Earth of moving faster than the others, a characteristic which led the Greeks to name it Hermes, after the messenger of the gods. The Romans, in turn, called the planet Mercury after their own deities' wing-footed messenger.

In the eighteenth century, Johann Hieronymus Schroeter (1745-1816) became the first astronomer to record his observations of Mercury's surface detail, but his drawings, like those of Giovanni Schiaparelli (1835-1910) more than a century later, were ill-defined and turned out to be inaccurate. The great American astronomer Percival Lowell (1855-1916) reported that he had observed streaks on Mercury's surface similar to those that he and Schiaparelli had both observed on Mars. Schiaparelli had called these Martian features *canali* (channels) and Lowell decided they were *canals*, built by intelligent life. Both astronomers agreed, however, that the streaks on Mercury's surface were of natural origin.

In 1929 Eugenios Antoniadi (1870-1944), a Greek-born astronomer working in France, completed a chart of Mercury's surface that stood for nearly half a century as the accepted map of the planet. Using one of the world's best telescopes, he identified a number of major surface features and proved that the streaks seen by Schiaparelli and Lowell were optical illusions. He agreed with the earlier astronomers, however, on the idea that Mercury's rotational and sidereal periods were identical, and thus that the planet always had the same hemisphere turned toward the Sun. It was not until 1962 that this was shown to be untrue.

The major milestone in the observation of Mercury came in March 1974 when the American spacecraft Mariner 10 began a series of three flybys at a distance of about 12,000 miles, in which it was able to photograph in great detail, objects as small as 325 feet across.

The photos returned by Mariner 10 revealed a planet whose surface features might easily be mistaken for those on the Earth's Moon. Like the Lunar surface, that of Mercury is pocked by thousands of craters. With the exception of the relatively smooth Caloris Basin, Mercury's surface is characterized almost exclusively by craters, overlapping craters and craters within craters. The Lunar surface, by contrast, has more larger open areas known as *maria*, or seas. The Caloris Basin, which is itself pocked by hundreds of relatively smaller craters, is the only major open plain comparable to the Moon's maria. Unlike the Lunar seas, which are ancient lava flows, it is believed that the Caloris Basin was created by a massive, ancient impact, as is indicated by the presence of mountains and ridges around its periphery, possibly caused by seismic waves. Other ridges and escarpments are to be seen on the surface, and are possibly due to the expansion and contraction of Mercury's core as it cooled and shrank. Some of the cliffs produced by this effect rise as much as 6300 feet above the adjacent valley floors. There is some evidence of ancient volcanic activity on Mercury, but less than that of the Moon.

Because of Mercury's overall density, its core is thought to be largely (70 percent) composed of iron, with the surface crust being silica rock, like that of the Earth or Lunar surfaces. Due perhaps to its slow rotation, Mercury has a relatively weak magnetic field, despite its being composed mostly of iron.

Unlike the other three inner terrestrial planets, Mercury has virtually no atmosphere. Faint traces of gaseous helium form 98 percent of the 'atmosphere,' with the remainder being composed mostly of hydrogen, with minute traces of argon and neon also being present. The helium was probably captured from the Sun, because any gasses emanating from the interior of the planet would have long ago dissipated into space.

Because of its virtually non-existent atmosphere, Mercury's surface temperatures vary widely. The midday temperature on the side facing the Sun can be as hot as 610 degrees Fahrenheit, while at night temperatures can plummet to −346 degrees Fahrenheit because there is no atmosphere to hold the heat.

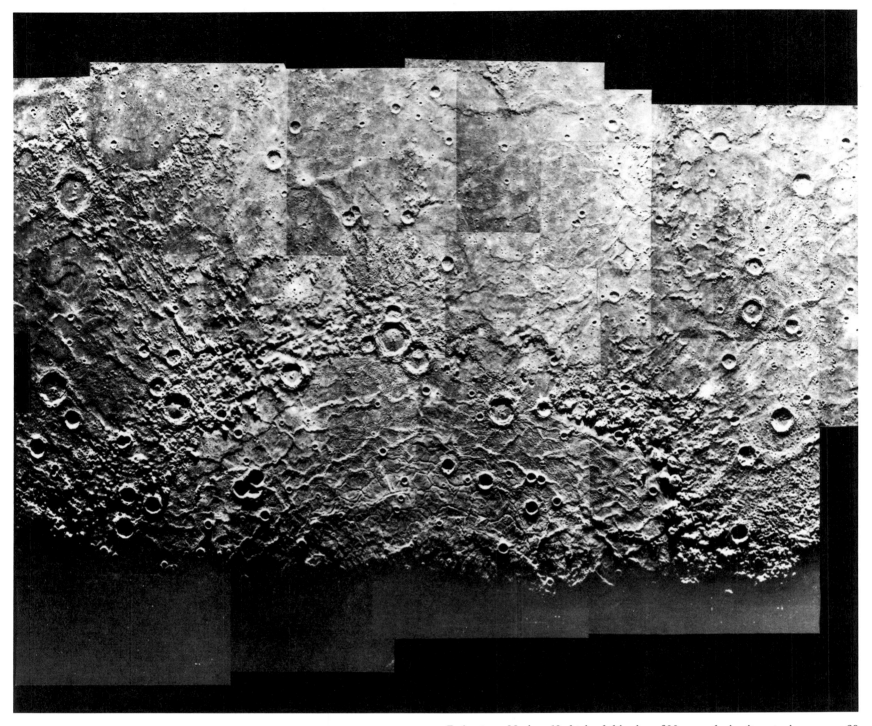

Facing page: Mariner 10 obtained this view of Mercury during its outgoing pass on 29 March 1974. *Left:* This photomosaic taken by Mariner 10 was constructed to show a terrain unique to Mercury—where hills and ridges cut across many of the craters and the inter-crater areas. The left half of the photomosaic *above* shows the largest structural feature on Mercury—the 800-mile wide Caloris Basin.

MERCURY
Diameter: 3031 miles (4878 km)
Distance from Sun: 43,309,572 miles (69,700,000 km) at aphelion
28,520,937 miles (45,000,000 km) at perihelion
Mass: 1.501×10^{23} lb (3.302×10^{23} kg)
Rotational period (Mercurian day): 58.65 Earth days
Sidereal period (Mercurian year): 87.97 Earth days
Eccentricity: 0.206
Inclination of rotational axis: 0°
Inclination to ecliptic plane (Earth = 0): 7°
Albedo (100% reflection of light = 1): .06
Mean surface temperature: 407° F
Maximum surface temperature: 620° F
Minimum surface temperature: 194° F (-346° F on dark side)
Largest known surface feature: Caloris Basin
840 miles in diameter (1350 km)
Major atmospheric component: Trace amounts of Helium (98%)
Other atmospheric components: Hydrogen
Argon
Neon

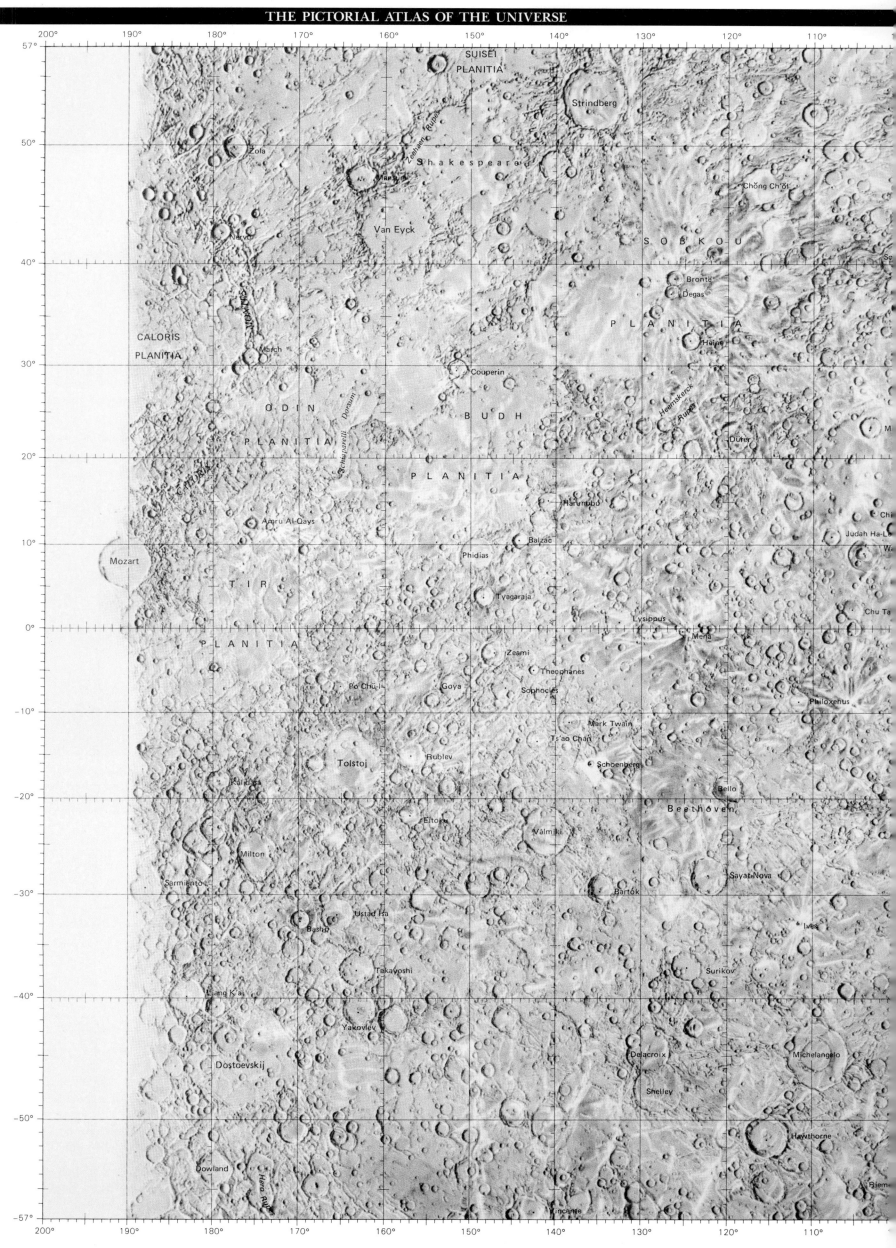

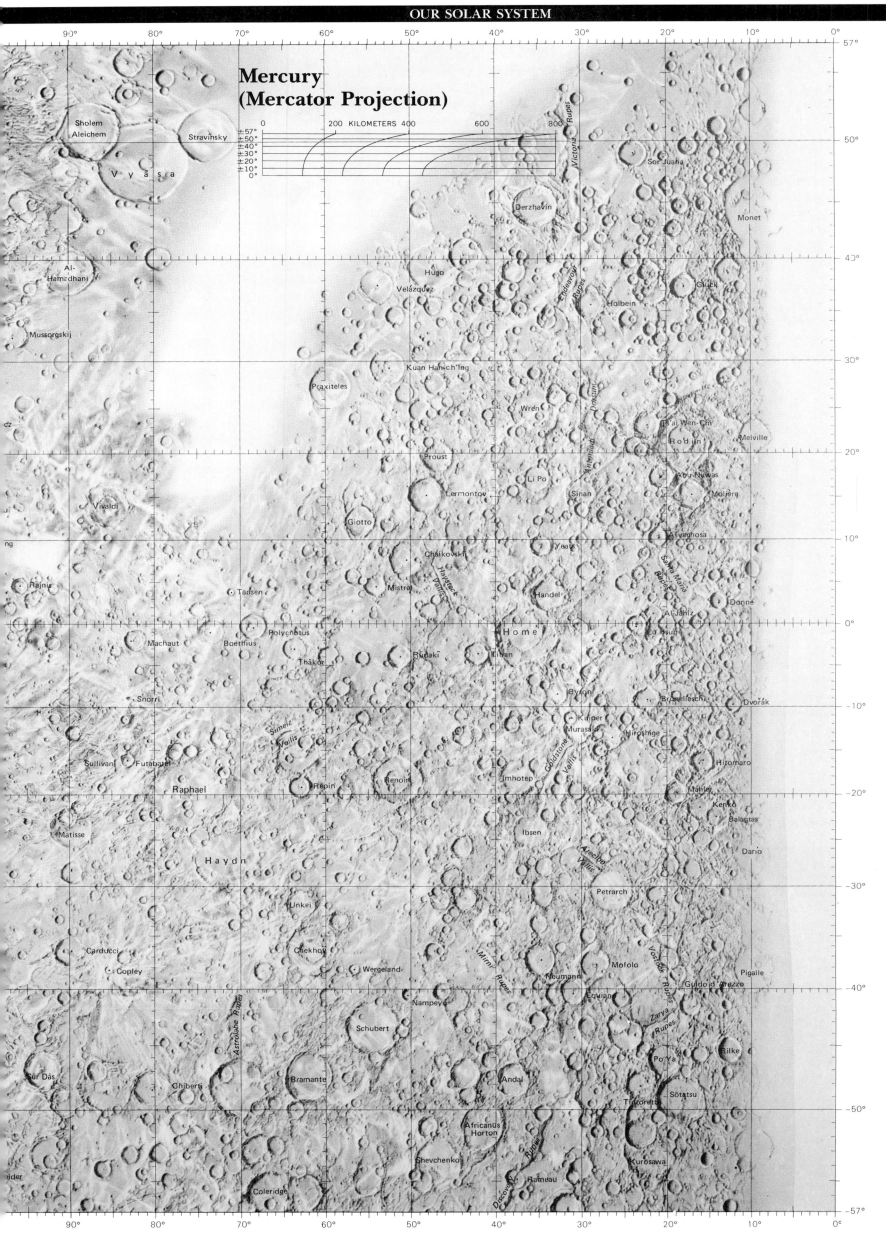

Mercury
(Mercator Projection)

0   200 KILOMETERS 400   600   800

±57°
±50°
±40°
±30°
±20°
±10°
0°

Sholem Aleichem
Stravinsky
V y ā s a
Al-Hamadhani
Mussorgskij
Vivaldi
Rajnis
cz
ng
Sür Däs
eider

Victoria Rupes
Sor Juana
Derzhavin
Monet
Hugo
Velázquez
Gück
Holbein
Kuan Han-ch'ing
Doskan
Wren
Tsai Wen-Chi
Praxiteles
Rodin
Melville
Proust
Li Po
Abu Nuwas
Lermontov
Sinan
Molière
Giotto
Asvaghosa
Chaikovskii
Yeats
Santa Maria Rupes
Mistral
Handel
Donne
Tansen
Al-Jahiz
Polycnotus
Home
Lu Hsun
Machaut
Boethius
Rudaki
Titian
Thakor
Brunelleschi
Dvořák
Snorri
Byron
Simeiz Vallis
Kuiper
Murasaki
Hiroshige
Sullivani
Goldstone Vallis
Futabatei
Imhotep
Hitomaro
Raphael
Repin
Renoir
Mahler
Kenko
Balagtas
Matisse
Ibsen
Dario
H a y d n
Arecibo Vallis
Petrarch
Unkei
Carducci
Chekhov
Copley
Wergeland
Mofolo
Pigalle
Mirni Rupes
Neumann
Guido d'Arezzo
Astrolabe Rupes
Nampeyo
Eqviano
Vostok Rupes
Schubert
Zarya Rupes
Po Ya
Bilke
Sür Däs
Ghiberti
Bramante
Andal
Tintoretto
Sotatsu
Discovery Rupes
Africanus Horton
Kurosawa
Shevchenko
Rameau
Coleridge

VENUS

The second planet from the Sun, Venus is a near twin of the Earth in terms of size, with a diameter 95 percent that of our own planet. As viewed from Earth, Venus is the brightest celestial object in the sky except for the Sun and Moon. The Greek poet Homer even went so far as to call it the most beautiful star in the sky, while the Romans named it Venus after their goddess of beauty.

Like the Moon, Venus is seen to go through a series of phases as it orbits the Sun and is viewed from Earth. *Transits*— in which the planet passes directly between the Earth and the Sun—are characterized by an effect similar to an eclipse, although Venus appears as a mere tiny black dot creeping across the face of the Sun. Transits are rare, occurring in pairs eight years apart—and then not at all, for well over a century. The last pair of transits, for example, occurred in 1874-82, and the next will occur in 2004-12.

Early attempts at mapping the surface features of Venus were frustrated by the fact that the entire surface is covered by a thick cloud layer, a fact not known to early astronomers. Giovanni Cassini (1625-1712) produced the first 'map' in 1667, but as cloud patterns changed he could no longer find the features he had drawn. Johann Hieronymus Schroeter (1745-1816) was also fooled and reported having seen mountains on the surface. Schroeter, however, *was* the first to observe a very real phenomena, that of the 'ashen light' seen in the Venusian atmosphere on the dark side of the planet. This faint light was at one time thought to be the city lights of Venusian civilization, but is now attributed to lightning which occurs during the planet's frequent electrical storms.

By the early twentieth century, it had been determined that the Venusian surface was obscured by clouds, and various theories evolved regarding the actual nature of the surface beneath those clouds. The nineteenth century idea that the planet was covered by lush jungles was dismissed in favor of the two schools of thought that suggested either a vast desert or a vast ocean of water.

It had been established that the surface would be extremely hot because carbon dioxide in the thick atmosphere would prevent solar heat from escaping the surface, thus producing what is referred to as a 'greenhouse effect.'

The atmosphere of Venus has long been known to consist primarily of carbon dioxide, and the instruments of Pioneer Venus and Venera have pinpointed the proportion of carbon dioxide at 96 percent. Nitrogen constitutes more than three percent of the Venusian atmosphere, and there are also traces of neon and several isotopes of argon.

There is some water vapor present in the Venusian cloud cover, where it has a density of 200 ppm—ten times the density of water vapor in the clear air near the surface. In the clouds the water vapor combines chemically with traces of sulphur dioxide to produce droplets of sulfuric acid, which give the Venusian cloud cover its distinctive yellowish color.

The Venusian cloud cover is complete and unbroken. The cloud layer is roughly 15 miles thick, with its base about 30 miles above the surface of the planet, relatively higher than the thinner cloud cover on Earth. The air at the surface is probably quite clear and the air relatively still. The clouds, however, are pushed by winds with speeds up to 200 mph and circulate around the entire planet once every four Earth days, in contrast to the rotation period of Venusian 'day,' or 243 Earth days. Electric storms are common within the clouds and lightning has been detected by both American and Soviet spacecraft.

The most notable visible feature in the Venusian atmosphere, and one that misled so many would-be mapmakers in earlier days, is the Y Feature, whose tail sometimes stretches around the planet. The feature is actually the prevailing winds in the northern and southern hemi-

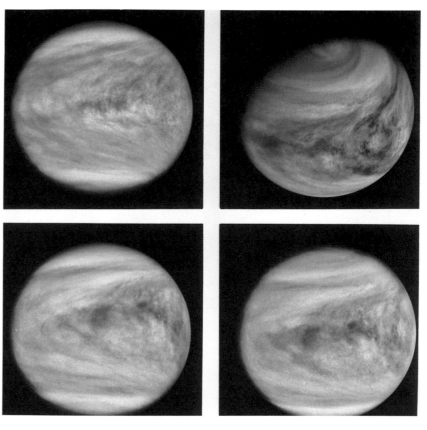

The four ultraviolet photographs *above* taken by the Pioneer Venus Orbiter spacecraft show a variety of cloud formations over the planet Venus. The planet's clouds circle Venus completely once every four hours. Taken between 2 May and 4 May 1980, the views cover a period of 38 hours. The time sequence is as follows: *Lower left:* 2 May 1980, 7:58 am PDT. *Upper left:* 9.5 hours later. *Upper right:* 4.5 hours after upper left. *Lower right:* 24 hours after the one above. All views show different versions of the planet's Y feature, which usually covers more than one hemisphere. Note that the Y feature varies its form with some regularity.

Below, left: A cutaway view of Venus, showing the complexity of its dense atmosphere and planetary surface and a diagram of the same *(below)*, which names various constituent features.

Right: A photo of Venus taken by NASA's Pioneer Venus on 27 December 1980.

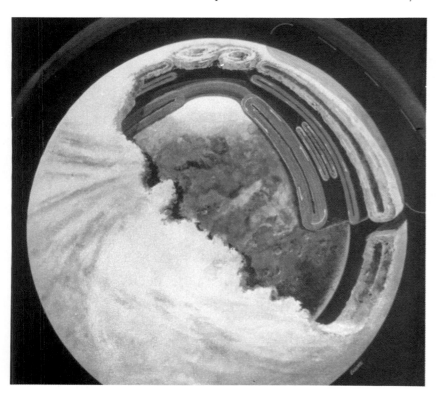

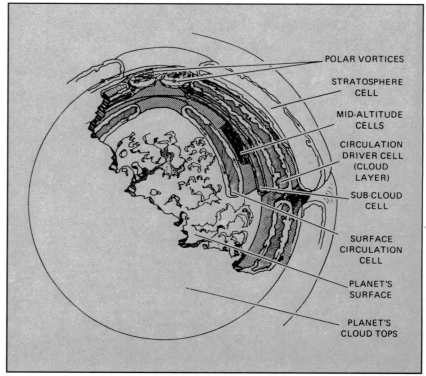

POLAR VORTICES

STRATOSPHERE CELL

MID-ALTITUDE CELLS

CIRCULATION DRIVER CELL (CLOUD LAYER)

SUB-CLOUD CELL

SURFACE CIRCULATION CELL

PLANET'S SURFACE

PLANET'S CLOUD TOPS

spheres as they diverge at the equator. This pattern is constantly changing, and sometimes it is seen as a reversed C. It always, however, retains an approximate north-south symmetry.

The first successful expedition to the vicinity of Venus came in December 1962 when the American unmanned spacecraft Mariner 2 traveled to within 21,600 miles of the planet. The flight of Mariner 2 was a major milestone in unlocking the secrets of the mysterious planet. Among its achievements were confirmation that Venus has no detectable magnetic field, confirmation of the planet's exact rotational period—243 Earth days—and confirmation that it rotates from east to west, rather than the opposite as previously supposed.

Mariner 2 also provided a more accurate reading of the planet's surface temperature, which at 900 degrees Fahrenheit is too hot for the existence of an ocean, because water could exist there only as steam. Water vapor is in fact present in the atmosphere, and some astronomers have theorized that at an early stage in the evolution of Venus, oceans *may have* in fact existed on the surface.

In 1978 the United States undertook the Pioneer Venus project as a follow-on to several earlier Mariner probes. The project consisted of an orbiter spacecraft and a multiprobe spacecraft. The former undertook the detailed radar mapping of the Venusian surface that made possible the maps on these pages, and which gave us much of the information we now have about the planet's terrain. The multiprobe was actually five probes designed to return data about the Venusian atmosphere as they plunged toward the surface. One of the Pioneer Venus multiprobes continued to return data from the surface for just over an hour after impact.

The Soviet Union, meanwhile, prepared a series of spacecraft to conduct soft landings on the Venusian surface, which returned the only photographs ever taken of the Venusian surface. The Soviet Venera 9 and Venera 10 spacecraft each returned a single black and white image in 1975, and the Venera 13 and Venera 14 spacecraft returned color photos in March 1982.

While the Soviet Venera spacecraft provided the first photographs of specific points on the Venusian surface, the American Pioneer Venus

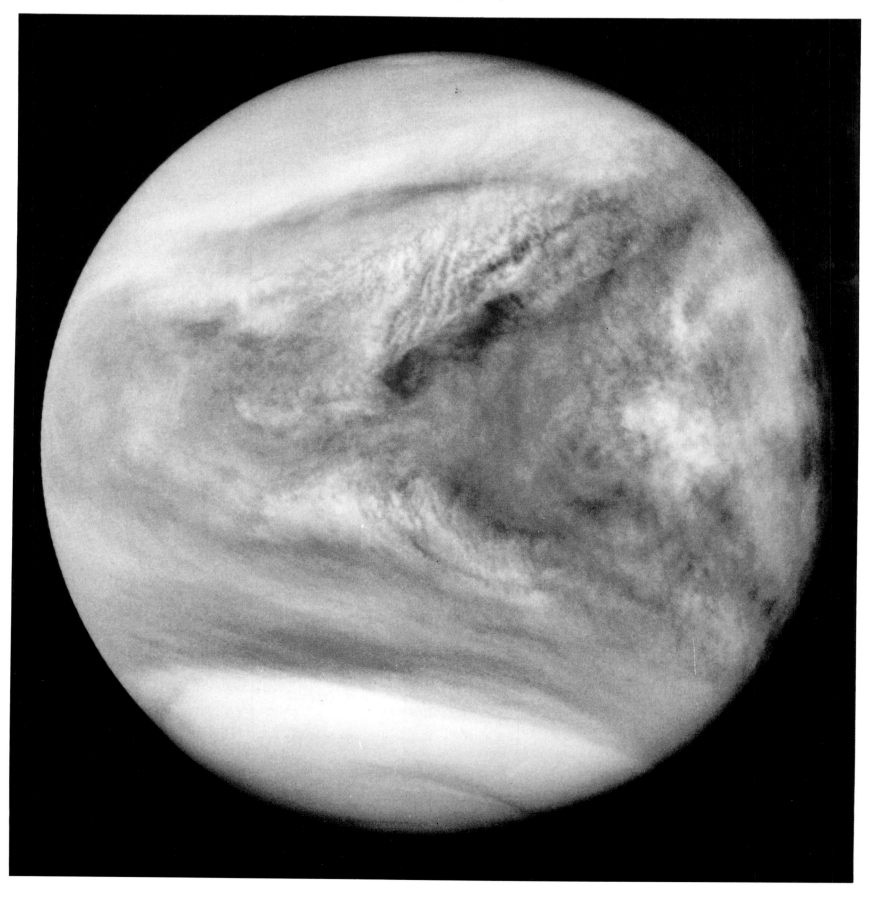

Orbiter provided our first clear look at the overall global surface features of Venus.

Using a radar altimeter, Pioneer Venus was able to obtain the data necessary to produce a topographical map of 90 percent of the planet's surface, from 73 degrees north latitude to 63 degrees south latitude.

This data showed that the surface was generally smoother than those of the other three terrestrial planets, with much less variation in altitude than is seen on Earth. For instance, 60 percent of the Venusian surface is within 1600 feet of the planet's *mean radius* of 3752 miles. It has been suggested that this is due to the deeper lowlands having been filled with sand and other wind-blown material. Because there are no seas on Venus, the mean radius is used as a reference point in the same way that sea level is used on Earth.

Most of the surface of Venus is characterized as rolling uplands, rising to an altitude of roughly 3000 feet, while 20 percent of the surface is identified as lowlands and 10 percent as mountainous. The two largest upland regions, or continental masses, are Aphrodite Terra (roughly the size of Africa), near the equator in the Southern hemisphere, and Ishtar Terra (roughly the size of Australia), in the northern hemisphere near the North Pole. These two features constitute the Venusian 'continents' and are named respectively for the ancient Greek and ancient Babylonian goddesses of love.

The highest points on the mapped surface of Venus are in the Maxwell Mountains (Maxwell Montes) in Ishtar Terra. High enough to have been identified by Earth-based radar prior to the Pioneer Venus project, the Maxwell Mountains, which may actually be a single mountain, rise to more than 35,000 feet above mean radius, or roughly 20 percent higher than Mount Everest rises above Earth's *sea level*. If viewed from the surface they would be an impressive sight, rising nearly 27,000 feet above Lakshmi Planvin, the surrounding plateau which is roughly the same elevation as the Tibetan plateau on Earth.

Data obtained from Pioneer Venus indicates that the Maxwell Mountains may be the rim of an ancient volcano whose caldera had a diameter of roughly 60 miles. The lava flows, however, have long since been worn away by wind erosion, and the slopes of the Maxwell Mountains are strewn with rocks and debris.

Another important upland region is Beta Regio with its great shield volcanos, Rhea Mons and Theia Mons, which are larger than the great shield volcanos of Hawaii on Earth. The mountainous Beta Regio is still in the process of formation and may possibly contain active volcanos. As such, it is the newest major surface feature on Venus.

The lowest point on the Venusian surface is actually a canyon, Diana Chasma, located within central Aphrodite Terra. At just 9500 feet below mean radius, Diana Chasma is much shallower than the corresponding lowest point on Earth, the Marianas Trench. The largest and lowest lowland region on Venus is the Atalanta Plain (Atalanta Planitia) located northeast of Aphrodite Terra and due east of Ishtar Terra. It is roughly the same size as the Earth's North Atlantic Ocean, although it is shallower by comparison.

VENUS
Diameter: 7521 miles (12,104 km)
Distance from Sun: 67,580,000 miles (109,000,000 km) at aphelion
66,588,000 miles (107,400,000 km) at perihelion
Mass: $2.213 - 10^{24}$ lb ($4.8689 - 10^{24}$ kg)
Rotational period (Venusian day): 243.0 Earth days (retrograde)
Eccentricity: 0.007
Sidereal period (Venusian year): 224.7 Earth days
Inclination of rotational axis: 3°
Inclination to ecliptic plane (Earth = 0): 3.39°
Albedo (100% reflection of light = 0): .76
Mean surface temperature: 866.9° F
Maximum surface temperature: 900° F
Minimum surface temperature: 833° F
Highest point on surface: Maxwell Mountains
Largest surface feature: Aphrodite Terra
6025 × 1990 miles (9700 × 3200 km)
Major atmospheric components: Carbon dioxide (96%)
Other atmospheric components: Nitrogen, Water vapor, Carbon monoxide, Hydrogen chloride, Hydrogen fluoride, Sulphur dioxide

In March 1982, the Soviet Union's Venera 13 and 14 spacecraft transmitted the only color photos ever taken of the Venusian surface. The use of a super wide angle lens resulted in some distortion, but Venus' horizon can be seen in the upper corners of the photos at the *top left* and in the *middle*. The two shots *on the left* were taken by Venera 13.

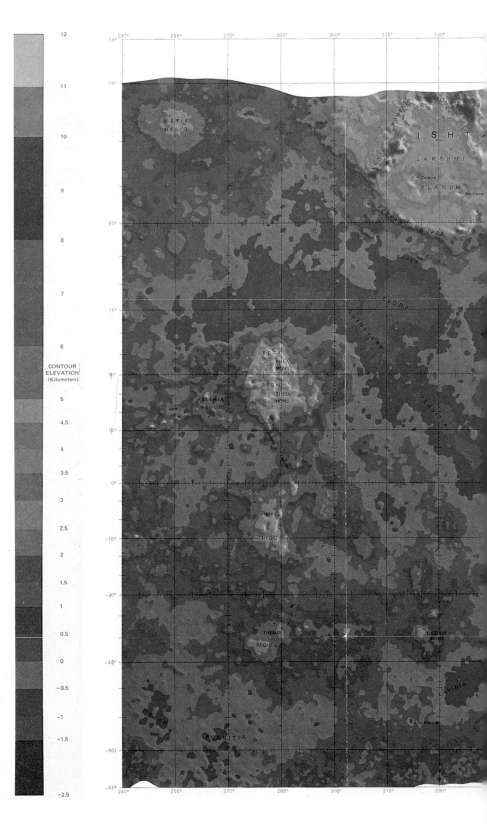

Venus (Radar Mercator Projection)

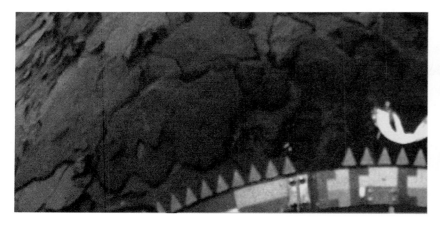

The photos in the *middle* and *on the right* give the total Venera 14 view. The atmospheric pressure on the planet's surface makes landings extremely difficult and therefore photographs of the surface are quite rare. Immediately after Venera took these photographs the spacecraft was crushed under its own weight. *Below:* The radar Mercator projection details the Venusian surface. The Maxwell Mountains on Ishtar Terra (indicated in red) are the highest points on the mapped surface of Venus. An impressive sight indeed, the Maxwell Mountains rise to more than 35,000 feet above mean radius—or 20 percent higher than Mount Everest rises above Earth's sea level.

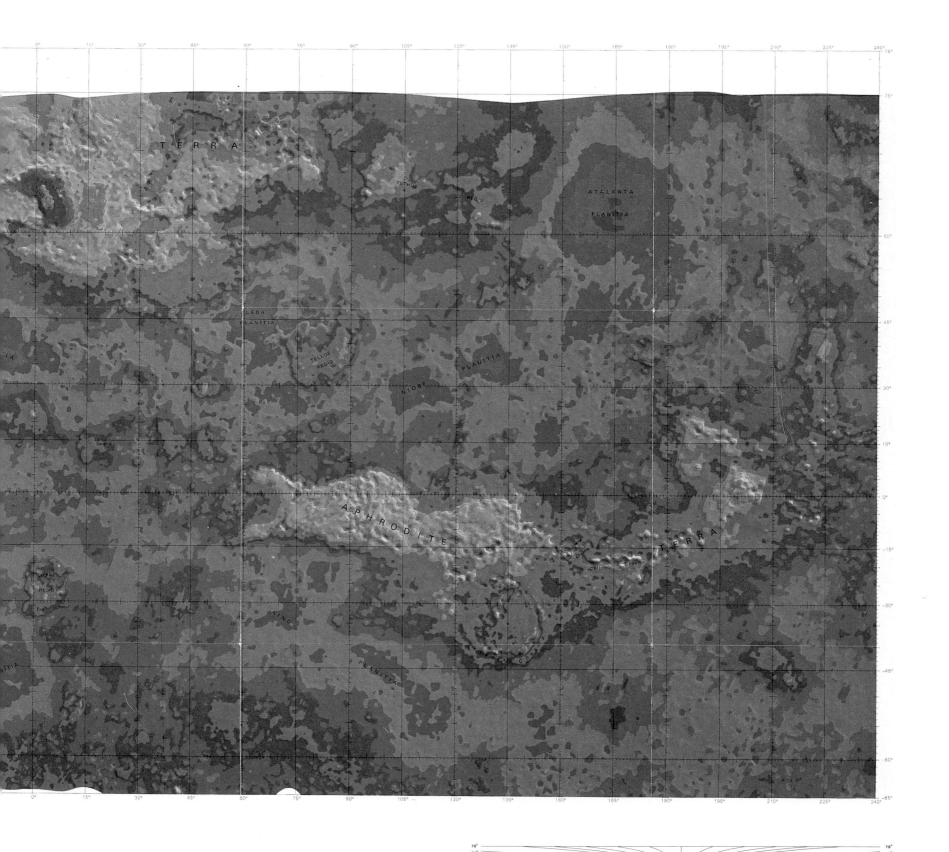

Venus (Mercator Projection)

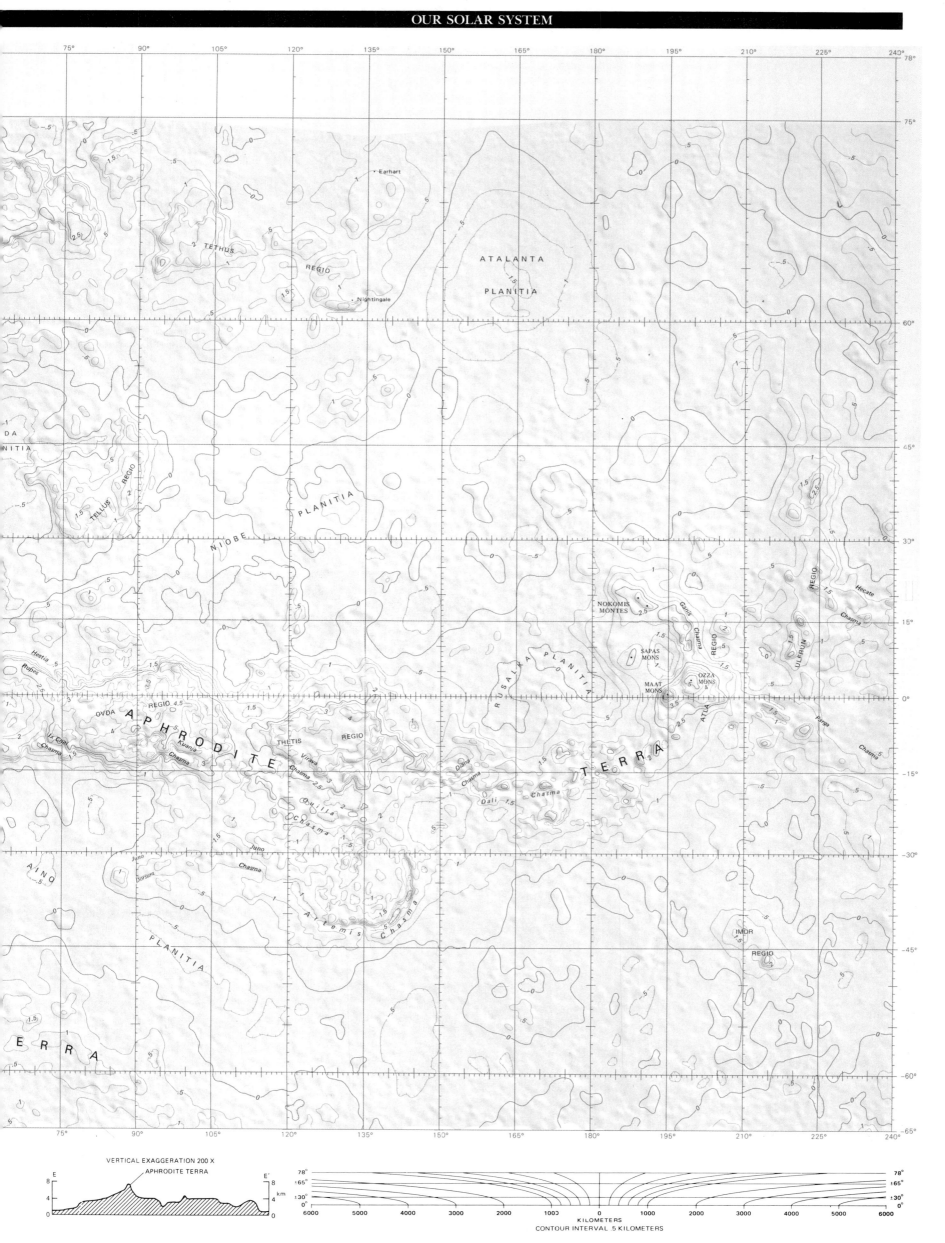

VERTICAL EXAGGERATION 200 X
APHRODITE TERRA

KILOMETERS
CONTOUR INTERVAL .5 KILOMETERS

THE EARTH

The third planet from the Sun, the Earth is the largest of the four terrestrial planets. The Earth is the only planet in the Solar System where life is known to have evolved, and because it is our home planet, we know more about its physical characteristics than we do of the other planets.

At the time the Solar System was formed 4.6 billion years ago, the Earth was probably solid throughout, but 500 million years later radioactive decay heated the Earth, and gradually metallic material melted and separated from nonmetallic silicate material and sank toward the center of the Earth just as the silicate floated up. This molten metallic material, consisting mostly of iron with some nickel, survives today as the Earth's *core*, which is approximately 4200 miles in diameter. At temperatures of approximately 11,000 degrees Fahrenheit, the core is mostly molten, although a solid inner core, perhaps 200 miles in diameter, is thought to exist at the center of the Earth. The constant motion of the molten core gives the Earth its magnetic field.

Outside the core is the layer known as the *mantle*. Composed largely of both solid and molten silicate rock, the mantle is roughly 1800 miles thick. Covering the mantle is a thin *crust*, which ranges from 25 to barely five miles thick. Occasionally, hot molten rock from the mantle forces its way through the crust in the form of lava during volcanic eruptions. So thin is the crust that it exists as a group of separate continental plates that literally float on the semi-liquid mantle, a phenomenon called *continental drift*. The edges of the continental plates are the faults and rift zones where volcanic activity and Earthquakes are most common.

The Earth's major *continents*, or land masses, are, in order of size: Eurasia (21.3 million square miles), Africa (11.7 million square miles), North America (9.4 million square miles), South America (6.9 million square miles), Antarctica (6 million square miles) and Australia (3 million square miles). Prior to the Triassic period (200 million years ago), the continents were combined in a single massive supercontinent called Pangaea. Over the next 160 million years, a continent called Gondwana (Antarctica/Australia) drifted away from Pangaea on the semi-liquid mantle, and Eurasia/Africa gradually separated from North America/South America. Since the Cenozoic period (60 million years ago), Antarctica and Australia separated and the space between Eurasia/Africa and the Americas increased. It was through continental drift that the continents came into their present position on the Earth's surface and it will be through this same process that the continents will continue to move apart.

The continents, however, are merely the uplands of the Earth's crust and together they comprise less than a third of the Earth's total surface area. Approximately 70 percent of the crust is covered by water in the form of four major oceans and a number of smaller bodies known as seas and lakes. The four major oceans are, in order of size, the Pacific (64 million square miles), the Atlantic (31.8 million square miles), the Indian (25.3 million square miles) and the Arctic (5.5 million square miles). The largest seas are the Mediterranean (1.2 million square miles) and Caribbean Sea/Gulf of Mexico (1.7 million square miles).

The Earth's oceans provide a convenient means of reckoning mean surface altitude (mean radius), which is referred to on Earth simply as *sea level*. The highest region on the continental mass of the Earth is the Tibetan plateau and the accompanying Himalaya Mountains, which are located within the Eurasian Continent. No fewer than the 47 tallest mountain peaks on Earth are located in this region. The tallest of these, Mount Everest, stands 5.5 miles above sea level. By comparison, the

Below: This composite photo from the Landsat 1 satellite taken from an altitude of 568 miles (914 kilometers) shows part of the mountainous terrain of Nepal. The high plains at the bottom of the photo give way to hills and then mountains. Mount Everest appears at the right corner. *Right:* The Earth gleams brightly against the stark backdrop of space as seen by the Apollo 16 astronauts during their Earth-Moon round trip.

Maxwell Mountains on Venus rise to 6.6 miles above mean radius, while Mount Olympus on Mars towers 15.5 miles above mean radius.

The lowest point on the Earth's surface is the Challenger Deep in the Marianas Trench of the Pacific Ocean, which is seven miles below sea level. Again, by comparison, the floor of the Diana Chasma on Venus is 1.8 miles below mean radius and the Hellas Basin is 1.9 miles below the mean radius of Mars.

Because of the effects of wind and water erosion, the meteor impact craters common to such other inner terrestrial bodies as Mercury, Mars and the Earth's own Moon are rare on the Earth. The effect of water alternately freezing and thawing also has a tendency to break up the rocks of the Earth's mountains. Consequently, the newly formed ranges on the Earth, such as the Rocky Mountains (which are between 70 and 300 million years old), tend to be higher than the more ancient ranges—such as the Appalachians, which are at least 400 million years old. The Earth's mountains were originally formed by the pressure of the continental plates moving against one another, and through volcanic action. Most of the ranges were formed by the former process, although the latter takes a relatively shorter time and is a good deal more spectacular. The sea mounts (mountains whose base is on the ocean floor, but whose top may be above sea level) of the Hawaiian Island chain are a good example of the latter and the Island of Hawaii, with its two active volcanos (Mauna Loa and Kiluea) is a good example of a sea mount that is still in the process of growing.

After the Jovian moon Io, the Earth is the second most volcanically active body in the Solar System, with Venus being the only other body where volcanic activity is thought to be occurring at this time. The most volcanically active area on Earth is the Pacific Basin, with volcanos active not only in Hawaii but also in an arc around the north Pacific rim, that stretches from Indonesia to Japan and Alaska and down the west coast of North America to the Cascades range, where the 1980 eruptions of Mount St Helens in Washington were very spectacular. Other volcanically active regions include the Italian peninsula and the North Atlantic (particularly Iceland).

Above the surface of the Earth is its atmosphere, which is comprised of several layers of gasses roughly 120 miles thick and weighing 5700 trillion tons. Composed primarily of nitrogen (78 percent) and oxygen (21 percent), the Earth's atmosphere is divided into five layers. The *troposphere* is the thickest and closest layer, covering the Earth to a depth of seven miles. Next are the *stratosphere* or *ozonosphere* (7 to 30 miles), the *mesosphere* (30 to 50 miles) and the *ionosphere* (50 to 150 miles). Roughly 80 percent of the Earth's atmospheric molecules and most atmospheric pressure are concentrated in the *troposphere*. The atmosphere becomes much thinner above the *mesosphere*, so that 120 miles altitude is generally recognized as the edge of outer space. However, some remnants of Earthly atmosphere exist above 120 miles, so that the upper *ionosphere* and the region beyond is subdivided into the *thermosphere* (60 to 400 miles) and the *exosphere* (beyond 400 miles).

The Earth's atmosphere serves to shield the planet from much of the Sun's radiation. The visible spectrum penetrates all the atmospheric layers, but infrared and radio waves are partially blocked by the *stratosphere*. Ultraviolet radiation is almost entirely blocked by a layer of ozone in the *stratosphere*, and x-rays do not penetrate the *mesosphere*.

While the composition of the Earth's atmosphere is the same at all altitudes, clouds of water vapor are concentrated only in the troposphere. Here they are subdivided into low, middle and high clouds. Low clouds are typically the billowy *cumulus*, as well as *stratus* and *nimbo stratus* types, and exist up to an altitude of roughly 2.5 miles. Middle clouds are the thinner *altostratus* and patchy *altocumulus* types, and exist between 2.5 and 4.5 miles. High clouds include the thin *cirrostratus* and *cirronimbus* types, as well as the distinctive, wispy *cirrus*.

At any given moment, half the Earth's surface is covered with clouds. This compares to 100 percent of the surface of Venus, less than 10 percent of the Martian surface, and *none* of the surface of Mercury.

The Earth's cloud cover is constantly moving in global weather patterns. The Earth's water is always being recycled through the clouds. When clouds encounter cold air masses, water falls to Earth in the form of rain (liquid), snow (crystalline solid) or occasionally as hail (solid). Once on Earth it flows into streams, and from there to rivers, and ultimately into the oceans and other large bodies of water, from which it evaporates back into the atmosphere to once again help form a cloud.

During certain seasons, cyclonic storms (typhoons in the Pacific or hurricanes in the Atlantic), characterized by high winds, can form in the Earth's cloud cover. By comparison, the cloud cover on Venus moves as

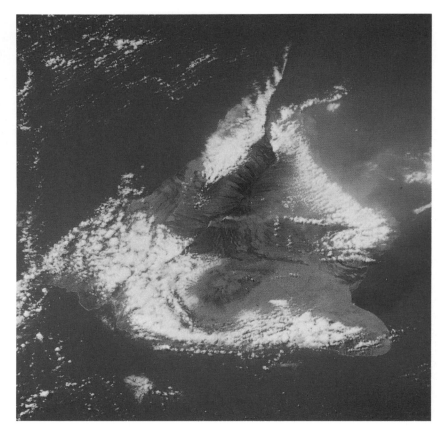

Above: **Fumes and steam rise from the river of hot lava pouring down the side of the Muana Loa volcano on the island of Hawaii. The rough surface of the mountain tells the story of past lava flows. Kilauea (lower center of photo), also active at the time of the photo, is largely under clouds. The view *below*, however, gives quite a different view of Kilauea as a fountain of flame erupts from the earth's surface.**

The San Francisco Bay Area in natural color *(right)* as photographed by Skylab 2 with a 70mm Hasselblad camera and in infrared *(left)*. The infrared 'false color' image was shot by Landsat 2 satellite from an altitude of 575 miles. Three colors—green, red and infrared—are seen and recorded separately by the satellite and combined by NASA's Goddard Space Flight Center. Healthy, dense vegetation appears as bright red; suburbs and areas of cultivation appear pink and red. Central city and industrial areas appear light to dark gray, and desert areas appear light gray to blue. Clear water is various shades of blue. The gray area clustered around the San Francisco Bay (blue in center of photo) is San Francisco, Oakland and numerous other communities. The narrow strip of red in the gray near the top of the peninsula is Golden Gate Park in San Francisco.

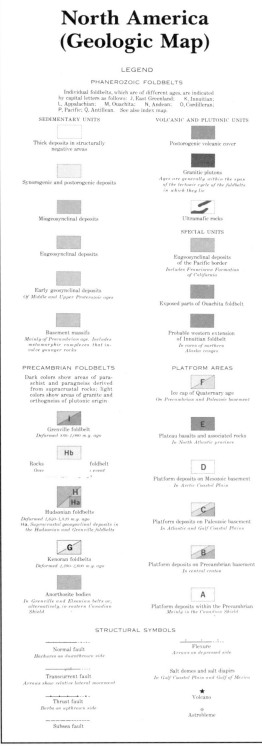

North America (Geologic Map)

LEGEND

PHANEROZOIC FOLDBELTS

Individual foldbelts, which are of different ages, are indicated
by capital letters as follows: J, East Greenland; K, Innuitian;
L, Appalachian;   M, Ouachita;   N, Andean;   O, Cordilleran;
P, Pacific; Q, Antillean.   See also index map.

SEDIMENTARY UNITS

Thick deposits in structurally
negative areas

Synorogenic and postorogenic deposits

Miogeosynclinal deposits

Eugeosynclinal deposits

Early geosynclinal deposits
Of Middle and Upper Proterozoic ages

Basement massifs
*Mainly of Precambrian age. Includes
metamorphic complexes that involve younger rocks*

PRECAMBRIAN FOLDBELTS

Dark colors show areas of para-
schist and paragneiss derived
from supracrustal rocks; light
colors show areas of granite and
orthogneiss of plutonic origin

I

Grenville foldbelt
Deformed 880–1,000 m.y. ago

Hb

Rocks   foldbelt
Over   event

H
Ha

Hudsonian foldbelts
Deformed 1,640–1,820 m.y. ago
*Ha, Supracrustal geosynclinal deposits in
the Hudsonian and Grenville foldbelts*

G

Kenoran foldbelts
Deformed 2,390–2,600 m.y. ago

Anorthosite bodies
*In Grenville and Elsonian belts or,
alternatively, in eastern Canadian
Shield*

VOLCANIC AND PLUTONIC UNITS

Postorogenic volcanic cover

Granitic plutons
*Ages are generally within the span
of the tectonic cycle of the foldbelts
in which they lie*

Ultramafic rocks

SPECIAL UNITS

Eugeosynclinal deposits
of the Pacific border
*Includes Franciscan Formation
of California*

Exposed parts of Ouachita foldbelt

Probable western extension
of Innuitian foldbelt
*In cores of northern
Alaska ranges*

PLATFORM AREAS

F

Ice cap of Quaternary age
On Precambrian and Paleozoic basement

E

Plateau basalts and associated rocks
In North Atlantic province

D

Platform deposits on Mesozoic basement
In Arctic Coastal Plain

C

Platform deposits on Paleozoic basement
In Atlantic and Gulf Coastal Plains

B

Platform deposits on Precambrian basement
In central craton

A

Platform deposits within the Precambrian
Mainly in the Canadian Shield

STRUCTURAL SYMBOLS

Normal fault
Hachures on downthrown side

Transcurrent fault
Arrows show relative lateral movement

Thrust fault
Barbs on upthrown side

Subsea fault

Flexure
Arrows on depressed side

Salt domes and salt diapirs
In Gulf Coastal Plain and Gulf of Mexico

Volcano

Astrobleme

The mountains of North America, formed when the continental plates collided, have been further shaped by eons
of wind and water erosion. The Rockies in Glacier
National Park *(above)* are an example of postorogenic
volcanic cover as indicated in orange on the map *at right*.
Water, as harsh waves and rain, also played a part in
shaping the Oregon coast *(below)*, an example of the
eugeosynclinal deposits of the eastern Pacific rim.

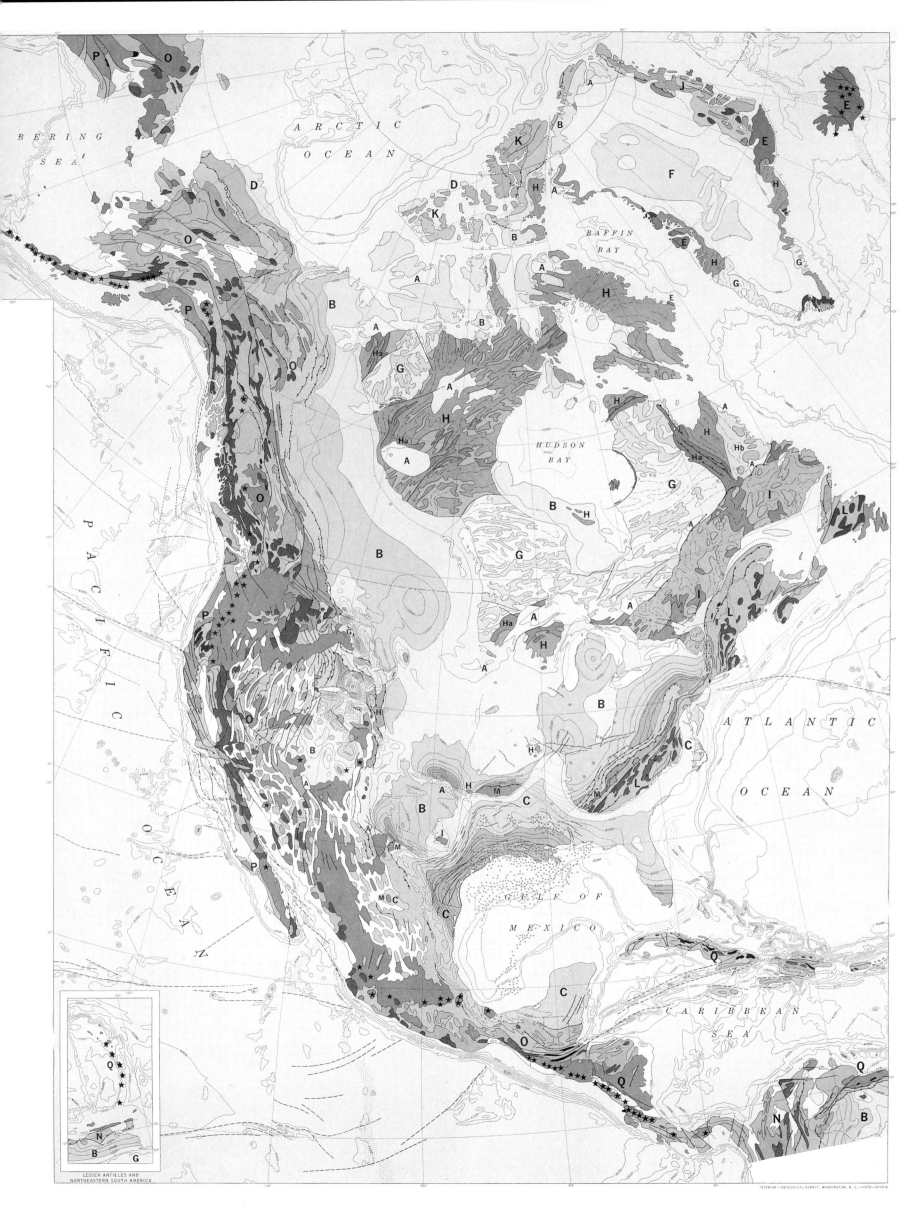

LESSER ANTILLES AND
NORTHEASTERN SOUTH AMERICA

INTERIOR—GEOLOGICAL SURVEY, WASHINGTON, D.C.—1972—G7-2516

a single, unified mass with its constant Y feature, while the cloud cover on Jupiter is characterized by numerous cyclonic storms. While such storms on Earth have a lifespan of a few days, however, those on Jupiter can last for dozens or even hundreds of years.

The Earth's atmosphere acts as a modulator of temperatures. Had the Earth been slightly warmer, it would have suffered the same sort of greenhouse effect that befell Venus and would today also have a carbon dioxide atmosphere.

The Earth's 23.4 degree inclination of its axis produces the *seasonal* effect, wherein the northern and southern hemispheres are alternately closest to the Sun. Only twice each Earth year, on the *vernal* and *autumnal* equinoxes, will the Sun shine directly on the Earth's equator. In the northern hemisphere, for example, the inclination toward the Sun increases from the *vernal equinox* (21 March) until the *summer solstice* (21 June). At the summer solstice, the northern hemisphere is oriented so that it receives the most sunlight of the year, while the southern hemisphere receives the least. From the summer solstice until the *autumnal equinox* (23 September), the amount of sunlight gradually decreases in the northern hemisphere and increases in the southern, as the Sun is perceived to cross the equator. On the autumnal equinox the Sun 'crosses' the equator and the trend continues until the *winter solstice* (21 December), when the most sunlight reaches the southern hemisphere and the least sunlight reaches the northern hemisphere. After the winter solstice, the Sun's warmth once again moves north toward the equator, and the northern hemisphere and the seasonal cycle goes around again and again. The Sun is directly overhead only at the equinoxes. This regular annual pattern determines the *climate* of all the regions of the Earth.

Changes in the axial inclination, which varies by as much as 2.5 degrees in 100,000 years, can produce such dramatic changes in climate as the Ice Age, which covered 25 percent of the Earth's land area with ice until 15,000 years ago.

Throughout the Earth's annual seasonal cycle, its equator receives more sunlight than any other part of the planet, while the poles receive the least. For this reason, the Earth's poles have permanent ice caps which recede slightly with their respective warmer seasons, but which are always present. In the south polar region there is the ice covered continent Antarctica, while in the north polar region there is the ice covered Arctic Ocean. The Antarctic ice cap contains an average of 6.3 million cubic miles of frozen water, while the Arctic ice cap and associated North American and Eurasian glaciers (including Greenland) contain 680,000 cubic miles of water.

The inclination of the Earth to its axis and the resulting seasonal effect produce annual changes in temperature and pressure. These, in turn, control the Earth's global weather pattern and the movement of the clouds. The mountains on the Earth's continents can, in turn, affect weather by triggering precipitation on their windward side.

The complex interrelationship of axial inclination, chemical composition and geographical composition that is unique to the Earth probably played an important role in the development of the phenomena of life.

At any given time, about half of the Earth's surface is covered with clouds, which can take the form of wispy cirrus hanging high in a peaceful summer sky—or a typhoon *(below)* brewing in the Pacific, 1200 miles north of Hawaii; thunderclouds over the Amazon Basin in Brazil *(right)*, or a thunderhead with lightning *(far right)*.

EARTH
Diameter: 7926 miles (12,756 km)
Distance from Sun: 94,240,000 miles (152,000,000 km) at aphelion
                91,140,000 miles (147,000,000 km) at perihelion
Mass: 2.7155×10^{24} lb (5.9742×10^{24} kg)
Rotational period (Earth, or sidereal, day): 23.93 Earth hours
                               23 hrs, 56 min
Sidereal period (Earth year): 365.2 Earth days
Eccentricity: 0.017
Inclination of rotational axis: 23.45°
Inclination to ecliptic plane (Earth = 0): 0°
Albedo (100% reflection of light = 1): .39
Mean surface temperature: 60.53° F
Maximum surface temperature: el Azizia, Libya 136.4° F
                                  Death Valley, CA USA 134° F
Minimum surface temperature: Vostok, Anarctica −126.9° F
Highest point on surface: Mt Everest
                           29,028 ft
Largest surface feature: Pacific Ocean
                        64,186,000 sq mi (166,883,600 sq km)
Major atmospheric components: Nitrogen (76.08%)
                                      Oxygen (20.95%)
                                      Argon (.934%)
                                      Carbon dioxide (.031%)
                                      Water (up to 1%)
Other atmospheric components: Neon
                                 Helium
                                 Methane
                                 Krypton
                                 Hydrogen
                                 Nitrous oxide
                                 Carbon monoxide
                                 Xenon
                                 Ozone
Atmospheric depth: 120 miles

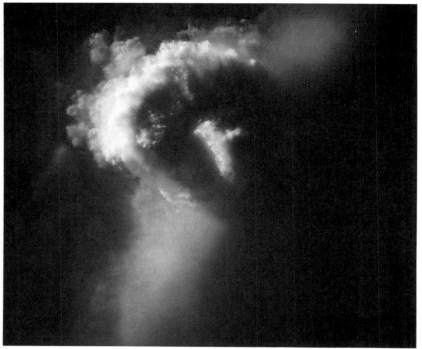

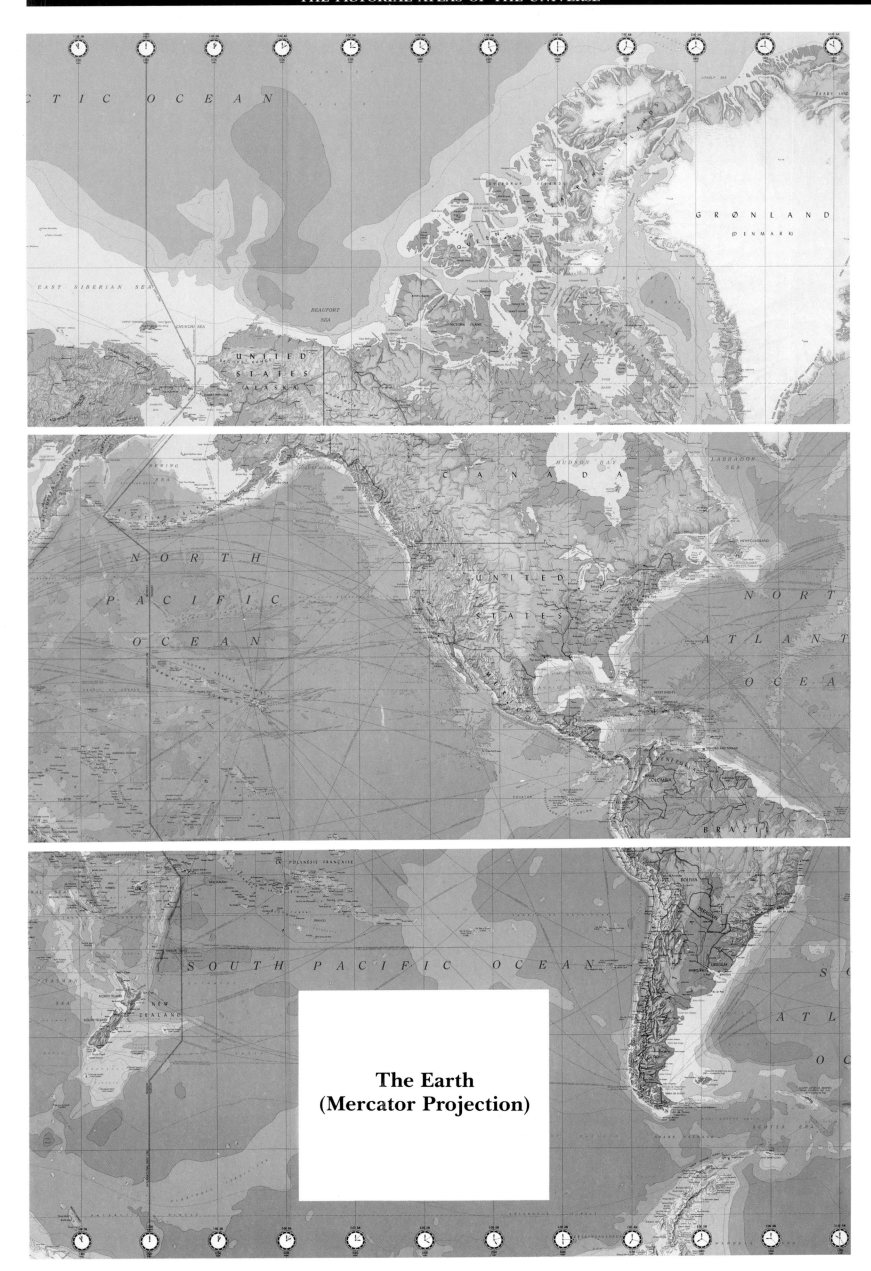

**The Earth
(Mercator Projection)**

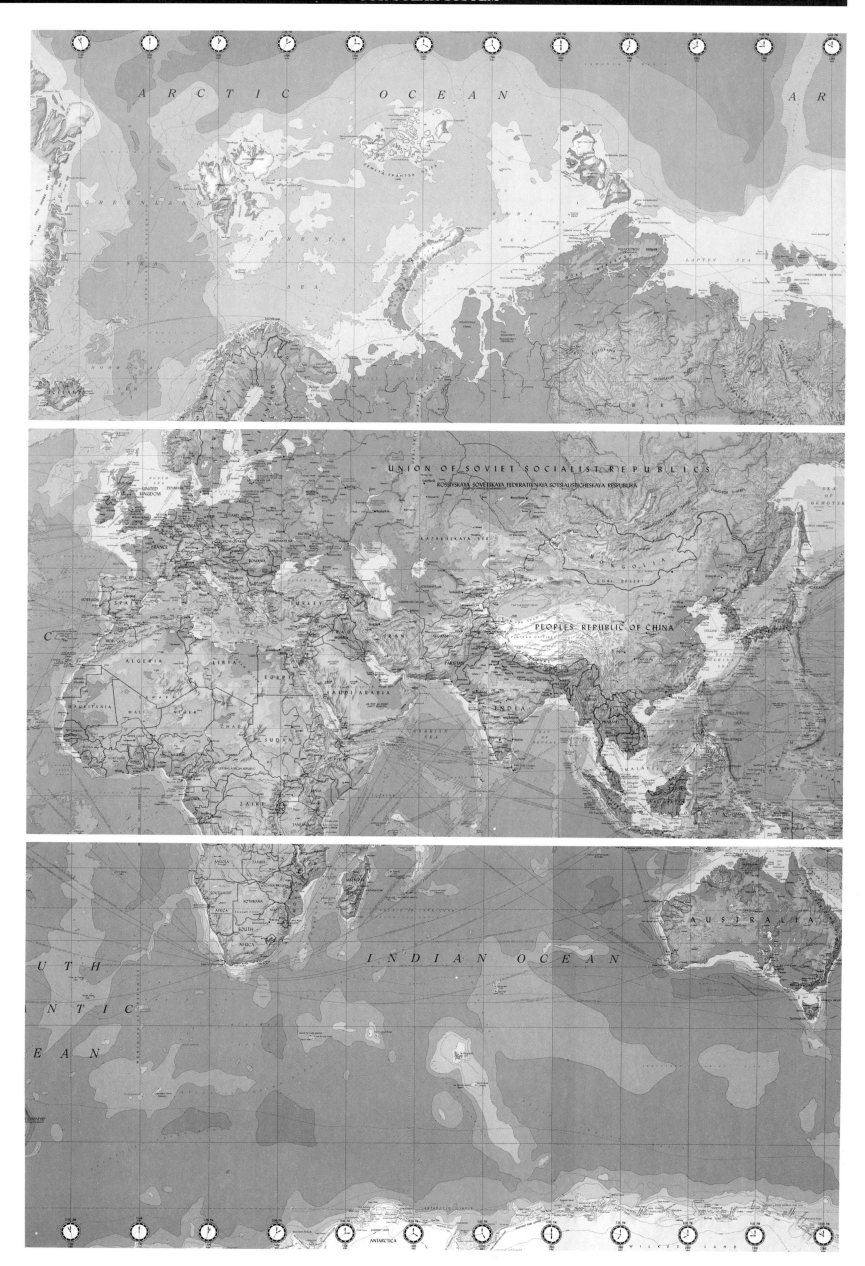

THE EARTH'S MOON

Though it is simply called 'the Moon,' the Earth's single satellite is mythologically associated with Luna (or Diana), the Roman goddess of the hunt, who was also their goddess of the Moon. The sixth largest moon in the Solar System, the Moon is closer in size to its mother planet than any other except Pluto's moon Charon. For this reason the Earth and the Moon (like Pluto and Charon as well) are occasionally described as being a *double planet*. While the larger planets have on the order of a thousand times the mass of their moons, the Earth has 81 times the mass of the Moon and four times the diameter.

Though it is the second brightest object in the sky, all of the Moon's light is reflected from the Sun. Some tiny portion of the Moon's light could be called *Earthshine*, as noticed during a crescent phase when the 'dark' part of the Moon is slightly illuminated. It is light from the Sun reflected by the Earth to the Moon, which, in turn, reflects it back to

Below: A stunning shot of a full moon taken during the flight of Apollo 17, the last manned lunar flight. A third of the photo provides a rare glimpse at the far side of the moon. *Facing page:* The Apollo 12 Lunar Module *Intrepid* heads for its landing site in the Ocean of Storms. The large crater on the right side of the photo is Hershel.

Earth. As perceived from Earth, the Moon appears to go through a series of phases depending upon its reflection of light from the Sun. These phases, which constitute the Lunar 'day,' go through a complete cycle every 29 days, 12 hours and 44 minutes. The cycle is also known as the *synodic*, or *Lunar month*, as seen on Earth.

When the Moon is fully illuminated it is said to be 'full.' As the visible face of the Moon rotates away from the Sun it is said to be 'waning.' When exactly half the *face* of the Moon is illuminated, it is called a 'quarter Moon.' As it becomes less visible it is said to become a 'crescent Moon,' and when it becomes dark and the cycle is resumed, the Moon is said to be a 'new Moon.' From 'new,' the Moon waxes through the crescent phase to the quarter phase, and once again to full. The Sun always illuminates one-half the Moon. Depending upon the relative angle between the Earth and Moon, we see portions of the sunlit side. At full Moon we see the entire sunlit side, and at new Moon none of the the sunlit side is facing the Earth.

The Moon's period of rotation is 27 days, 7 hours and 43 minutes— exactly the same as the period of its revolution around the Earth, so the same side always faces the Earth. Because of the Moon's slight wobbling, we are able to see slightly more than half of its surface from

the Earth. The Moon's mysterious far side had been a mystery to mankind for centuries, and it was not until the Soviet Luna 3 spacecraft returned photographic images of the 'dark side of the Moon' in October 1959 that actual detailed information of the Moon's 'other half' was revealed to mankind. Though the 41 percent of the Lunar surface that is never visible from the Earth is frequently referred to as the 'dark side,' it actually receives as much light from the Sun as the near side.

The Moon's surface is characterized by rugged mountain ranges and by thousands of meteorite impact craters. In this sense it is very much like the planet Mercury. Unlike Mercury, however, the Moon has large open areas that are called seas (or in Latin, *maria*) because to the eye they appear darker than the surrounding terrain, and were once thought by Galileo to resemble seas. Almost entirely concentrated on the side facing the Earth, the maria cover 15 percent of the Lunar surface, and were probably once 'seas' of molten rock that flowed out of the Moon's interior. The gravitational effect of the Earth probably has a

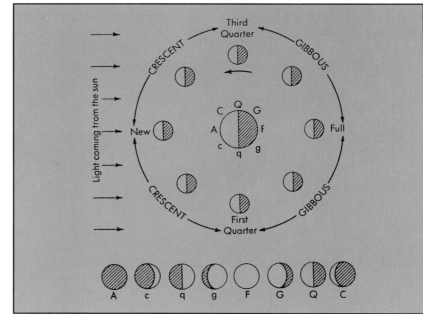

Right: **The Phases of the Moon. The circles at the bottom of the diagram (A, c, q, etc) show how the moon appears when viewed from a corresponding position (A, c, q, etc) on Earth (represented by the central circle). The shaded part of a circle represents the dark part of the moon.**

great deal to do with the fact that such features are concentrated on the Earthward side.

Unlike the Earth, the Moon has neither magnetic poles nor a significant magnetic field, although rocks in the Lunar crust are weakly magnetized. Probably due to its low mass and density, the Moon never developed an atmosphere, although trace amounts of hydrogen and helium, as well as hints of argon and neon were detected as escaping from the Lunar surface in 1972 by the Apollo 17 crew.

The Apollo program studies revealed that the Lunar interior was quite active, with moonquakes being more common on the Moon than earthquakes are on the Earth, although they have not been recorded in excess of two on the Richter scale.

The Moon formed about the same time as the Earth—4.6 billion years ago—and is composed of the same basic materials, but their early relationship is unclear. One line of thought theorizes that the Moon was formed out of the Earth, either in a single piece that broke loose (perhaps from the Pacific Basin) or in the form of debris that was knocked loose in a collision with an asteroid, and which eventually congealed into the Lunar mass. Another theory holds that the Moon was a separate planet 'captured' by the Earth's gravitational field. A third notion has it that the Earth and Moon were formed in the same way and in the same place and time. Because the Earth was 81 times larger, the Moon became enslaved to its gravity.

Once in place, the Moon's geology evolved much like that of the Earth. Originally molten, the crust gradually cooled, leaving a molten core like that of the Earth. In the meantime, it was being bombarded by debris from the formation of the Solar System. In addition to smaller craters, huge basins were hammered into the surfaces of both bodies. Some of the first basins to be formed in the Moon were Mare Fecunditatus and Mare Tranquilium; they probably formed 4.4 billion years ago. The last basins to be formed were the Mare Imbrium and Mare Orientale. Dating from 3.85 billion years ago, Mare Imbrium is the largest of the Lunar Seas, and its origin concludes the *Pre-Imbrian* Period of Lunar geologic evolution.

When the *Imbrian* Period began 3.85 billion years ago, the Lunar surface was probably pocked entirely and uniformly with impact craters. The semicircular mountain ranges found around the periphery of the maria are the only remnants of the enormous impacts that created them. During this period, however, intense interior heating resulted in vast flows of darker basalt from deep within the Moon. Part of the heating came from meteor impacts, and part from radioactive decay. These flows filled the huge basins, and the Lunar Seas briefly were seas—of lava!

When the Moon cooled, and the lava flows ended 3.3 billion years ago, small scale volcanic activity continued for approximately 1.3 million years through what is called the *Ratosthenian* Period. During this period, interplanetary debris crashed into the Moon, creating newer, smaller impact craters on the Lunar Seas themselves. One of the major craters now visible on the surface, Copernicus, was probably formed one billion years ago, marking the climax of the third period of Lunar geology. Since the formation of Copernicus there has been very little geologic activity on the Moon. This fourth period, the present *Copernican* Period, has also been marked by very little in the way of impact crater formation, although the crater Tycho is thought to have been formed as recently as one million years ago, and the formation of the great crater Giordano Bruno is believed to have been witnessed from Earth in 1178 AD. In July 1972, a 2200 pound meteorite was recorded as having struck the Moon. Throughout the billion years of the *Copernican* Period the Moon's surface has remained relatively unchanged because there is no air, no wind and no water to cause erosion of the type that has greatly altered the surfaces of such bodies as the Earth and Mars.

Being the first person to study the Lunar surface with a telescope, the great Italian astronomer Galileo Galilei (1564-1642) was the first to publish a systematic Lunar Map (in 1610). In 1651 the Jesuit astronomer Father Joannes Riccioli (1598-1671) published a map of the Moon that is important because the names he assigned to Lunar features on this map are used by astronomers to this day. In the nineteenth century photography came into play as a tool of Lunar cartography, and in 1935 the International Astronomical Union published the definitive map of the Lunar near side. Early spacecraft confirmed the Earth-based observations, and in 1959 the Soviet Luna 3 added the far side to what was known about Lunar geography.

The next major step in Lunar mapping came with the American Lunar Orbiter project. Between August 1966 and August 1967, five Lunar Orbiter spacecraft conducted high-resolution photography of 99 percent of the Lunar near side and 80 percent of the Lunar far side. Between June 1966 and February 1968, a series of five (out of seven launched) American Surveyor spacecraft were successfully landed on the Lunar surface to conduct remote sampling of Lunar surface material. The Lunar Orbiter and Surveyor projects increased our knowledge of the Moon far beyond what had been known before, but they were soon to be overshadowed by the project for which they had been designed to pave the way.

In 1968 the United States began the Apollo project, a series of space flights during which the Moon became the first body in the Solar System beyond Earth to be explored firsthand by human beings.

The Moon was surveyed by human beings from Lunar orbit for the first time by means of two circumlunar manned flights in December 1968 and May 1969, which began the operational phase of the Apollo program. In July 1969 the Apollo 11 spacecraft became the first vehicle to land human beings on the moon. The initial landing was followed by six others between November 1969 and December 1972. (A seventh mission was aborted because of hardware failure in April 1970.)

During the Apollo program, 12 American astronauts conducted detailed surveys of the Lunar surface and seismic studies of the Lunar interior. The Apollo program completed detailed mapping of the Moon and provided a wealth of information about its composition and its geologic history.

EARTH'S MOON
Diameter: 2159.89 miles (3476 km)
Distance from Earth: 252,698 miles (406,676 km)
Mass: 3.34×10^{22} lb (7.34×10^{22} kg)
Rotational period (Lunar day): 27.32 Earth days
Sidereal period (Lunar year): 27.32 Earth days
Inclination of rotational axis: 1.53°
Inclination to ecliptic plane (Earth=0): 4° 58' to 5° 9'
Mean surface temperature: 0° F
Maximum surface temperature: 279° F
Minimum surface temperature: −273.2° F
Highest point on surface: The rim of the crater Newton
Largest surface feature: Mare Imbrium
384,400 sq mi (1,000,000 sq km)
Major atmospheric components: Traces of Hydrogen

Below: An Apollo 10 westward view across Landing Site 3 in the Central Bay. The prominent crater Bruce near the bottom of this photo is 3.7 miles (roughly 6 km) wide.
Below right: A photomicrograph of a thin section of an Apollo 12 lunar rock sample, a fine- to medium-grained heledrystalline basalt.

The Earth's Moon (Geologic Map)

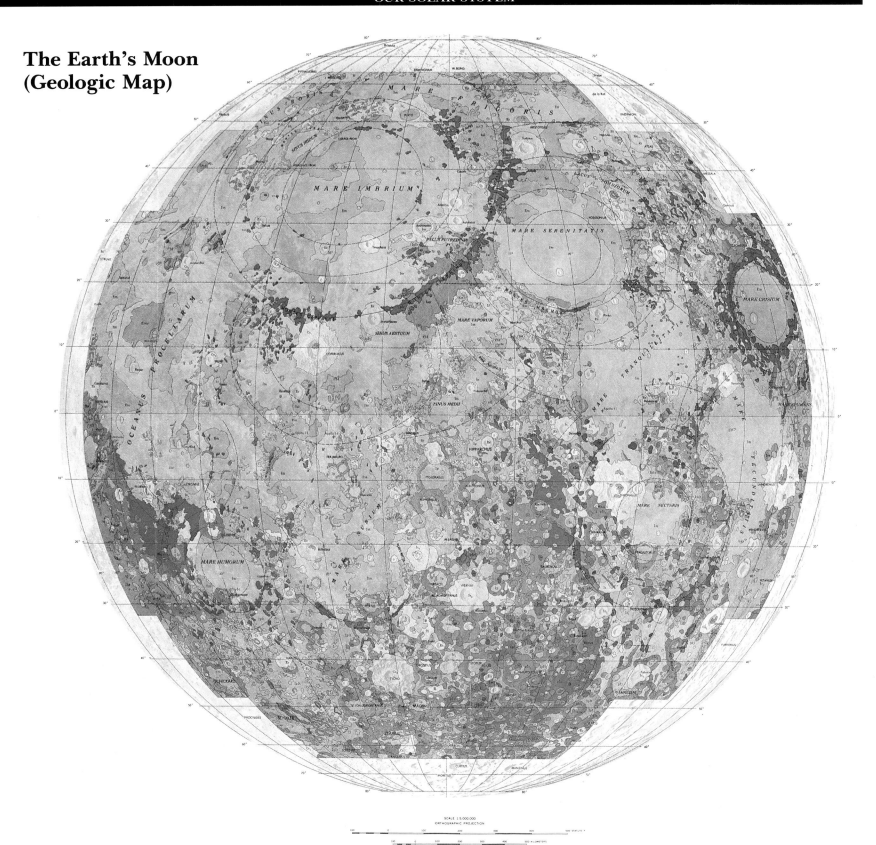

SCALE 1:5,000,000
ORTHOGRAPHIC PROJECTION

SCALE AT CENTER OF MAP

DESCRIPTION OF MAP UNITS

CRATER MATERIALS
(Only craters 20 km or more in diameter are mapped)

Cc

Ec — MATERIAL OF VERY SHARP-RIMMED RAYED CRATERS

Ic₂ — MATERIAL OF SHARP-RIMMED CRATERS

Ic₁ — MATERIAL OF SINGLE CRATERS—Orientale basin age or younger

Ifc — MATERIAL OF SINGLE CRATERS—Older than Orientale basin and younger than Imbrium basin

Ica — MATERIAL OF IMBRIAN CRATERS, UNDIVIDED

Icc — MATERIAL OF ELONGATE CLUSTERS OF CRATERS APPROXIMATELY RADIAL TO ORIENTALE BASIN—*Interpretation:* secondary craters of the Orientale basin

Ifc — MATERIAL OF ELONGATE AND IRREGULAR CLUSTERS OF CRATERS—Some not obviously related to any particular Imbrian basin or crater, others secondary craters of adjacent Imbrian crater to which they are approximately radial

Nc — FURROWED, RAISED CRATER FLOOR OR FILL MATERIAL—Most are convex upward. Texture equally sharp in Nectarian and Imbrian craters. *Interpretation:* Postimpact filling, probably lava

Ncc — MATERIAL OF SUBDUED CRATERS—Older than Imbrium basin and younger than Nectaris basin

pNc — MATERIAL OF ELONGATE CLUSTERS OF SUBDUED CRATERS—Craters approximately the same size. *Interpretation:* secondary craters of the Nectarian basin to which they are adjacent and (or) approximately radial

MATERIAL OF SUBDUED TO VERY SUBDUED CRATERS—Older than Nectaris basin

BASIN MATERIALS

Nb — (Multiringed circular structures 300 km or more in diameter as measured across most prominent ring)

Nbl — MATERIAL OF RAISED RIMS AND SLUMPED WALLS OF BASINS—Primarily the outermost ring. *Interpretation:* disrupted bedrock largely covered by ejecta

NpNbm — LINEATED MATERIAL SURROUNDING BASINS—Linear elements approximately radial to basin; locally only weakly developed. *Interpretation:* basin ejecta deposited ballistically and as massive flows

NpNbr — MATERIAL OF NECTARIAN BASIN MASSIFS—Massive mountain blocks, mainly form part of outermost basin rings; inner ring in Korolev. *Interpretation:* uplifted and structurally complex blocks of prebasin bedrock; may be covered by basin ejecta

pNb — MATERIAL OF RUGGED MOUNTAINS AND MOUNTAIN SEGMENTS OF NECTARIAN BASINS—Smaller than massifs (unit NpNbm); mainly form inner rings. *Interpretation:* uplifted and complexly faulted prebasin bedrock; may be covered by basin ejecta

PRE-NECTARIAN BASIN MATERIAL, UNDIVIDED—Subdued, eroded mountain rings and arcuate segments of rings

pNbm — MATERIAL OF PRE-NECTARIAN BASIN MASSIFS—Relatively massive single mountain blocks or part of continuous ring. *Interpretation:* same as unit NpNbm

pNbr — RUGGED MATERIALS OF PRE-NECTARIAN BASINS—Discontinuous blocky mountains forming arcuate ring segments; smaller than massifs (unit NpNbm). *Interpretation:* same as unit NpNbr

OTHER MATERIALS

Im — MARE MATERIALS OF DARK PLAINS—*Interpretation:* basaltic lavas, by analogy with returned Apollo samples. STIPPLED PATTERN: light streaks and swirls in Mare Ingenii. *Interpretation:* Surficial markings of uncertain origin, probably not related to underlying mare rocks

Ip — MATERIAL OF GROOVES AND MOUNDS—Covers craters and other terrae of pre-Nectarian through Imbrian age. Craters have mainly radial grooves on rim and walls; some mounds. Level terra has mounds and grooves. Particularly well developed around Mare Ingenii and crater Van de Graaff. *Interpretation:* origin uncertain; general area antipodal to Imbrium basin; therefore could be depositional site of Imbrium ejecta that traveled around the Moon, or mass-wasting caused by Imbrium seismic shaking; alternatively, may be some unidentified local phenomenon unique to this area

INp — SMOOTH LIGHT PLAINS—Generally higher density of craters than on maria. *Interpretation:* may be related to formation of an Imbrian basin

Np — LIGHT PLAINS—Higher density of craters than unit Ip. *Interpretation:* may be related to various Imbrian and/or Nectarian basins

It — HIGHLY CRATERED LIGHT PLAINS—*Interpretation:* may be related to Nectarian basins

Nt — RELATIVELY FRESH-APPEARING, IRREGULAR TERRA—Low relief; low density of superposed craters. *Interpretation:* probably a complex mixture of local erosional debris and crater and basin ejecta

NpNt — ROLLING TERRA—Moderately high density of craters, particularly craters of diameter less than 20 km. *Interpretation:* same as unit It

pNt — IRREGULAR TERRA—Covers large areas and has high density of craters larger than 20 km wide. *Interpretation:* same as unit It

CRATERED TERRA—High density of arcuate low hills or crater segments, and pre-Nectarian craters. *Interpretation:* same as unit It except contains erosional remnants of pre-Nectarian craters

67

The Earth's Moon (North and South Polar Projections, Mercator Projection)

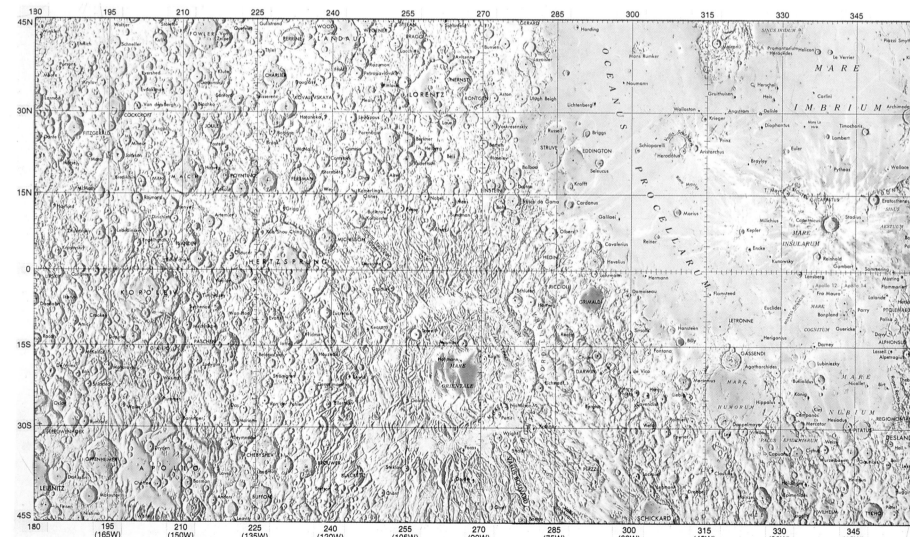

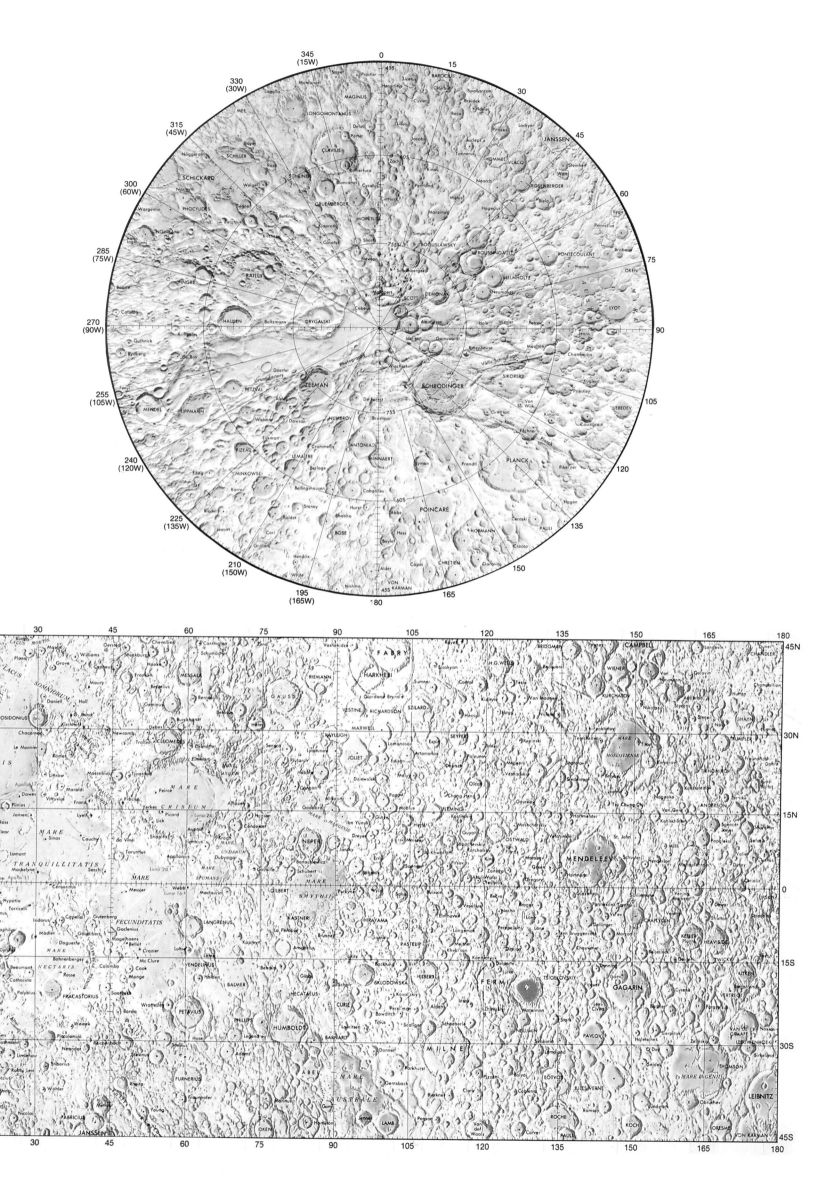

MARS

Known as 'The Red Planet' because of its distinctive iron oxide coloration, Mars reminded early observers of a distant bloody battlefield; therefore the Romans named it Mars after their god of war. Because of its perceived similarity to Earth, Mars has interested and intrigued Earthbound observers for centuries, and that is certainly still the case in the twentieth century.

Venus may be the Earth's near twin in terms of size, but Mars has more specific characteristics in common with the Earth than does any other planet. The Martian year lasts 23 Earth months, but the Martian day is only 41 minutes longer than the Earth day, and its inclination of 24 degrees of its rotational axis is very close to the Earth's 23.4 degrees. As a result, Mars has four seasons that parallel those that we experience on Earth. The Martian summer is relatively warmer than its winter, which is characterized in the temperate zones by occasional light snow or frost. Mars is the only planet in the Solar System besides the Earth that has polar ice caps, and these can be seen to expand and recede seasonally like those on Earth. The south polar cap is composed of water ice and carbon dioxide ice (dry ice). The north polar cap is composed only of water ice with merely a residual carbon dioxide snow cover that evaporates in summer.

Mars is a good deal smaller and less dense than Earth. Because of this, Mars has less gravity and a much thinner atmosphere than Earth. It is also colder than the Earth, with temperatures in the polar regions rarely rising above the −200 degrees Fahrenheit level. The midsummer temperature near the Martian equator can, however, reach a comfortable 80 degrees Fahrenheit, closer to an Earthly temperature range than can be found anywhere else in the Solar System.

The characteristic rust-red Martian surface is indicative of the global high concentration of iron oxide in its soil and rocks. The surface of Mars is covered by the types of volcanic and impact craters that are found on Mercury or on the Earth's moon, but there are also vast lightly cratered plains (or *planitia*), particularly in the northern hemisphere. While there are no currently active volcanos on Mars, those dormant volcanos which do exist are the tallest volcanos yet discovered in the Solar System.

The dormant shield-type volcano, Olympus Mons (Mount Olympus), is the tallest mountain on Mars, soaring 15.5 miles above the mean radius, or standard elevation, of the Martian surface. Mount Olympus stands ten miles higher than the Earth's Mount Everest and encompasses more than 50 times the volume of Hawaii's Mauna Loa, the largest shield volcano on Earth. Southeast of Mount Olympus, across the plain of the Martian Tharsis Region, stands a neat row of three other large and important shield volcanic mountains—Arsia, Pavonis and Ascraeus. Ancient lava flows from the Martian volcanos helped to create Mars' vast open plains.

Another feature common to other bodies in the inner Solar System are fault rifts and seismic fracture zones. One such large fracture is Valles Marineris (Mariner Valley), a huge canyon stretching east by southeast from the Tharsis Region across the Martian equator. More than 3000 miles in length, Valles Marineris is the largest single surface feature on the planet. More than four times deeper than the Grand Canyon on Earth, it is a network of roughly parallel rift canyons with an overall width of up to 400 miles and a main canyon 125 miles wide at its widest.

In addition to craters and rift canyons, the Martian surface is marked by vast networks of dry riverbeds, huge channels cut by former streams of running water. These features defy explanation on a planet whose water is frozen in polar ice caps or trapped deep below the surface in subterranean permafrost. There is no liquid water visible at any place on the surface of the red planet, nor is Mars' atmospheric pressure high enough to permit it to exist. Yet the riverbeds bear silent witness to the fact that a great deal of water may have once flowed there. The channels can be divided into three categories: run-off channels with networks of tributaries; outflow channels that flowed from underground sources; and wide, flat-floored fretted channels or flood plains. While there is no clue as to where the water disappeared, the evidence suggests large scale and widespread flooding. While some riverbeds cut across craters, there are other craters superimposed upon them, thus indicating that the flooding took place over a long period of time.

Beneath the Martian surface is a rigid crust 31 miles thick which probably contains water ice permafrost. The Martian mantle, composed of basalt rock, is roughly 125 miles thick. Beneath the mantle is a partially-molten transition zone leading to a formerly molten core that is between 800 and 1300 miles in diameter.

Like that of Venus, the Martian atmosphere is almost entirely composed of carbon dioxide, with traces of nitrogen, argon and oxygen also present. The atmosphere is divided into three layers, which are (from the densest and closest): the *troposphere*, which rises to an altitude of 22 miles; the *stratosphere* (22 to 80 miles), and *thermosphere* (80 to 140 miles). The *exosphere* accounts for the residual martian atmospheric gases that exist above an altitude of 140 miles altitude. Unlike the Earth's atmosphere, which generally circulates laterally with little interaction between the weather patterns of the northern and southern hemispheres, the Martian atmosphere has distinct north-south weather patterns that cross the equator. Circulating in what is called a Hadley cell (after its discoverer) warm Martian air rises in the hemisphere experiencing summer and moves to the opposite hemisphere at high altitude, where it sinks and returns to the original hemisphere at low altitude. The Earth has Hadley cells too, but they don't cross the equator.

Mars has much less cloud cover than the Earth's roughly 50 percent coverage, but the cloud types are similar. These include cirrus and gravity wave clouds, as well as cyclonic storms that on Earth would be referred to as hurricanes or typhoons. Low lying areas, such as deep valleys or canyons, develop ground fog as a result of frost being vaporized by the early morning Sun, a phenomenon not uncommon on the Earth.

While most of the Martian cloud cover is composed of water vapor (like the clouds of the Earth's atmosphere), carbon dioxide clouds exist at high altitudes and in the polar regions during the winter. Such clouds may result in precipitation in the form of dry ice snowstorms that play a role in replenishing the polar ice caps. The ice caps are also replenished by carbon dioxide condensation. While the carbon dioxide that is present in the ice caps as dry ice vaporizes and circulates within the Martian atmosphere, polar temperatures are such that most of the water ice present in the Martian ice caps remains frozen continuously, even in summer.

Winds that are raised as a result of atmospheric circulation and seasonal or daily temperature fluctuation can result in huge dust storms in the Martian atmosphere. In 1977, for example, 35 major dust storms were recorded, and two of these developed into global storms.

In 1659 the Dutch astronomer Christiaan Huygens (1629-1695), who was the first to identify a Martian surface feature (Syrtis Major), also calculated the Martian day to be almost the same as the Earth's, which it is. Seven years later the Italian astronomer Giovanni Domenico Cassini (1625-1712) discovered the Martian ice caps. By 1783 William Herschel (1738-1822) had correctly calculated the exact length of the Martian day and the exact inclination of Mars' axis of rotation to the plane of its orbit.

By the middle of the nineteenth century the picture painted of Mars was that of a hospitable place that 'certainly' supported life in some form, probably similar to that of Earth. After all, their days were the same length and their seasons were parallel to ours. The darker areas on

Below: **This computer enhanced photo was taken by Viking 2 Orbiter in August of 1976. Visible features are, from left to right, the large, frosty crater basin called Argyre; the great rift canyon, Valles Marineris; and ice cloud plumes on the western flank of Ascreaus Mons, one of the giant Martian volcanoes.**

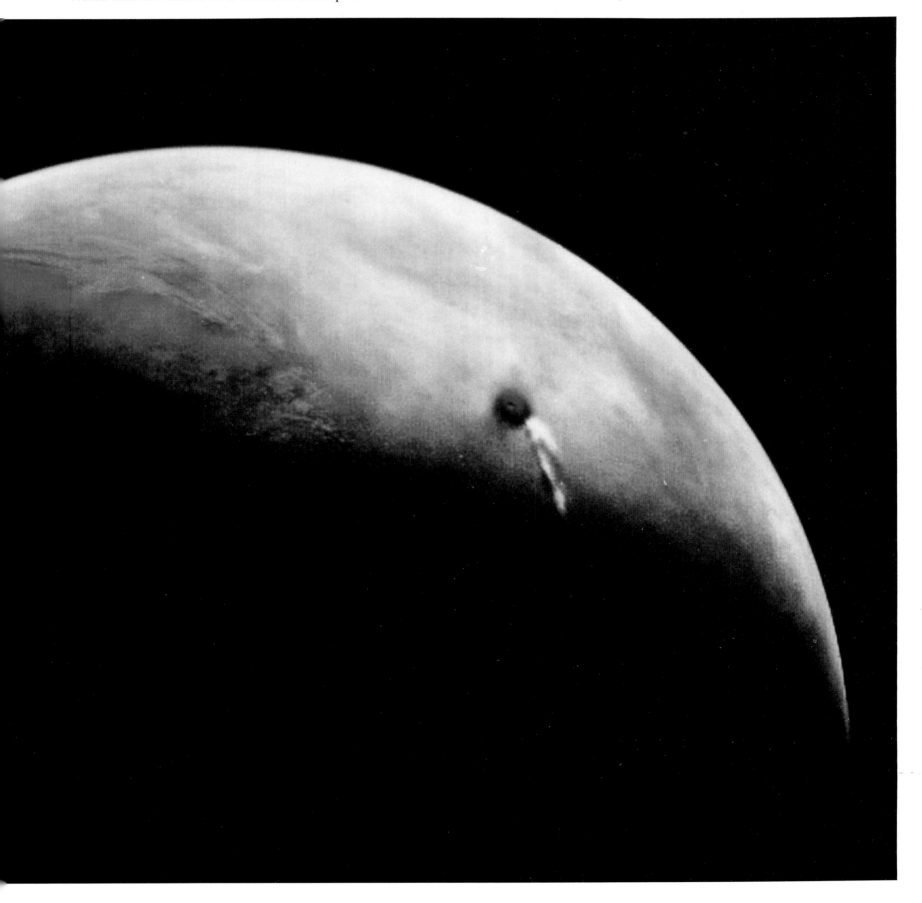

Mars were thought to represent 'vegetation,' and some observers recorded that this 'vegetation' waxed and waned with the Martian seasons.

In 1877 the Italian astronomer Giovanni Schiaparelli (1835-1910) made a startling discovery. There were channels, or *canali*, on the surface of Mars! Translated into English as 'canals,' the features were quickly ascribed to artificial origin. It was thought that intelligent creatures had constructed an intricate system of irrigation canals on Mars to bring water from the polar ice caps to the warmer equatorial region.

In 1894 the American astronomer Percival Lowell (1855-1916) opened his observatory at Flagstaff, Arizona primarily for the purpose of studying Mars. Lowell carefully observed and mapped the Martian surface and became a leading exponent of the idea that the canals were constructed by living creatures to irrigate their crops.

In the 1930s Eugenios Antoniadi, a Greek-born astronomer working in France, produced a map of Mars which was quite accurate for its day, but one which rejected the earlier notion of artificially constructed canals. By the late twentieth century the canal theory had been thoroughly discredited as having been an optical illusion, but the idea of Martian vegetation survived until spacecraft visited the red planet.

The first spacecraft to pass near Mars was the American Mariner 4 in 1965, and it was followed by Mariner 6 and Mariner 7, four years later. The data returned by these flybys seemed to confirm the notion that Mars was a dull and lifeless place, roughly cratered and more like Mercury than the Earth.

In 1971, however, the Mariner 9 spacecraft was placed into orbit around Mars. For the first time the full range of the planet's wonders, such as the great shield volcanos and the vast networks of river beds, was revealed. Mariner 9 remained in service until October 1972, by which time the entire Martian surface had been mapped.

In August and September 1975 the United States launched the two identical Viking spacecraft toward Mars. Each Viking consisted of an orbiting module and a landing module designed to make a soft landing on the Martian surface. The Viking project was an outstanding success. The Viking 1 Lander alighted in the Chryse Planitia on 20 July 1976 and continued to transmit data until November 1982. The Viking 1 Orbiter conducted a close-up reconnaissance of the Martian moon Phobos and continued in its orbit around Mars until August 1980. The Viking Lander touched down in the Utopia region on 3 September 1976 and

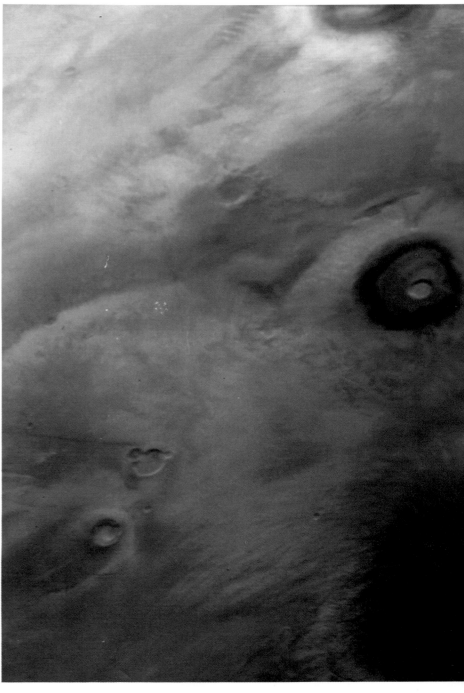

Left: A thin layer of water ice coats the rocks and soil of the Utopia Planitia, the landing site for the Viking 2 Lander. *Above:* This view of the Tharsis Ridge, the major volcanic province of Mars, was taken by the Viking 1 Orbiter on 13 July 1980. The three Tharsis volcanoes—Arsia Mons, Pavonis Mons and Ascraeus Mons—rise an average of 10.8 miles (17 kilometers) above the 6.2 miles (10 kilometers) high Tharsis Ridge.

MARS
Diameter: 4212.28 miles (6794 km)
Distance from Sun: 154,380,000 miles (249,000,000 km) at aphelion
127,720,000 miles (206,000,000 km) at perihelion
Mass: 2.9178×10^{23} lb (6.4191×10^{23} kg)
Rotational period (Martian day): 24.62 Earth hours
Sidereal period (Martian year): 687 Earth days (1.88 Earth years)
Eccentricity: 0.093
Inclination of rotational axis: 23.98°
Inclination to ecliptic plane (Earth = 0): 1.85°
Albedo (100% reflection of light = 1): .16
Maximum surface temperature: 78.8° F
Minimum surface temperature: −193.3° F
Highest point on surface: Mt Olympus (Olympus Mons)
Largest surface feature: Valles Marinaris (over 3000 miles long & 450 miles at the widest point)
Major atmospheric components: Carbon dioxide (95.32%), Nitrogen (2.7%), Argon (1.6%), Oxygen (.13%), Carbon monoxide (.07%), Water vapor (.03%)
Other atmospheric components: Neon, Krypton, Xenon, Ozone

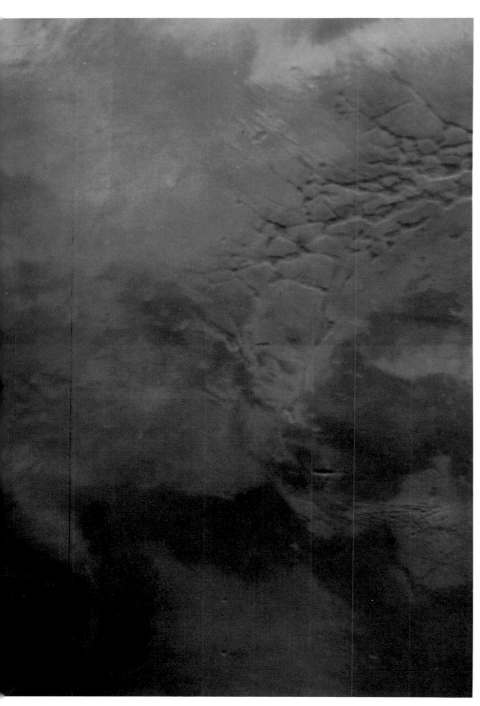

continued to transmit data until April 1980. The Viking 2 Orbiter surveyed the Martian moon Deimos and continued to operate until it was powered down by Earth-based technicians in July 1978.

The Viking project expanded our knowledge of Mars manyfold and returned spectacular close-up photographs of the Martian surface that spanned Mars' seasonal changes for more than a Martian year. Viking answered a great many questions about Mars, but the notion of Martian life remains an enigma. There were three biology experiments aboard the Viking landers that were specifically designed to detect evidence of Martian life, but the answer returned was a resounding 'maybe not.' In each experiment, samples of Martian soil were scooped up by the landers' remote surface sample arms and brought aboard the spacecraft.

The Pyrolytic Release Experiment was designed to determine whether Martian organisms would be able to assimilate and reduce carbon monoxide or carbon dioxide as plants on Earth do. The easily monitored isotope carbon-14 was used and the results were described as 'weakly positive.' While the experiment could not be repeated by Viking on Mars, parallel experiments on Earth showed that the same results could possibly be explained by chemical, rather than biological, reactions.

In the Labeled Release Experiment an organic nutrient 'broth' was prepared and 'fed' to some samples of Martian soil, again using carbon-14 as the trace element. If microorganisms were present, they would 'breathe out' carbon dioxide as they 'ate' the nutrients. Carbon dioxide was, in fact, detected! However, the outgassing of carbon dioxide stopped and could not be restarted. This could have indicated some sort of chemical reaction or that a microbe *had* been present, but that it had died while 'eating' the 'broth.' To distinguish a chemical reaction from a biological reaction, the mixture was heated. This process stopped whatever it was that was producing the carbon dioxide, which *should* have ruled against the notion of a chemical reaction, but which might confirm that it had been caused by a now-deceased organism. In the end, the Labeled Release Experiment was labeled 'inconclusive' because the activities of whatever produced the carbon dioxide had no exact parallel with known reactions of Earth life.

The Gas Exchange Experiment was designed to examine Martian soil samples for evidence of gaseous metabolic changes, by again mixing a sample with a nutrient 'broth.' Because the Martian environment is so dry, it was decided to gradually humidify the samples before plunging

The summit caldera *(right)* of Olympus Mons is comprised of a series of craters formed by repeated collapses after centuries of eruptions. The volcano, the highest point on Mars, towers 16 miles above the planet's surface. In contrast, Hawaii's Muana Loa, the largest comparable feature on Earth, rises a mere 5 miles above the ocean floor. Olympus Mons is higher even than Mount Everest—by 10 miles!

PHOBOS
Diameter: $12.4 \times 14.3 \times 17.4$ miles ($20 \times 23 \times 28$ km)
Distance from Mars: 5760.11 miles (9270 km)
Mass: 4.36×10^{15} lb (9.6×10^{15} kg)
Rotational period (Phobian day): 7.66 Earth hours
Sidereal period (Phobian year): 7.66 Earth hours
(7 hrs, 39 min, 27 sec)
Inclination to Martian equatorial plane: 1.1°
Largest surface feature: Stickney (a large crater)
6 miles in diameter
Major atmospheric component: None

DEIMOS
Diameter: $6.2 \times 7.5 \times 9.9$ miles ($10 \times 12 \times 16$ km)
Distance from Mars: 14,540 miles (23,400 km)
Mass: 9.10×10^{15} lb (20×10^{15} kg)
Rotational period (Deimosian day): 30.35 Earth hours
(1 day, 6 hrs, 21 min, 16 sec)
Sidereal period (Deimosian year): 30.35 Earth hours
(1 day, 6 hrs, 21 min, 16 sec)
Inclination to Martian equatorial plane: 1.8°

Above: **For many years, the Argyre Planitia (the large smooth plain surrounded by heavily cratered terrain) has been observed from Earth. This view, looking across Argyre toward the horizon, was taken by the Viking 1 Orbiter on 11 July 1976. The clouds seen above the horizon are thought to be crystals of frozen carbon dioxide.**

them into the 'broth' so as not to 'shock' any of the life forms that might be present. A major shock came instead to the Earth-based experimenters as the sample was being humidified—there was a sudden burst of oxygen! When the nutrient 'broth' itself was added, there was some evidence of carbon dioxide but no more oxygen. Once again the results were described as 'inclusive' because the results could not be explained by known biological reactions. Subsequent studies have been done to attempt to determine whether some type of oxidizing agent exists in the Martian soil which could provide a 'chemical reaction' explanation of the strange results of the Gas Exchange Experiment.

The three Viking biology experiments raised some curious questions, but there remain no conclusive answers to the question that has intrigued Earth-bound observers. Perhaps the answer lies closer to the Martian poles where there is more water, or perhaps the question might be restated as whether life *might have existed* at one time on Mars.

THE MARTIAN MOONS

In 1877 as Schiaparelli was astounding the world with his discovery of *canali* on the Martian surface, the American astronomer Asaph Hall (1829-1907) made an even more important discovery. Observing Mars from the US Naval Observatory in Washington, DC, Hall determined that the red planet was accompanied by two tiny moons. Named Deimos (terror) and Phobos (fear) after the characters of (some sources say 'the horses of') the mythological war god *Mars*, the two moons are irregularly shaped rocks pocked with numerous craters. Phobos, the larger of the pair, is just over 17 miles in length, while

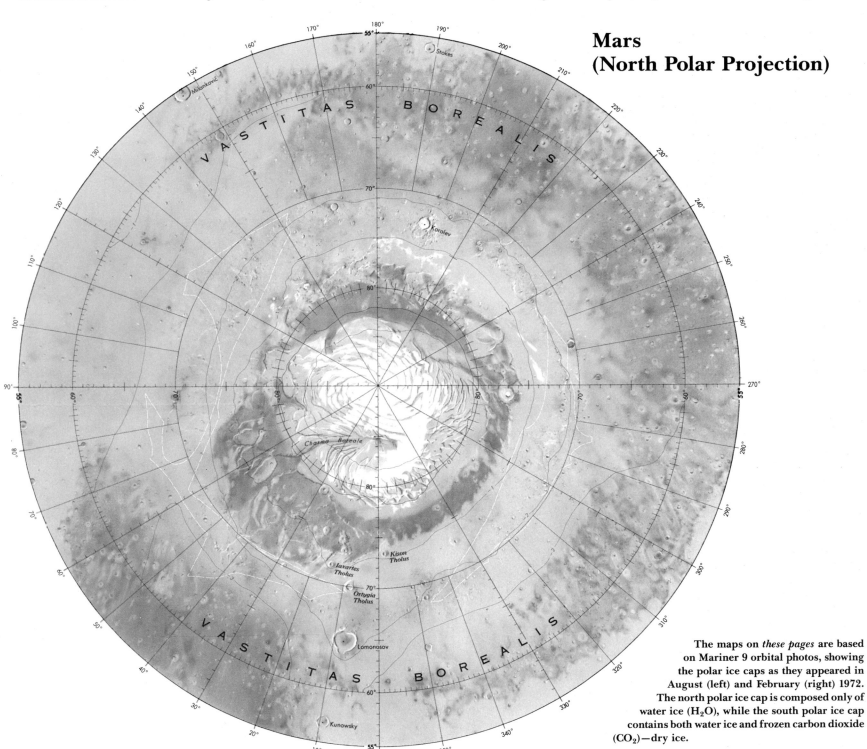

Mars
(North Polar Projection)

The maps on *these pages* are based on Mariner 9 orbital photos, showing the polar ice caps as they appeared in August (left) and February (right) 1972. The north polar ice cap is composed only of water ice (H_2O), while the south polar ice cap contains both water ice and frozen carbon dioxide (CO_2)—dry ice.

Deimos is less than nine miles long. Because of their shape, size and texture, it is thought that they originated among the asteroids and became trapped in Martian orbit at the time of the formation of the Solar System. Neither Deimos nor Phobos have the mass to allow them to hold an atmosphere, but they exert sufficient gravity to retain a thin layer of dust on their surfaces—which is perhaps residue from the meteorite impacts that caused the cratering.

Both are relatively small, and Deimos would appear no larger from the Martian surface than Venus does from the Earth. Phobos, however, would appear as if it were one third the size of the Earth's Moon. Though both moons revolve around Mars in the same direction, Phobos would *appear* to revolve in the *opposite* direction because it revolves in less than eight hours, a third of the time that it takes Mars to rotate on its axis.

Phobos is characterized by a number of large craters, the largest of which, Stickney (the maiden name of Asaph Hall's wife), is six miles across. The next largest craters are Hall and Roche, which are about half the size of Stickney, while the average Phobos crater diameter is about 500 feet. Other features include surface fractures that were probably induced by Martian gravitational effects.

Deimos has a much smoother surface than its larger brother, with fewer craters and none with diameters greater than two miles. In other words, the ratio of longest overall dimension to largest crater diameter is 2.8 to 1 on Phobos and 5.3 to 1 on Deimos. Because Deimos is more than twice as far from the parent planet than is Phobos, it shows no evidence of surface fracturing that has been induced on the latter by the tidal effects of Martian gravity.

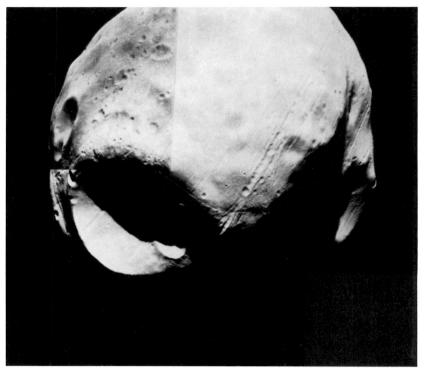

Above: **This photomosaic taken by the Viking 1 Orbiter shows the side of Phobos that always faces Mars. Stickney, the largest crater on Phobos, is at the left near the morning terminator. Kepler Ridge is casting a shadow in the southern hemisphere, which partially covers the large crater, Hall, at the bottom.**

Mars
(South Polar Projection)

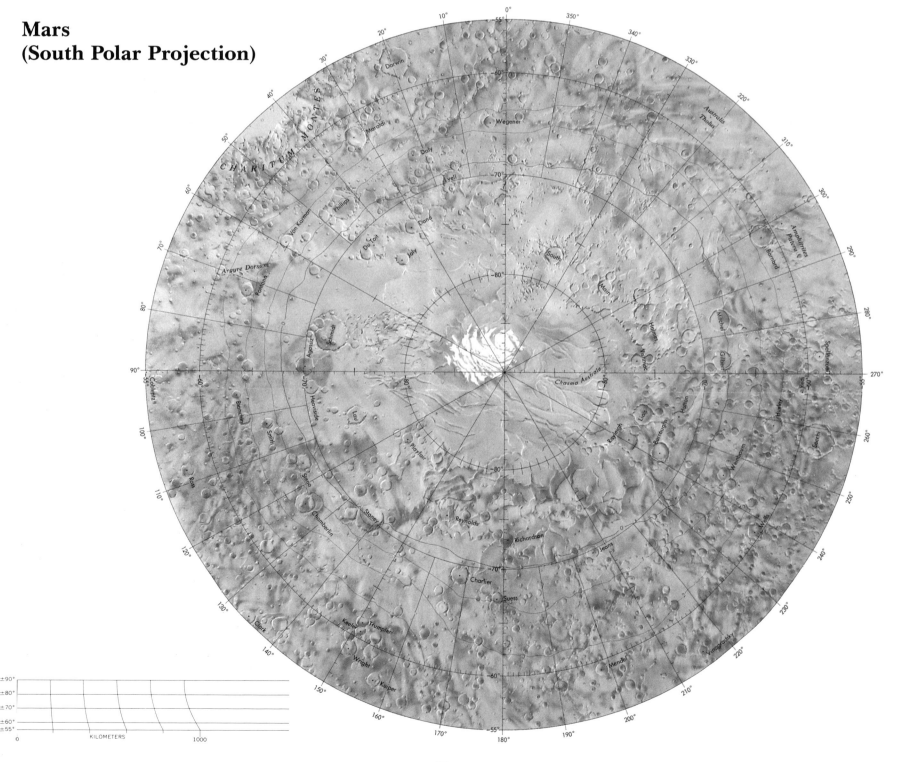

Mars (Mercator Topographical Projection)

Right: An early Martian map, dating from Percival Lowell's time. Note the now familiar regions such as Argyre and the Tharsis ridge. Compare this with the contemporary map *below.*

Facing Page: This late winter picture, taken in the Utopia Planitia (*see map*), by the Viking 2 Lander, shows traces of the white frost that covered most of the planet's surface during the Lander's winter on Mars. This thin layer is composed of water or carbon dioxide ice, or a combination of the two.

Some scientists believe that it *could* have risen out of the surface by a process called cryopumping. Most of the rocks average 20 inches in size and were probably thrown out as a result of meteor impacts long ago. The small pits in some of the rocks are either wind eroded or were caused by trapped gas bubbles as the rocks formed.

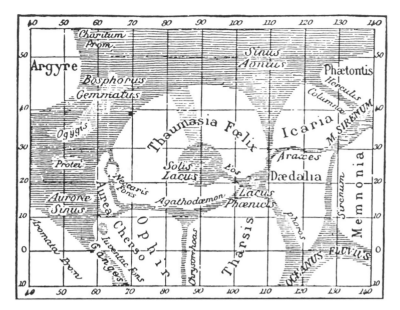

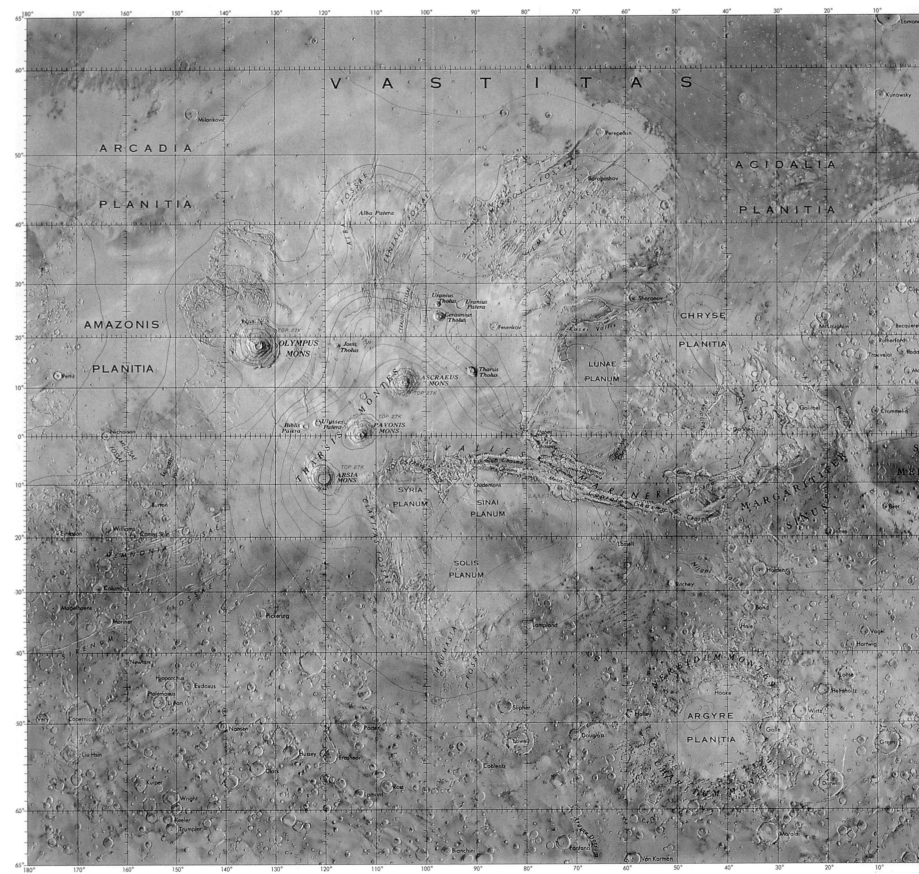

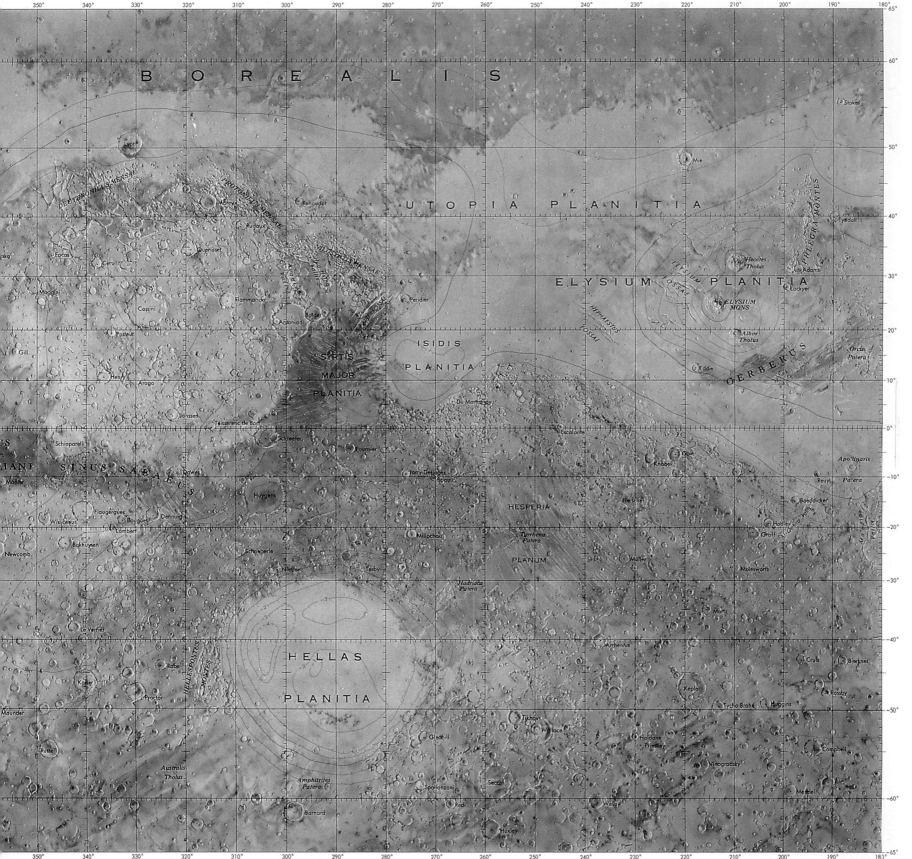

Mars (Mercator Geological Projection)

Right: Viking unlocks the secrets of the mysterious red planet—The orange-red rocks are probably limonite (hydrated ferric oxide) and the reddish cast to the sky is likely a scattering and reflection from reddish sediment suspended in the atmosphere. *Facing page (from left to right):* Valles Marineris, the huge (over 3000 miles) seismic rift canyon; and Olympus Mons, the tallest mountain in the solar system.

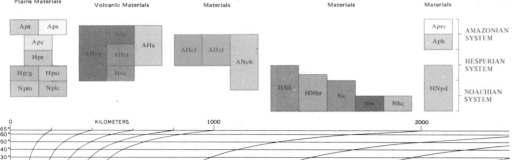

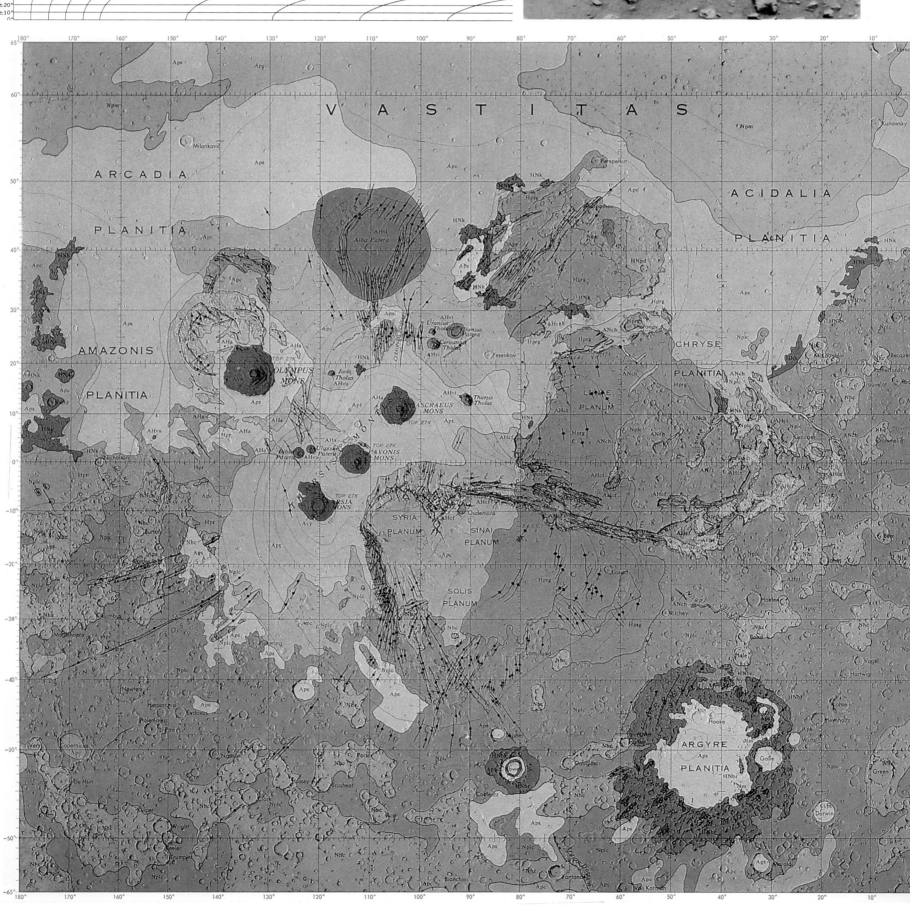

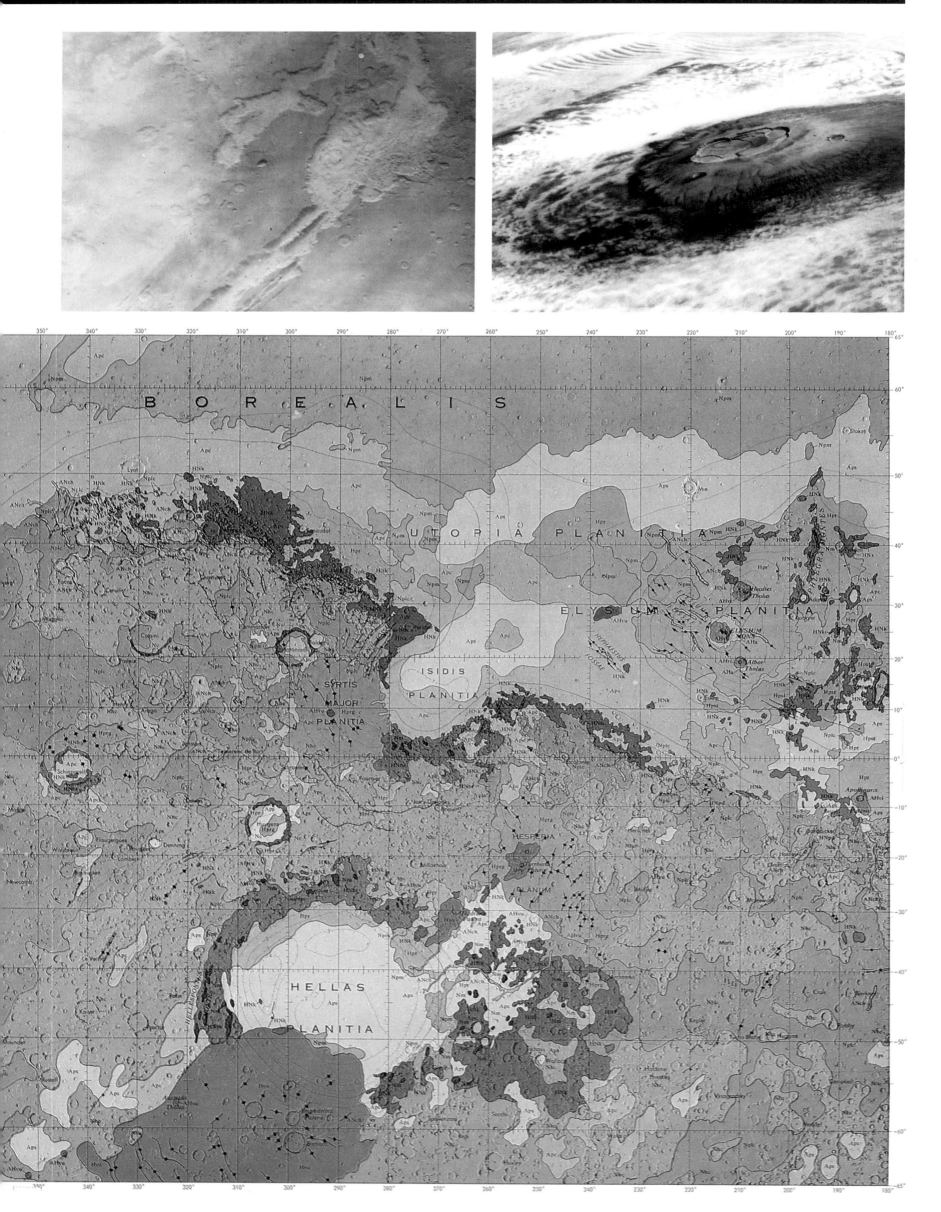

THE ASTEROIDS

In the 342 million mile interval between the orbits of Mars and Jupiter is a vast collection of small planet-like objects called *asteroids*. While their name translates as implying a star-like character, the asteroids are more accurately described as planetoids or minor planets. Literally they are fragments of rock that may have their origin in the cataclysmic destruction of one or several terrestrial planets, or they may be debris left over from the origin of the Solar System itself. The largest asteroid, Ceres, is 485 miles in diameter, but there are only six known asteroids with diameters greater than 100 miles.

The discovery of the field of minor planets that we know as the *Asteroid Belt* dates to the theoretical work of German astronomer Johann Elert Bode (1747-1826) of the Berlin Observatory. In 1772 Bode authored Bode's Law, which took into account the regular intervals between the known planets and postulated that a planet should, by his law, exist between Mars and Jupiter. Little did Bode realize that this interval was not filled by a single planet, but rather by thousands of planetoids. In 1800 Bode's countryman Johann Hieronymus Schroeter (1745-1816) organized what he called the Celestial Police, an association of astronomers dedicated to finding the planet whose existence had been postulated by Bode (and by Titius of Wittenberg before him).

Ironically, the first asteroid, Ceres, was not discovered by a member of Schroeter's Celestial Police, but was discovered on New Year's Day in 1801 by Giuseppe Piazzi (1746-1826), director of the observatory at Palermo, Sicily. Though Piazzi later joined the Celestial Police, the most successful member of the 'force' would have to be Heinrich Olbers (1748-1840), a German amateur astronomer who was able to 'recover,' or rediscover, Ceres in 1802. Olbers then went on to discover the asteroids Pallas and Vesta in 1802 and 1807 respectively. It would be over 30 years, however, before a fifth asteroid would be discovered.

In 1830 another German amateur astronomer, Karl Ludwig Hencke (1793-1866), went on a search for further asteroids which finally bore fruit in 1845 with the discovery of Astraea. Two years later Hencke discovered a sixth asteroid, Hebe. Both Iris and Flora were discovered in 1847, the same year that Hencke found Hebe, and after that several were found each year. By the 1890s photography was brought into play as a tool and suddenly the search for new asteroids took on a whole new flavor. Within ten years, 48 asteroids had been discovered, and by 1899 there were 451 known asteroids. By 1930, the year that Clyde Tombaugh discovered Pluto, there were more than 1000 known asteroids. After World War II the International Astronomical Union set up a cooperative program of asteroid research. By 1980 there were more than 2000 known asteroids, and by the end of 1985 the number exceeded 3450.

Because it is now possible to detect smaller and smaller asteroids, the number of known asteroids is likely to increase indefinitely. The total number of asteroids is estimated at 30,000, but theoretically they can range down to sand grain-sized specks that will probably never all be counted.

With the flurry of discovery in the nineteenth century, the convention was adopted to number the asteroids in the order they were discovered, and it is also conventional to incorporate the assigned numeral into the official name. Because of differences in magnitude owing to composition and distance from Earth, the numbers denoting order of discovery don't necessarily list the asteroids in the order of their size. For example, 1 Ceres and 2 Pallas are the two largest asteroids, but the third largest is 4 Vesta, while 3 Juno is actually sixth in size order.

The naming of the first asteroids followed the same pattern of classical mythology used with the planets and their moons: 1 Ceres was named for the tutelary goddess of Sicily, 2 Pallas for the goddess Pallas Athena, 3 Vesta for the Roman goddess of the hearth, 4 Juno for the sister of Jupiter and the principal goddess of the Roman pantheon, 5 Astraea for the Greek goddess of justice, 6 Hebe for the Greek goddess of youth and spring, 7 Iris for the Greek messenger and goddess of the rainbow, while 8 Flora was named for the Roman goddess of flowers. Since the mid-nineteenth century, however, the naming convention has been stretched to include, among the classical goddesses, such names as those of astronomers and Earthly geographical locations. Today, asteroids can be named after anything, usually at the prerogative of the discoverer. In some cases asteroids have been assigned names already assigned to other objects in the Solar System. For example, the asteroids 52 Europa and 1036 Ganymede coexist with the Jovian moons Europa and Ganymede. Some asteroids have simply been assigned unromantic code numbers, but recently named asteroids also include 2309 Mr Spock (formerly 1971 QX²), named for a character on the *Star Trek* television series, and the asteroids numbered 3350 through 3356, which were renamed in March 1986 for the seven persons killed two months earlier in the accident involving the American spacecraft *Challenger*.

Few asteroids have anything approximating the staid, near-circular orbits of most planets. In fact, asteroid orbits are extremely elliptical. It is for this reason that we have chosen to use Astronomical Units (AU) rather than miles/kilometers for most of the tables in this section. Astronomical Units (1 AU = 93 million miles) can be used as a sort of shorthand to allow us to easily grasp the immensity of the eccentricity of these orbits without an overwhelming blizzard of digits. While 1 Ceres has an elliptical orbit that varies between 2.55 AU and 2.94 AU from the Sun, 944 Hidalgo varies between 2.00 AU and 9.61 AU, and the amazing 2060 Chiron has a perihelion of 18.50 AU and an aphelion of 8.50 AU. This translates as a difference of 930 million miles between its closest and furthest approach to the Sun!

While the greatest concentration of asteroids is in the Asteroid Belt between Mars and Jupiter, there are a number of interesting exceptions to this rule, and 2060 Chiron is only one. In 1898 it was discovered that the elliptical orbit of 433 Eros brought it within the orbit of Mars, and in 1931 and 1975 it came within .15 AU of the Earth. By the mid-twentieth century, a fairly large number of asteroids were found to cross the orbit of Mars. These include 1566 Icarus and 1862 Apollo, which actually cross the *Earth's* orbit and come as close to the Sun as .19 AU and .65 AU respectively! The names for these two are well chosen. Apollo was the Greek god of the Sun, while Icarus was the character from Greek mythology who attempted to escape from Crete using homemade wings, but who crashed into the sea when the wax on his wings melted because he came *too close to the Sun*. After the discovery of 1862

Schematic Map of the Asteroid Belt

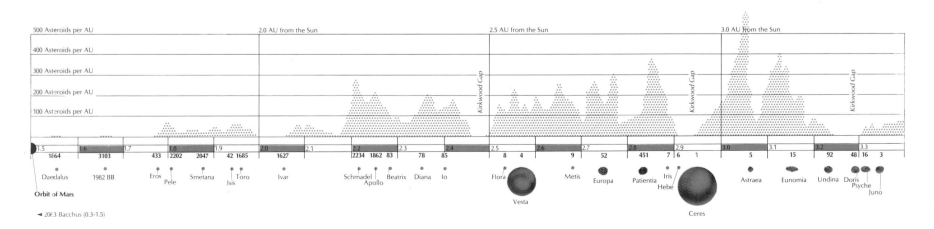

Apollo in 1932, it was 'lost' for 41 years. After its rediscovery in 1973, the name Apollo has been applied as a class name to *all* asteroids whose elliptical orbits cross the orbit of the Earth.

While 2060 Chiron, whose aphelion of 8.50 AU never even brings it within the orbit of Jupiter, is hardly in the Apollo class, it opens up a whole area of speculation about asteroids because of its incredible eccentricity and the fact that it never comes near the Asteroid Belt. Some astronomers have suggested that it might actually be a tailless comet nucleus, while others have suggested that it might be the harbinger of a whole new Asteroid Belt awaiting discovery in the distant reaches of the Solar System.

Another interesting class of asteroids are the Trojan asteroids, which exist at the outer edge of the Asteroid Belt and, in fact, travel in the same orbital path as Jupiter. Traveling at the speed of the Jovian revolution around the Sun, a group of *Leading Trojans* precede Jupiter in its orbit by 60 degrees, while the *Trailing Trojans* follow at the same speed, remaining 60 degrees behind.

Some of the asteroids are observed to be characterized by other interesting peculiarities. At least two of them, 2 Pallas and 12 Victoria, actually have smaller satellite asteroids orbiting around them like moons around a planet! The 'moon' associated with 2 Pallas bears the same size relationship to 2 Pallas that the Moon does to the Earth. Meanwhile, 8 Flora has a mass of at least 13 tiny bodies that accompany it in its orbit, and five of these have diameters in excess of 18 miles.

Asteroids vary widely in their shapes and other characteristics. Most of the well-known larger ones, such as 1 Ceres, 3 Juno and 4 Vesta, are roughly spherical or just slightly oblique like 2 Pallas. Many, however, are as eccentric in their shapes as they are in their orbits: some, such as 41 Daphne, 44 Mysa, 107 Camilla and 349 Dembowska are so elongated as to appear almost cigar-like.

One very oddly shaped asteroid is 624 Hektor. One of the Trojan asteroids sharing Jupiter's orbit, 624 Hektor might be a dogbone-shaped object, or it may actually be *two* asteroids. If it is the latter, it would be the only known instance where two asteroids may actually be touching one another. If 624 Hektor is such a *contact binary*, 624A and 624B would probably be identical in size and mass.

Asteroids are also varied in their color and composition, with the very dark carbonaceous *C-types* accounting for three-quarters of the known asteroids. The C-types include 1 Ceres, 2 Pallas, 10 Hygiea, 65 Cybeie and 624 Hektor. Roughly 15 percent of known asteroids are the rust red *S-types*, rich in iron and magnesium silicates. These include 3 Juno, 6 Hebe, 7 Iris and 15 Eunomia, as well as 8 Flora and its associated family. About five percent of the asteroids are classed as *M-types*, with characteristics suggestive of metallic substances. The remaining asteroids vary widely from 4 Vesta, which is composed of light gray basalt, to the metallic 16 Psyche, to the bright and olivine-rich 349 Dembowska.

Because of their size, none of the asteroids have the mass to permit the holding of an atmosphere or the more complex features noted on planets, but they are potentially rich in data about the origin of the Solar System.

The Fifteen Largest Asteroids

Size Order	Number	Name	Diameter (Miles)	Diameter (Km)	Year Discovery
1	1	Ceres	622	1003	1801
2	2	Pallas	377	608	1802
3	4	Vesta	334	538	1807
4	10	Hygiea	279	450	1849
5	31	Euphrosyne	229	370	1854
6	704	Interamnia	217	350	1910
7	511	Davida	200	323	1903
8	65	Cybele	192	309	1861
9	52	Europa	179	289	1858
10	451	Patienta	171	276	1899
11	15	Eunomia	169	272	1851
12	16	Psyche	155	250	1851
	48	Doris	155	250	1857
	92	Undina	155	250	1867
13	324	Bamberga	153	246	1892
14	24	Themis	145	234	1853
15	95	Arethusa	143	230	1867

The First Ten Asteroids

Number	Name	Absolute Magnitude	Discovery		(AU)	Farthest Distance from Sun (Miles)	(Km)	(AU)	Number Closest Distance to Sun (Miles)	(Km)	Diameter (Miles)	(Km)
1	Ceres	4.5	Piazzi	1 Jan 1801	2.94	273,420,000	440,206,200	2.55	237,150,000	381,811,500	622	1003
2	Pallas	5.0	Olbers	23 Mar 1802	3.42	318,060,000	512,076,600	2.11	196,230,000	315,920,300	377	608
3	Juno	6.5	Harding	1 Sep 1804	3.35	311,550,000	501,595,500	1.98	184,140,000	296,465,400	155	250
4	Vesta	4.3	Olbers	29 Mar 1807	2.57	239,010,000	384,806,100	2.15	199,950,000	321,919,500	334	538
5	Astraea	8.1	Hencke	8 Dec 1845	3.06	284,580,000	458,173,800	2.10	195,300,000	314,433,000	63	117
6	Hebe	7.0	Hencke	1 Jul 1847	2.92	271,560,000	437,211,600	1.93	179,490,000	288,978,900	121	195
7	Iris	6.8	Hind	13 Aug 1847	2.94	273,420,000	440,206,200	1.84	171,120,000	275,503,200	130	209
8	Flora	7.7	Hind	18 Oct 1847	2.55	237,150,000	381,811,500	1.86	172,980,000	278,497,800	94	151
9	Metus	7.8	Graham	25 Apr 1848	2.68	249,240,000	401,276,400	2.09	194,370,000	312,935,700	94	151
10	Hygiea	6.5	DeGasparis	12 Apr 1849	3.46	321,780,000	518,065,800	2.84	264,120,000	425,233,200	279	450

Below, these pages: The Asteroid Belt between the orbits of Mars and Jupiter is here charted, with the stalagmite-like formations above the bar representing concentrations of asteroids per Astronomical Unit. The images below the bar represent some of the more prominent, or better known, asteroids.

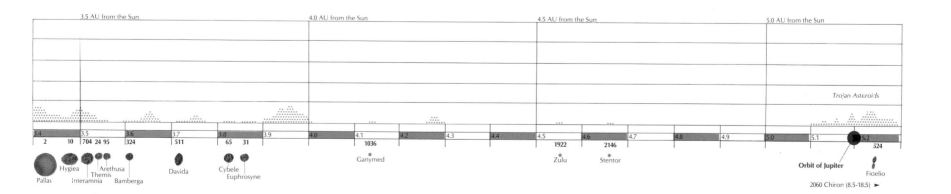

JUPITER

Justifiably named for the king of all the Roman gods, Jupiter is the largest planet in the Solar System, and second in mass only to the Sun. This 'king' of planets has 1330 times the volume of the Earth and 318 times the mass. As the Solar System was being formed 4.6 billion years ago, Jupiter may have had the makings of becoming a star. At that time it was 10 times its present diameter and heated by gravitational contraction. It may have blazed like a second Sun. Had the nuclear reactions within Jupiter become self sustaining as they did in the Sun, the two objects may have become a double star of the type that exist elsewhere in the galaxy and the Solar System would have been a vastly different place than it is today. But Jupiter failed as a star and gradually began to cool and to collapse to its present size. As Jupiter cooled it became less brilliant, so that after a million years the 'star that might have been' went from one hundred thousandth the luminosity of the Sun to one ten billionth. Today, however, as much energy is still radiated from *within Jupiter itself* as it *receives from the Sun*.

Jupiter's magnetic field is more than 4000 times greater than that of the Earth, leading observers to postulate the existence of a metallic core. Strangely, the center of Jupiter's magnetic field is not located at the planet's center, but at a point 6200 miles offset from the center and tipped by 11 degrees from the rotational axis. This point is also the center of Jupiter's vast magnetosphere, which is six million miles across. Three million miles from Jupiter the plasma reaches the hottest temperatures recorded in the Solar System, roughly 17 times as hot as the interior of the Sun.

Like the Sun, Jupiter is composed almost entirely of hydrogen and helium and, unlike the terrestrial planets, it may be composed almost entirely of gases and fluids with no solid surface. If there is a solid rocky surface, the solid diameter of Jupiter may actually be just slightly larger than the Earth. Above this rocky surface, if it exists, there may be a layer of ice more than 4000 miles thick which is kept frozen by *pressure* rather than temperature, as the *temperatures* would be frightfully hot.

There is almost certainly a sea of liquid metallic hydrogen that makes up the bulk of Jupiter. Above the liquid metallic hydrogen is a transition zone leading to a layer of fluid molecular hydrogen. Jupiter's atmosphere is characterized by colorful swirling clouds that cover the planet completely. These clouds form in Jupiter's troposphere, at the altitude where convection takes place. The lower clouds, like those of the Earth, are thought to be composed of water vapor, with ice crystals being present at higher altitudes. Above these, higher clouds are composed of ammonium hydrosulfide, with Jupiter's high cirrus composed of ammonia. At a point 40 miles above the ammonia cirrus, where the Jovian *troposphere* gives way to the *stratosphere*, temperatures can dip to

colder than −150 degrees Fahrenheit. Above that, in the *ionosphere*, however, temperatures increase again.

Jupiter's atmosphere is a complex and dynamic feature characterized by distinct horizontal 'belts,' or darker bands of clouds, that exist at semi-symmetrical intervals in the northern and southern hemispheres, and which alternate with lighter colored 'zones.'

The most outstanding feature on Jupiter is certainly the Great Red Spot. First observed in 1664 by the astronomer Robert Hooke (1635-1702), it is a brick red cloud three times the size of the Earth. Described as a high pressure system, the Great Red Spot resembles a storm and exists at a higher and colder altitude than most of Jupiter's cloud cover, although traces of ammonia cirrus are occasionally observed above it. It rotates in a counterclockwise direction, making a complete rotation every six Earth days, and it varies slightly in latitude. The exact nature of the Great Red Spot is uncertain, but one theory is that it is above an updraft in the Jovian atmospheres in which phosphine, a hydrogen-phosphorus compound, rises to high altitudes—where it is broken down into hydrogen and red phosphorus-4 by solar ultraviolet radiation. The pure phosphorus would give the Great Red Spot its characteristic color. Another theory has the Great Red Spot as the top of a column of stagnant air that exists above a topographical surface feature far below, within Jupiter. The Great Red Spot is almost certainly the top of some sort of high altitude updraft plume from below the Jovian cloud cover, but the divergent flow from it is quite small. For example, one smaller feature was seen to circle the Great Red Spot for an Earth month without altering its distance.

The Great Red Spot may be an awesome feature, but it is a transient one. Any storm that has been raging for more than 300 years can certainly be termed as an impressive meteorological phenomenon, but it hasn't been constant in its intensity. Between 1878 and 1882 it was seen as very prominent, but thereafter it dimmed markedly until 1891. Since then, it has waned slightly several times—in 1928, 1938, and again in 1977.

Other intriguing meteorological phenomena have also been observed in the Jovian atmosphere, including smaller red spots in the northern hemisphere and some dark brown features that formed at the same latitude as the Great Red Spot. Designated as the South Tropical Disturbance, these features were first observed in 1900, overtook and 'leaped'

Right: **The king of the planets as photographed by Voyager 1. Jupiter's colorfully banded atmosphere displays complex patterns highlighted by the Great Red Spot, a large, circulating atmospheric disturbance.**
Below: **The ever-shifting face of Jupiter. These photos of Jupiter, taken four months apart by Voyagers 1 and 2, provide concrete evidence that the planet's atmosphere undergoes constant change. Although individual clouds in the Jovian atmosphere are long-lived, winds blow at greatly different speeds at different latitudes, causing clouds to move independently and pass each other. Note that one of the white oval-shaped storms located below and left of the Great Red Spot has drifted east (*right*).**

past the Great Red Spot several times and gradually began to fade in 1935, disappearing five years later.

In 1939 a group of large white spots formed near the Great Red Spot in the southern hemisphere. Like their larger red counterpart, they rotate counterclockwise. Similar but smaller features have been observed in the northern hemisphere, where they are seen to rotate in a clockwise direction. All of these features are oval in shape in the *tropical* and *temperate* latitudes, but are more rounded in polar regions. Like the Great Red Spot, the lesser white spots appear to be the tops of some sort of plumes, surrounded by darker filamentary rings.

Jupiter's equatorial band is characterized by regularly spaced features that resemble the type of convective storms that originate in the tropical latitudes on the Earth.

In the northern hemisphere, small brown counterclockwise-rotating storms race and tumble through the tropical and temperate zones. These playful features may collide, combine and later break apart.

The most notable interactions between Jovian clouds are in the region of the Great Red Spot. Other spots, or storms, caught on its outer edge

might break in two, with one piece remaining in the vortex and the second moving away in the same direction as that of the original storm. Occasionally, a ribbon of white clouds might form around the periphery of the Great Red Spot.

In the north polar region there is a very prominent aurora resulting from ultraviolet glows of atomic and molecular hydrogen. Nighttime observations by the Voyager spacecraft also observed widespread clusters of electrical storms at all latitudes in the Jovian atmosphere.

Unknown before the close-up observations by the Voyager spacecraft in 1979, Jupiter has a distinct ring system. Unlike the very visible Saturnian rings, the Jovian rings are very thin and narrow, and are not visible except when viewed from behind the night side of the planet, when they would be backlighted by the Sun. The ring system is divided into two parts that begin 29,000 miles above Jupiter's cloud tops, although some traces of ring material exist below that altitude. The two parts are a faint band 3100 miles across, feathering into a brighter band 500 miles across. The rings are composed of dark grains of sand and dust and are probably not more than a mile thick.

JUPITER
Diameter: 88,650 miles (142,984 km)
Distance from Sun: 505,734,000 miles (815,700,000 km) at
    aphelion
    459,358,000 miles (740,900,000 km) at
    perihelion
Mass: 8.632×10^{26} lb (1.899×10^{27} kg)
Rotational period (Jovian day): 9.84 Earth hours
Sidereal period (Jovian year): 4333 Earth days (11.86 Earth years)
Eccentricity: 0.048
Inclination of rotational axis: 3.12°
Inclination to ecliptic plane (Earth = 0): 1.3°
Albedo (100% reflection of light = 1): .34
Mean temperature: 26,637° F
Maximum temperature: 53,476° F
Minimum temperature: Great Red Spot: less than − 202° F
Largest feature: The Great Red Spot
    16,280 × 8,575 miles
Major atmospheric components: Hydrogen (<90%)
                     Helium (<10%)
Other atmospheric components: Methane, Ammonia, Ethane, Acetylene, Watervapor, Phosphine, Carbon monoxide, Germane, Tetrahydride

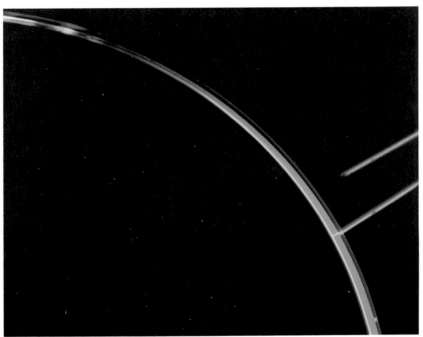

Above: Jupiter's faint ring system is shown as two light orange lines. To explain the fact that Jupiter gives off more energy than it receives from the sun, pre-Voyager theories postulated gravitational contraction as the cause, as illustrated in the cross-sectional model *below left*. The contrasting model *below right* is based on the Voyager's discoveries.

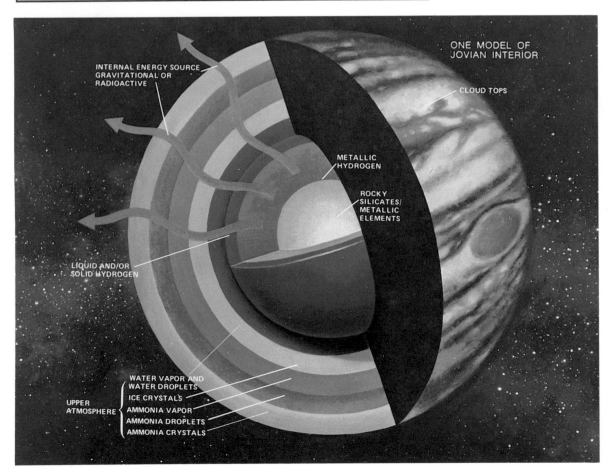

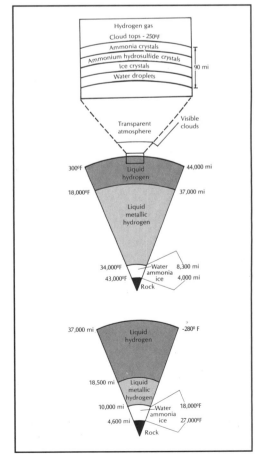

Each of Io's eruptions dumps 10,000 tons of sulfur onto the moon's surface. In extrapolation, this would account for 100 billion tons of sulfur deposits per year. This is enough to cover the entire surface with a layer of sulfur 'ash' a foot thick in 30,750 years. Combined with surface flows, Io could very well be completely resurfaced with a foot-thick layer in as short a period of time as 3100 years, giving this pizza-colored moon the youngest solid surface in the Solar System aside from Earth, and there are parts of Earth that change less over time than does much of Io. In fact, there were many noticeable changes in Io's surface—particularly around Pele—in just the four months between March and July 1979. This 'ever-youthful' surface accounts for the complete absence of meteorite impact craters on Io.

Surrounding the black volcanic caldera are black fan-shaped features that are the result of liquid sulfur that cools rapidly as it reaches Io's

Facing page: **This image of Io was made from several frames taken by Voyager 1 on 4 March 1979. The circular, donut-shaped feature in the center is the active volcano Prometheus. Io is the first body in the solar system (beyond Earth) where active volcanism has been confirmed. The two blue volcanic eruptions *(below)* originate from Amirani (upper) and Maui (lower). Io's volcanic activity appears to be of at least two kinds—explosive eruptions *(above)* that spew material as high as 160 miles above the moon's surface, and lava flows that smolder and gurgle across the surface.**

frigid surface. South of Loki the Voyager imaging team discovered a U-shaped molten sulfur lake 125 miles across that had partially crusted over. It was detected by its surface crust temperature of about 65 degrees Fahrenheit— compared to the surrounding surface temperature of less than −230 degrees Fahrenheit. This lake has certainly cooled and solidified by now, while other molten sulfur lakes have no doubt formed elsewhere.

Another common product of Io's eruptions is sulfur dioxide. In the atmospheres of Venus and Earth, sulfur dioxide gas mixes with water to form sulfuric acid. On Io, there is no water, and it is so cold that sulfur

dioxide exists as the fine white snow-like solid which is seen to dust various regions, or to form rings around some of the larger volcanic mountains.

While Io has no atmosphere in the usual sense, there is a donut-shaped torus, or tube, of electrically charged particles that exists in the path of its orbit around Jupiter. The torus apparently originates in the material from the eruptions, and consists of ionized sulfur and oxygen atoms.

Below: **The diffuse reddish and orangish colorations on Io are probably surface deposits of sulfur compounds, salts and possibly other volcanic sublimates. The dark spot with the irregular radiating pattern near the bottom of the photo is the Ra Patera Volcano with radiating lava flow. Voyager 1 took this photo on the morning of 5 March 1979 at a range of 77,100 miles.**

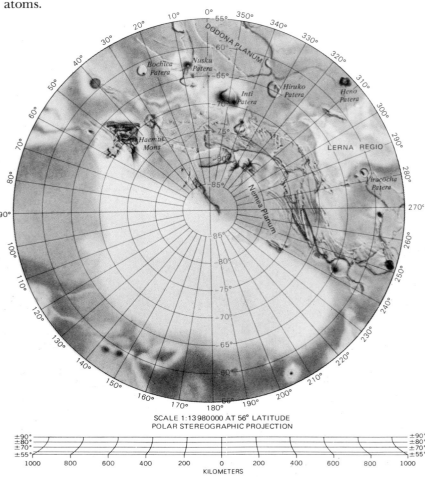

SCALE 1:13 980 000 AT 56° LATITUDE
POLAR STEREOGRAPHIC PROJECTION

KILOMETERS

SCALE 1:25 000 000 AT 0° LATITUDE
MERCATOR PROJECTION

KILOMETERS

Io
(South Polar and Mercator Projections)

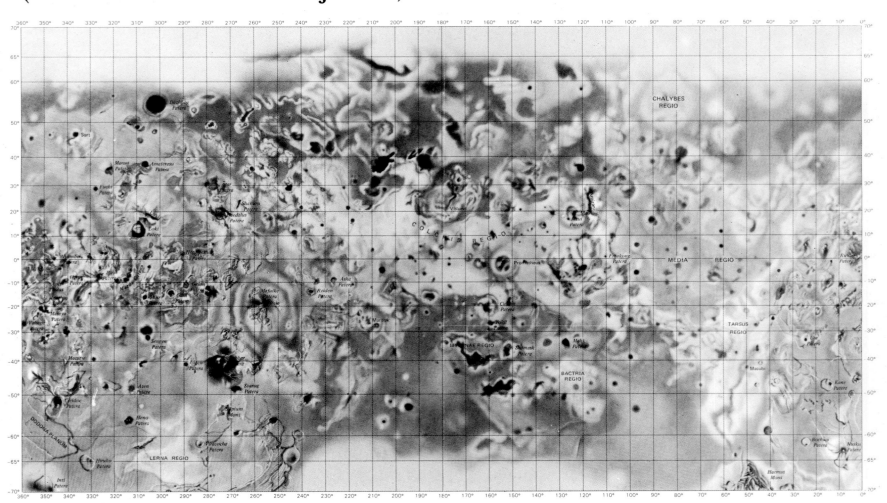

With a surface that is probably composed entirely of water ice and which is marred only by three definite impact craters, Europa is an enigma. The absence of impact craters on Io is explained by its violently active surface, but Europa has an extremely smooth and apparently inactive surface. Named for the Phoenician princess abducted to Crete by Zeus, Europa has a highly reflective surface that probably remained in a slushy semi-liquid state until relatively recently. This is at present the only explanation for its lack of meteorite craters.

The smooth surface is, however, not without features and these, too, present part of Europa's mystery. The features include long black *linea*, or lines, reminiscent of Percival Lowell's 'canals' on Mars. These features, which are up to 40 miles wide and stretch for thousands of miles across the surface, defy explanation. They appear to be cracks in the lighter surface, but they have no depth and thus they can only be described as 'marks' on the surface.

Another peculiar feature of Europa's icy surface is the presence of numerous dark *macula*, or spots, distributed across the surface. While the three impact craters range from 11 to 15.5 miles across, the macula are generally smaller than six miles.

The most unusual features on Europa are the *flexus*. Light colored, scalloped ridges, the flexus are much narrower and somewhat shorter than the linea. They are, however, more regular in width and in the regularity of their scallops or cusps.

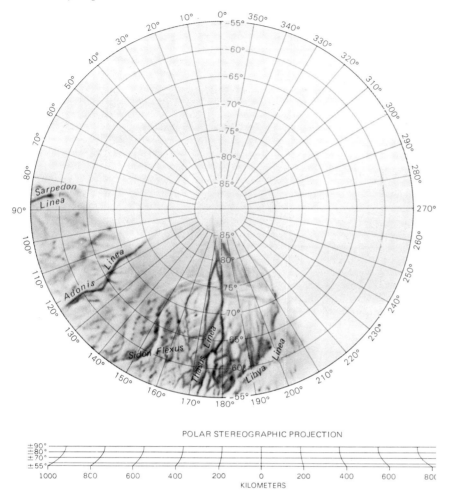

POLAR STEREOGRAPHIC PROJECTION

Europa
(South Polar and Mercator Projections)

IO
Diameter: 2257 miles (3632 km)
Distance from Jupiter: 261,970.09 miles (421,600 km)
Mass: 1.97×10^{23} lb (8.92×10^{22} kg)
Rotational period (Ioan day): 1.76 Earth days
Sidereal period (Ioan year): 1.76 Earth days
Inclination to ecliptic plane: 0°
Mean surface temperature: −243° F
Largest known surface feature: Pele (a volcanic plume)

EUROPA
Diameter: 1942 miles (3126 km)
Distance from Jupiter: 416,877 miles (670,900 km)
Mass: 5.25×10^{23} lb (4.87×10^{22} kg)
Rotational period (Europan day): 3.55 Earth days
Sidereal period (Europan year): 3.55 Earth days
Inclination to ecliptic plane: .5°
Mean surface temperature: Unknown
Largest surface feature: Entire surface covered with ice

MERCATOR PROJECTION
KILOMETERS

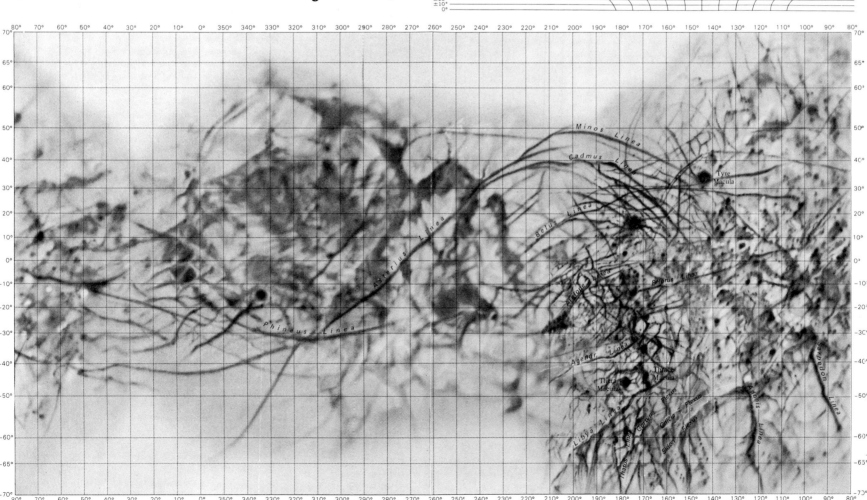

Europa is thought to have a relatively large silicate core with a layer of molten silicate above that, which is, in turn, covered by a layer of liquid water perhaps 60 miles deep. Above this is the strange, icy crust, which is roughly 40 miles thick.

Named for the cup-bearer of the Greek gods, Ganymede is the largest moon in the Jovian system and is, indeed, the largest moon in the entire Solar System. Ganymede, like Callisto, is composed of silicate rock and water ice, and thus these bodies came to be dubbed 'dirty snowballs.' Ganymede has an ice crust that is roughly 60 miles thick. This crust, in turn, floats upon a mantle of slushy, partially-liquid water that is roughly 400 miles deep. Beneath Ganymede's mantle is a heavy silicate core.

Like Earth's rocky crust, Ganymede's icy crust is divided into plates which shift and move independently, interacting with one another along fracture zones, resulting in geologic activity that is very much like what has been observed on Earth. Mountain ranges 10 miles across and 3000

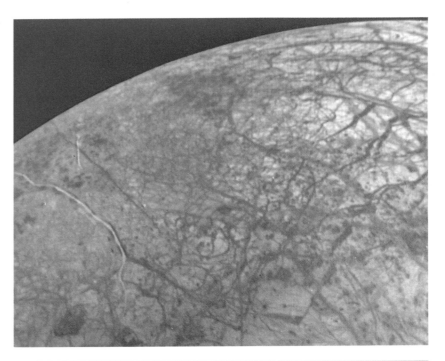

Below: Europa, Jupiter's smallest and brightest moon. Europa's crust evidently frac- tures *(above)*, but the pieces remain in approximately their original pieces. *Facing page, upper left:* In contrast, pieces of Ganymede's crust move in relation to one another. The photo *on the far right* provides an excellent view of the surface patterns and fault systems on Ganymede. *Facing page, below:* The ancient dark plains of Ganymede.

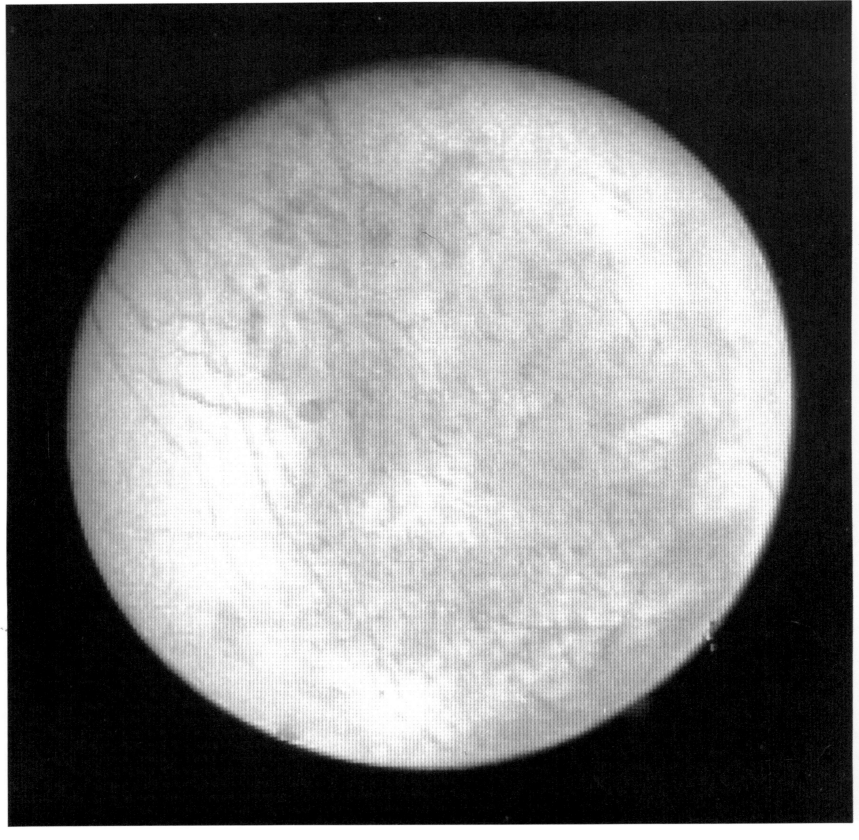

would be visible from Earth. It has since been determined that the cycle actually alternates between periods of 189 and 165 months. Huygens also discovered Saturn's largest moon, Titan.

In 1671 the Italian-born and naturalized French astronomer Giovanni Domenico (aka Jean Dominique) Cassini (1625-1712) began his own observations of the ringed planet. Cassini discovered a second moon of Saturn, Iapetus, in 1671, and in 1675 he determined that the 'ring' around Saturn was not a single band, but a pair of concentric rings. These two rings would come to be known as the A Ring and B Ring, with the space between them appropriately named the Cassini Division.

In 1837 Johann Franz Encke (1791-1865) at the Berlin Observatory tentatively identified a faint division in the A Ring. This division was confirmed in 1888 by James Keeler (1857-1900) of the Allegheny Observatory in the United States. Subsequently, this division is known as either the Keeler Gap or (more often) as the Encke Division.

The first spacecraft to venture close to Saturn was the American Pioneer 11 in September 1979. Prior to this time, there were only three known rings of Saturn, each lettered in the order of their discovery from A through C. Pioneer 11 helped Earth-based astronomers identify a fourth ring, which is now known as the F Ring. When the American Voyager Spacecraft first approached Saturn in November 1980, the spectacular photographs they beamed back to Earth revealed that there were not just four, six, or even a dozen rings in Saturn's ring system; rather, there were literally thousands of rings, with each known ring itself composed of hundreds or thousands of rings, with faint rings identified even within the Cassini Division.

In the new nomenclature of Saturn's ring system, the thousands of now known rings and ringlets are divided into seven *main rings* based on the older nomenclature. Closest to Saturn is a wide, but sparse and extremely faint ring known as the D Ring. At a point roughly 46,000 miles about Saturn's center and 8700 miles above Saturn's cloud tops, the D Ring merges into the more distinct C Ring. The C Ring is 10,850 miles wide, making it the second widest of the easily-visible main rings, though it is less prominent than the slightly narrower A Ring.

At a point 19,600 miles above Saturn's cloud tops, the C Ring merges into the B Ring without a major gap. The B Ring, which is 15,800 miles wide, is the brightest of Saturn's main rings and also the widest, except for the virtually invisible E Ring. The 2800 mile-wide Cassini Division separates the B Ring from the 9000 mile-wide A Ring, the second brightest of Saturn's rings.

The bright, yet tenuous F Ring is located just 2300 miles beyond the outer edge of the A Ring, and the narrow G Ring is located 20,700 miles

Above: Voyager's spectacular view flying over the Cassini Division. *Below:* A diagram of Saturn's system of rings and moons. *Right:* A false color image of Saturn. The largest violet colored cloud belt is the North Equatorial Belt.

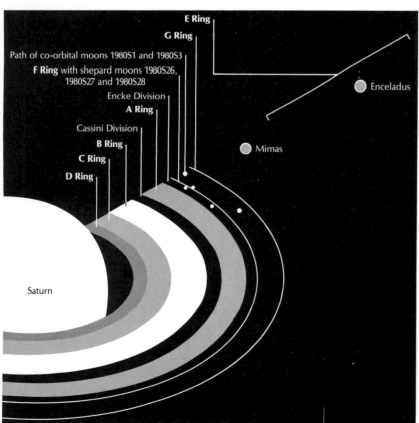

E Ring
G Ring
Path of co-orbital moons 1980S1 and 1980S3
F Ring with shepard moons 1980S26, 1980S27 and 1980S28
Encke Division
A Ring
Cassini Division
B Ring
C Ring
D Ring
Saturn
Enceladus
Mimas

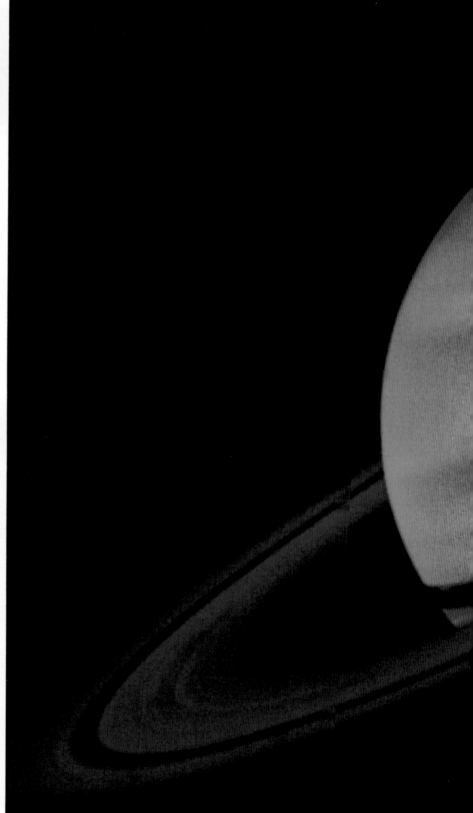

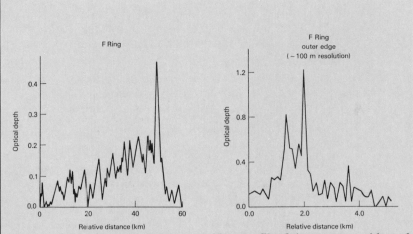

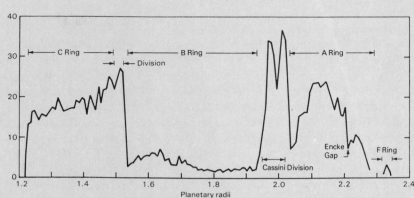

The occulation of a star by the rings provides a profile of ring structure with much higher resolution than could be obtained by imagery. *On the left* are two preliminary photopolarimeter plots of data from the occulation by the F Ring. The low resolution view *on the far left* shows a variety of faint ringlets in addition to the primary ring. The second graph, which is a more detailed presentation of the data, shows that the central part of the F Ring is broken up into finer structure.

The graph *on the right* represents ring brightness as seen from the unilluminated side of the rings. Seen from this angle, the brightest parts of the rings appear opaque. The brightest region is the Cassini Division, with the C Ring only slightly dimmer. The least brightness corresponds to the opaque B Ring as well as to the true gaps between the rings.

from the A Ring. The E Ring is a very, very faint 55,800 mile-wide mass of particles that begins 91,000 miles from Saturn's cloud tops and extends past the orbit of the moon Enceladus.

Saturn's rings are composed of silica rock, iron oxide and ice particles, which range from the size of a speck of dust to the size of a small automobile. They range in density from the nearly opaque B Ring to the very sparse E Ring.

Theories about the Ring system's origin generally fall into two camps. One theory, originating with Edward Roche in the nineteenth century, holds that the rings were once part of a large moon whose orbit decayed until it came so close to Saturn as to be pulled apart by the planet's tidal or gravitational force. An alternate to this theory suggest that a primordial moon disintegrated as a result of being struck by a large comet or meteorite. The opposing theory is that the rings were never part of a larger body, but rather they are nebular material left over from Saturn's formation 4.6 billion years ago. In other words, they were part of the same pool of material out of which Saturn formed, but they remained separate and gradually formed into rings.

Whatever their origin, however, Saturn's rings will continue to distinguish the planet and make it what Galileo described in 1610 as a 'most extraordinary marvel.'

Above: Voyager 2 leaving Saturn. *Right:* This awe-inspiring view of Saturn was assembled from photographs taken by Voyager 2 on 4 August 1981 from a distance of 13 million miles on the spacecraft's approach trajectory. Three of Saturn's icy moons are evident here. They are, in order of distance from the planet—Tethys, Dione and Rhea.

SATURN
Diameter: 74,565 miles (120,000 km)
Distance from Sun: 934,340,000 miles (1,507,000,000 km) at aphelion
835,140,000 miles (1,347,000,000 km) at perihelion
Mass: 2.5836×10^{26} lb (5.684×10^{26} kg)
Rotational period (Saturnian day): 10.25 Earth hours
Sidereal period (Saturnian year): 10,759 Earth days (29.46 Earth years)
Eccentricity: 0.056
Inclination of rotational axis: 26.73°
Inclination to ecliptic plane (Earth = 0): 2.49°
Albedo (100% reflection of light = 1): .33
Mean surface temperature: −284.8° F
Maximum surface temperature: −207.4° F
Largest surface feature: Anne's Spot (a large red spot)
3107 × 1864 miles
Major atmospheric components: Hydrogen (94%)
Helium (6%)
Other atmospheric components: Ammonia
Phosphine
Methane
Ethane
Acetylene
Methylacetylene
Propane

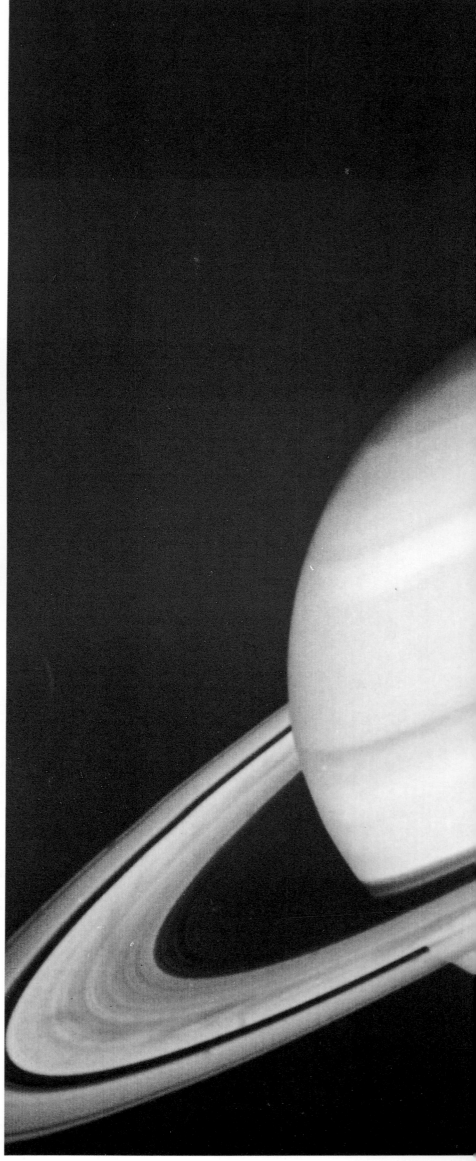

SATURN'S MOONS

Not only do its spectacular rings set Saturn apart from other planets, but so too does its complex system of more than 20 moons. Saturn's moons range in size from huge Titan, once thought to be the Solar System's largest moon, to the family of tiny moons that were discovered in photographs taken by the Voyager Spacecraft in 1980. Though the moons of Saturn are no less diverse in character than those of Jupiter, they are generally smaller and, with the exception of the two outermost (Iapetus and Phoebe), their orbital inclination is within 1.5 degrees of that of the rings. With the exception of Phoebe, the moons are synchronous, like Earth's moon, meaning that the same side faces Saturn at all times. The western hemispheres, which face in the direction of their orbital paths, are called *leading hemispheres*, while the eastern are called *trailing hemispheres*.

In 1977, when the two Voyager Spacecraft were launched from Earth, the ringed planet was known to have nine moons. Five of these were discovered prior to 1700 (with four found by Giovanni Cassini, the man who discovered that Saturn had multiple rings); only two were discovered after 1800. By the time that the Voyager data was digested in 1982, Saturn was known to have 17 moons and four to six additional Lagrangian co-orbital satellites. A co-orbital is one of a group of moons that share a single orbital path, while Lagrangian satellites (named after the eighteenth century astronomer whose mathematical theory postulated their existence) are small co-orbitals that exist in the orbit of a larger moon if they remain 60 degrees ahead or 60 degrees behind it in the orbital path.

Stephen Synnott of NASA's Jet Propulsion Laboratory has led the way in the identification of Lagrangian moons and in postulating the existence of others. Such moons have been found sharing the orbits of Mimas and Dione, and *four* such moons have been found with Tethys. There is also the possibility that Dione has a second co-orbital and that Tethys has a fifth.

Saturn's most recently discovered moons are so small and so close to the planet that it is almost hard to know where to draw the line between moons and ring particles. This also makes it harder to find such bodies visually against the brilliant rings.

The innermost of Saturn's moons is Atlas (originally 1980 S28), which is named for one of the Titans of Greek mythology who was condemned to support the weight of the universe on his shoulders. Atlas is also informally known as the A Ring Shepherd Moon because of its role in shepherding the nearby outer A Ring particles and, in a sense, *defining* the outer edge of the A Ring.

The next two moons, Prometheus and Pandora (originally 1980 S27

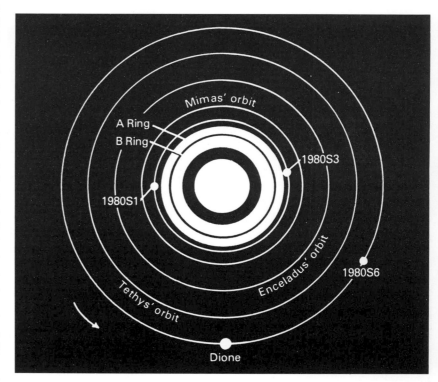

Above: **After the 1979 ring plane crossing and before the first Voyager Saturn encounter, a total of 12 Saturn moons were known—1980 S1 and 1980 S3 were co-orbital, and, as one was gaining on the other, it was expected that these two satellites would actually swap orbits as they closed upon one another sometime in 1981 or 1982. With no witnesses to this event, it's currently yet another incidence of 'the tree falling in the forest' syndrome. Did they or didn't they, and what was it like?**

The Inner Group of Saturn's Moons

JANUS (1980S1)
Diameter: 62 × 56 miles (100 × 90 km)
Distance from Saturn: 94,120 miles (151,472 km)
Rotational period (Janusian day): 16.67 Earth hours
Sidereal period (Janusian year): 16.67 Earth hours
Inclination to ecliptic plane: 0°

EPIMETHEUS (1980S3)
Diameter: 56 × 25 miles (90 × 40 km)
Distance from Saturn: 94,089 miles (151,422 km)
Rotational period (Epimethean day): 16.66 Earth hours
Sidereal period (Epimethean year): 16.66 Earth hours
Inclination to ecliptic plane: 0°

PANDORA (1980S26)
Diameter: 56 miles (90 km)
Distance from Saturn: 88,000 miles (141,700 km)
Rotational period (Pandoran day): 15.1 Earth hours
Sidereal period (Pandoran year): 15.1 Earth hours
Inclination to ecliptic plane: 0°

PROMETHEUS (1980S27)
Diameter: 136.7 miles (220 km)
Distance from Saturn: 86,589 miles (139,353 km)
Rotational period (Promethean day): 14.67 Earth hours
Sidereal period (Promethean year): 14.67 Earth hours
Inclination to ecliptic plane: 0°

ATLAS (1980S28)
Diameter: 24.9 × 12.4 miles (40 × 20 km)
Distance from Saturn: 85,500 miles (137,670 km)
Rotational period (Atlaen day): 14.4 Earth hours
Sidereal period (Atlaen year): 14.4 Earth hours
Inclination to ecliptic plane: Unknown

Schematic Map of Saturn's Moon System

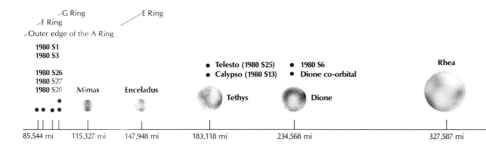

and 1980 S26) are named respectively for the Titan of Greek mythology who stole fire from Olympus to give it to man, and for the woman who was bestowed upon man as a punishment for Prometheus having stolen fire. Prometheus and Pandora are known informally as F Ring Shepherd Moons because of their positions on either side of the F Ring and their role in defining that ring. The two moons may also be responsible for the kinks and braiding observed in the F Ring.

Well beyond the F Ring, but inside of the G Ring, are Epimetheus and Janus (originally 1980 S3 and 1980 S1), which are the first of the several groups of co-orbital moons and the only group of co-orbitals not to be of the Lagrangian type. The centers of these two bodies, and hence the 'center lines' of their orbital paths, are offset by only 30 miles, a distance narrower than the radius of either! Epimetheus is named for the

brother, in Greek mythology, of Prometheus, who accepted Pandora (a gift from Zeus) as his wife, despite the warning of his brother. As Prometheus had warned, Pandora opened the infamous box, releasing all the evils within. Janus, the two-faced Roman god of doorways, became the namesake of a moon that was thought to have been identified in 1966 at distance of 105,000 miles from Saturn. The existence of this 'first' Janus was disproven, but the name was reassigned to 1980 S26, which was discovered in a nearby orbit.

Two satellites of Saturn share an orbit. The trailing co-orbital satellite, designated 1980 S3, but since named Epimetheus, is seen *below.* **The shadow of Saturn's F Ring was photographed transiting the moon in a series of six pictures; the colored stripes seen on the moon are a consequence of the shadow's motion as the images were taken through variably colored filters.**

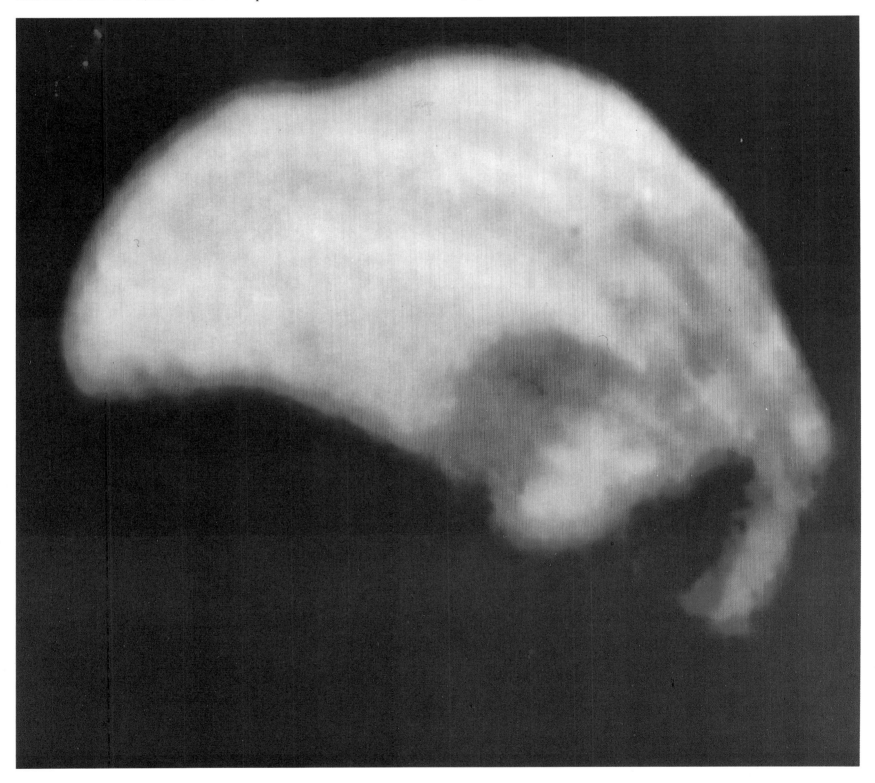

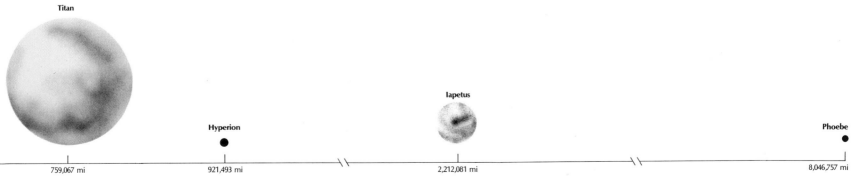

Titan

Hyperion

Iapetus

Phoebe

759,067 mi   921,493 mi   2,212,081 mi   8,046,757 mi

103

Discovered in 1789 by the German-born, but naturalized English, astronomer William Herschel (1738-1822), Mimas is scarred by a huge impact crater that bears his name. This huge crater is centered precisely on the equator and has a diameter one third the diameter of Mimas itself. The walls of the crater Herschel average 16,000 feet, and a huge mountain at the crater's center rises nearly 20,000 feet from its crater floor. Herschel is truly the standout feature on Mimas, as none of the other impact craters observed on the surface have anywhere near half its diameter. Mimas's surface is also characterized by valleys, or chasma, which tend to run in a parallel pattern from southwest to northwest. These uniform valleys are generally 60 miles long, one mile deep and six miles wide. They are thought to be fracture zones which date from the impact which formed Herschel.

Mimas is thought to be composed of 60 percent water ice with roughly 40 percent silicate rock, making it of the 'dirty snowball' class of moons found in much of the outer solar system. In 1982 Stephen Synnott identified a probable co-orbital moon within the orbit of Mimas.

Discovered by William Herschel (1738-1822) in 1789 at the same time that he identified Mimas, Enceladus is the most geologically active of Saturn's moons. It is named for the giant who rebelled against the gods of Greek mythology, and who was subsequently struck down and buried on Mount Etna.

Like Mimas, Enceladus is composed mostly of water, with the remaining roughly 40 percent of material being silicate rock. Enceladus, however, has a much more complex surface which is divided between vast and ancient fields of impact craters, large smooth plains and complex mountain ranges. The latter are typical of the type of fracture zones that characterize the surfaces of Jupiter's moon Ganymede or Uranus's moon Miranda. These features, including ridges and valleys, were possibly formed by the same sort of pressure between separate surface plates that is responsible for the silicate rock mountain ranges on Earth and the ice mountain ranges on Ganymede.

The smooth plains on Enceladus are further evidence of fracture zones because they were possibly formed by liquid water welling up from the interior and spilling out through fissures and faults, forming lakes in lowland areas. These lakes covered older fields of impact craters, and when the water froze the lakes became the relatively smoother and much newer plains which we see today.

Discovered in 1684 by Giovanni Domenico Cassini (1625-1712), Tethys is named for the Greek sea goddess who was both the wife and sister of Oceanus. Like the smaller Mimas and Enceladus, Tethys is a 'dirty snowball' composed mostly of water ice, with silicate rock as a secondary component. Most of its surface is marred by impact craters, but they appear somewhat softened—as though the surface had warmed slightly at some point since the formation of the craters and that partial melting had taken place.

The most notable feature on Tethys is the mysterious Ithaca Chasma, an enormous rift canyon that runs from near the north pole all the way to the south pole. With an average width of 60 miles and an average depth of three miles, Ithaca Chasma dwarfs the Earth's Grand Canyon in both scale and absolute terms. In the scale of the Earth, the equivalent of Ithaca Chasma would be like having a 40-mile deep trench as wide as

MIMAS
Diameter: 242.3 miles (390 km)
Distance from Saturn: 115,326 miles (185,600 km)
Mass: 1.70×10^{19} lb (3.76×10^{19} kg)
Rotational period (Miman day): 22.55 Earth hours
Sidereal period (Miman year): 22.55 Earth hours
Inclination to ecliptic plane: 1.5°
Largest surface feature: Herschel (a huge crater)
                       80.79 miles in diameter (130 km)

MIMAS CO-ORBITAL
Diameter: 6.2 miles (10 km)
Distance from Saturn: 115,326 miles (185,600 km)
Rotational period (Mimas co-orbital day): 22.55 Earth hours
Sidereal period (Mimas co-orbital year): 22.55 Earth hours
Inclination to ecliptic plane: 1.5°

ENCELADUS
Diameter: 310.7 miles (500 km)
Distance from Saturn: 147,948 miles (238,100 km)
Mass: 3.36×10^{19} lb (7.40×10^{19} kg)
Rotational period (Enceladian day): 1.37 Earth days (32.9 hours)
Sidereal period (Enceladian year): 1.37 Earth days
Inclination to ecliptic plane: 0°

TELESTO (a Tethys co-orbital)
Diameter: 9.3 miles (15 km)
Distance from Saturn: 183,100 miles (294,700 km)
Rotational period (Telestan day): 1.9 Earth days
Sidereal period (Telestan year): 1.9 Earth days
Inclination to ecliptic plane: 0°

CALYPSO (a Calypso co-orbital)*
Diameter: 9.3 miles (15 km)**
Distance from Saturn: 217,500 miles (350,000 km)
Rotational period (Calypsan day): 2.44 Earth days
Sidereal period (Calypsan year): 2.44 Earth days
Inclination to ecliptic plane: Unknown
    *The existence of another Tethys co-orbital has been theorized.
    **Some data suggests a diameter of 15.5 miles.

TETHYS
Diameter: 652.4 miles (1050 km)
Distance from Saturn: 1710 miles (1060 km)
Mass: 2.85×10^{21} lb (6.32×10^{21} kg)
Rotational period (Tethian day): 1.89 Earth days (45.3 hours)
Sidereal period (Tethian year): 1.89 Earth days
Inclination to ecliptic plane: 1.1°
Largest surface feature: Ithaca Chasma 1550 miles long × 62 miles
                     average width × 1.8 to 3.1 miles deep

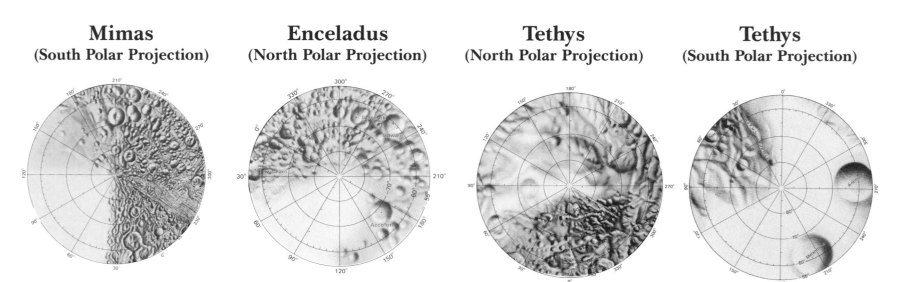

Mimas	Enceladus	Tethys	Tethys
(South Polar Projection)	(North Polar Projection)	(North Polar Projection)	(South Polar Projection)

Mimas (Mercator Projection)

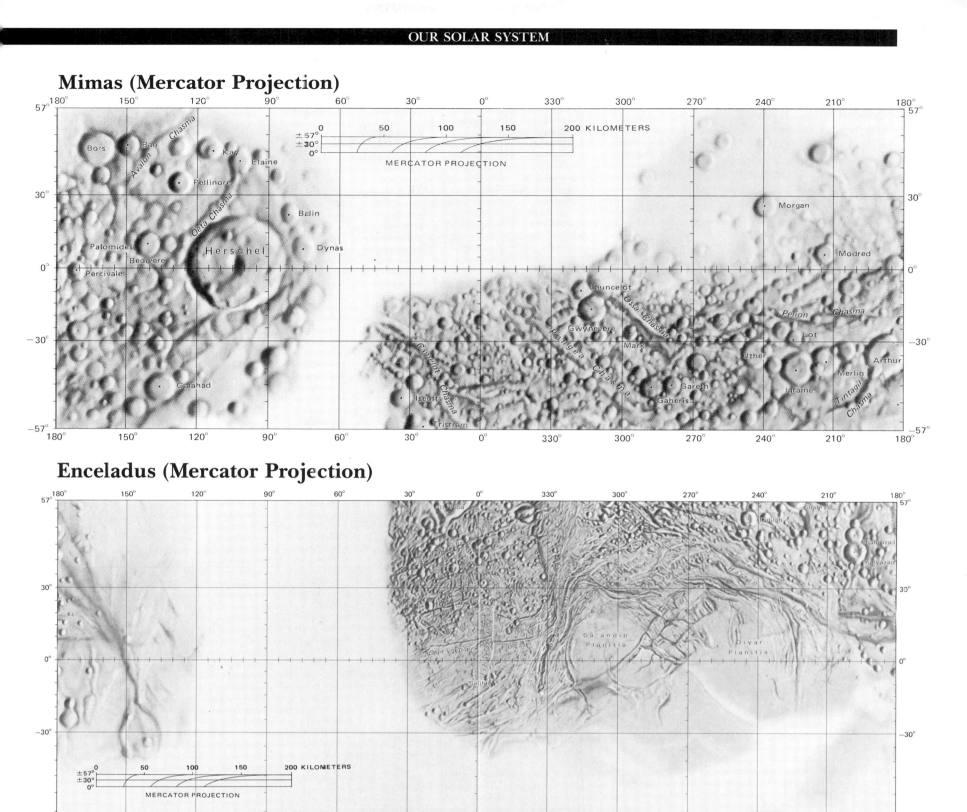

Enceladus (Mercator Projection)

Tethys (Mercator Projection)

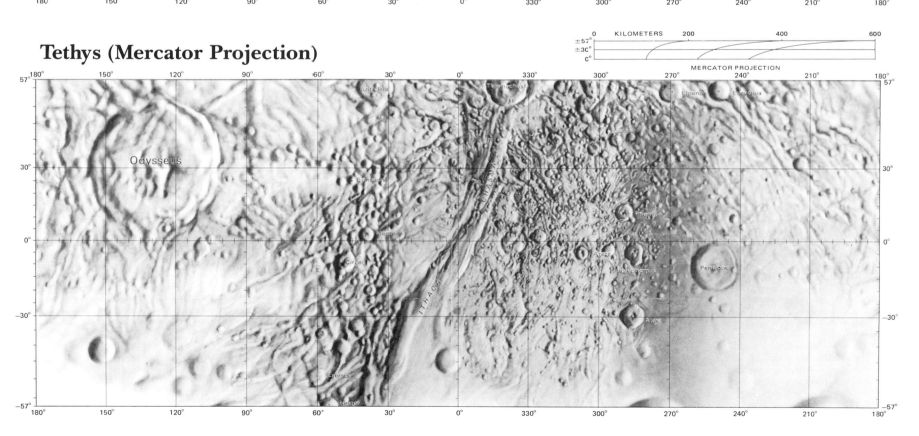

the state of Colorado, extending from Nome, Alaska, to the southern tip of Argentina. Of uncertain origin, this huge canyon was probably formed when Tethys cooled after it was first formed.

Tethys also has the distinction of being the 'parent,' both figuratively and *perhaps* literally, of a family of as many as *five* co-orbital moons. The larger of these are Telesto and Calypso (formerly 1980 S25 and 1980 S13). Calypso is named for the sea nymph of Greek mythology who delayed Odysseus and his men for seven years on her island. Calypso is derived from the Greek word *Kalupso*, meaning 'she who conceals'—an apt reference for a member of the group of co-orbitals which lurk in the shadow of Tethys.

The physical nature of the Tethys co-orbital family is unknown, but it would probably not be out of line to suggest that they are 'dirty snowballs' with surfaces that have been battered by meteorites.

Discovered by Giovanni Cassini (1625-1712) in 1684, Dione is named for the mother of the Greek goddess Aphrodite. Like the moons closer to Saturn, Dione is composed of silicate rock and water ice. However, while the inner moons have a predominance of water ice, Dione is at least half rock.

Dione's surface is darker than any of Saturn's other ice/rock moons, indicating that there are large regions of exposed rock. Dione's surface is characterized by impact craters common to both icy and rocky surface areas. The craters are generally smaller than twenty-five miles across, but Amata, the largest, measures nearly 150 miles in diameter. Amata is coincidentally located at the center of an eastern hemisphere pattern of unusual light colored streaks. While the streaks on Enceladus and Tethys are very sharply defined, as though cut with a knife, Dione's streaks are wispy—as though they were painted with an air brush. These streaks are probably cracks or fissures through which liquid water seeped and refroze over time. Amata appears to have been partially inundated by this seepage, and it has been suggested that whatever impact created Amata may have also played a role in the formation of the wispy streaks, because many of them seem to radiate from the crater.

Dione's family of co-orbitals includes 1980 S6, which is sometimes called Dione B. The largest of the Lagrangians, 1980 S6 is the same size as Phoebe, the outermost of Saturn's moons. It was discovered in 1980 by Lacques and Lecacheux in France and photographed by the Voyager spacecraft just a few months later. It was an interesting coincidence that Saturn's rings were oriented toward the Earth in such a way that it was possible for ground-based observers to discover 1980 S6 in the same year that the Voyagers made their own spectacular discoveries.

Stephen Synnott has identified a second Dione co-orbital that might actually be a 1980 S6 co-orbital, as the center lines of the orbits of these bodies are offset from Dione's path by about 300 miles, or exactly Dione's radius.

A third possible member, of either the Dione family or the Rhea family, is a body described by Synnott which is located about 57,000 miles beyond the orbital path of Dione and 1980 S6, and 35,300 miles inward from Rhea's orbit.

The second largest of Saturn's moons, Rhea was discovered by Giovanni Cassini (1625-1712) in 1672 and was named for the wife of Kronos, who according to Greek mythology, ruled the universe until dethroned by his son Zeus. In Roman mythology, as well as in astronomical nomenclature, Rhea is identified with Saturn because Saturn is the father of Jupiter, the Roman equivalent of Zeus.

Rhea the moon is composed of an equal mixture of water ice and silicate rock, with a possible core of denser material, or perhaps solid rock. The moon's leading hemisphere is solid water ice with intermittent patches of frost, while the darker, trailing eastern hemisphere shows signs of the same wispy surface detail that was observed more minutely by the Voyager spacecraft on Dione. The icy western hemisphere is characterized exclusively by thousands of impact craters, while there seem to be fewer craters in the eastern hemisphere and in the equatorial regions of both hemispheres. The largest crater, Izanagi, located deep in the southern hemisphere near the *prime meridian*, has a diameter of nearly 140 miles.

DIONE
Diameter: 695.9 miles (1120 km)
Distance from Saturn: 234,567 miles (377,500 km)
Mass: 4.77×10^{20} lb (1.05×10^{21} kg)
Rotational period (Dionian day): 2.74 Earth days (65.7 hours)
Sidereal period (Dionian year): 2.74 Earth days
Inclination to ecliptic plane: 0°
Largest surface feature: Amata (a basin with bright wispy features) 149.13 miles (240 km) in diameter

RHEA
Diameter: 950 miles (1530 km)
Distance from Saturn: 327,600 miles (527,200 km)
Mass: 1.0×10^{21} lb (2.28×10^{21} kg)
Rotational period (Rhean day): 4.52 Earth days (108 hours)
Sidereal period (Rhean year): 4.52 Earth days
Inclination to ecliptic plane: .3°

Below left: The surface of Enceladus is characterized by vast fields of impact craters, large smooth plains and complex mountain ranges. *Below:* Dione, too, has many impact craters—the record of the collision of cosmic debris. The largest crater is less than 62 miles in diameter and shows a well-developed central peak. Sinuous fault valleys break the moon's icy crust.

Dione (Mercator Projection)

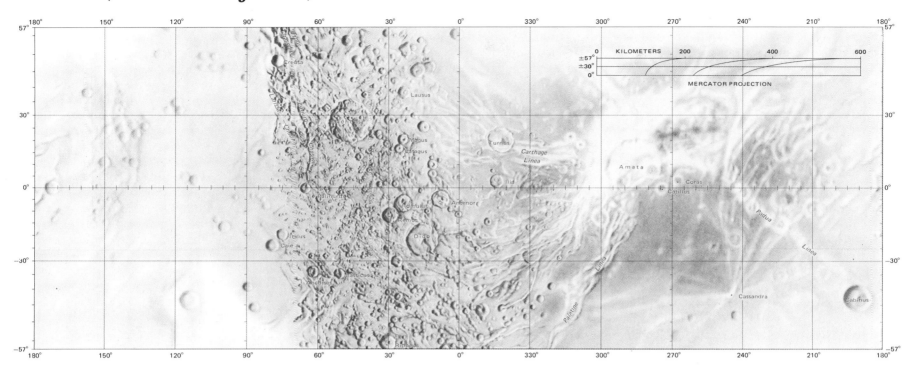

Rhea (Mercator Projection)

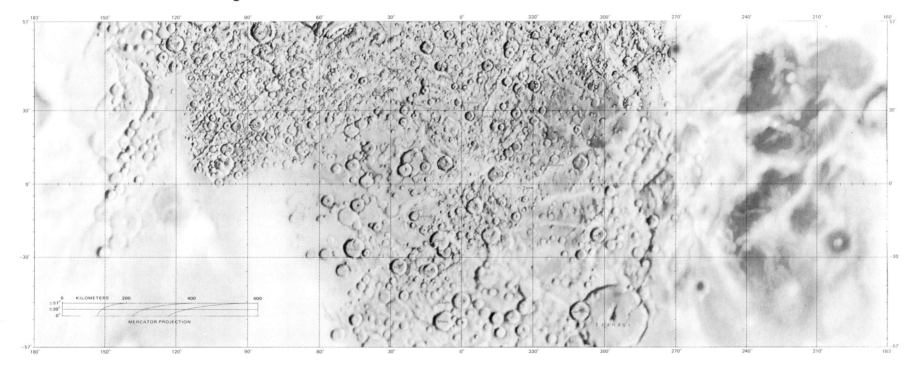

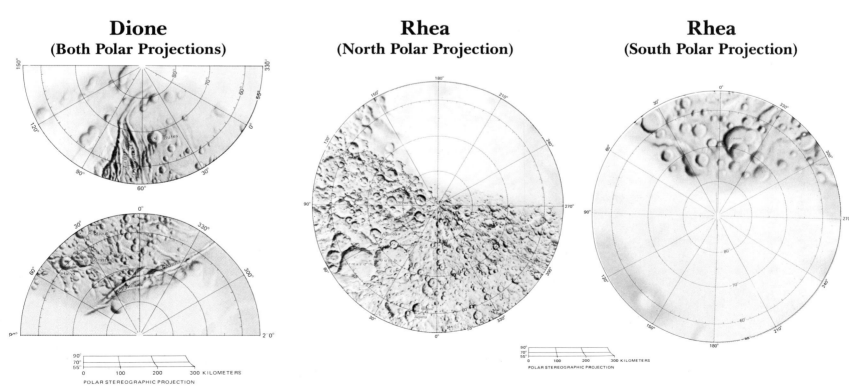

Dione
(Both Polar Projections)

Rhea
(North Polar Projection)

Rhea
(South Polar Projection)

Larger than either of the planets Mercury and Pluto, Titan is the second largest moon in the Solar System (after Ganymede). Once thought to be the largest, it was named for the family of pre-Olympian Greek gods whose name implies colossal size. Titan was discovered by the Dutch astronomer Christiaan Huygens in 1655, making it one of the first moons to be discovered in the Solar System. Though no longer on the throne as the Solar System's largest moon, it certainly must rank as one of the most spectacular.

Titan is the only known moon with a fully developed atmosphere that consists of more than simply trace gases. It has, in fact, a denser atmosphere and cloud cover than either Earth or Mars. This cloud cover, nearly as opaque as that which shrouds Venus, has prevented the sort of surface mapping that has been possible with the other major moons of the outer Solar System, but its presence has only served to make Titan all that much more intriguing. (Early astronomers mistook this dense atmosphere for Titan's actual surface, and it was through this mistake that Titan was once considered to be the Solar System's largest moon.)

Titan's atmosphere is extremely rich in nitrogen, the same element that makes up the greatest part of the Earth's atmosphere. Other major components of Titan's atmosphere are hydrocarbon gases, such as acetylene, ethane and propane, with methane being the most common of the hydrocarbons. While these gases are also to be found in Saturn's own atmosphere, Titan's atmosphere contains four times the concentration of ethane and 150 times the concentration of acetylene. Titan's atmosphere probably includes broken methane clouds at an altitude of about 25 miles, with the dense, smoggy hydrocarbon haze stretching up to an altitude of nearly 200 miles, where ultraviolet radiation from the Sun converts methane to acetylene or ethane.

Why Titan was able to develop an atmosphere, while Ganymede and Callisto (bodies of similar size) did not, is a matter of conjecture. It has been theorized that all the Solar System's largest moons had similar chemistry in the beginning, but Titan evolved in a colder part of the Solar System—farther away from the Sun and from Jupiter—when it almost became a primordial star. Thus the hydrocarbon gases were able to exist as solids on Titan, while the gases of Jupiter's Galilean moons dissipated into space, leaving only water and rock. Saturn's other moons meanwhile, were never large enough to have sufficient gravity to hold an atmosphere.

The view from Titan's surface is one of an exciting, but inhospitable, world. Covered by the opaque haze, the sky would appear like a smoggy sunset on Earth or like a view from the surface of Venus. The atmospheric pressure on on Titan's surface, while 1.6 times that of Earth is, however, a good deal less than that of Venus. Titan's surface tempera-

ture of nearly 300 degrees Fahrenheit would permit methane to exist not only as a gas, but also as a liquid or a solid, in much the same way that water does on Earth. A picture is thus painted of a cold, orange-tinted land where methane rain or snow falls from the methane clouds and where methane rivers may flow into methane oceans dotted with methane icebergs. There is evidence of a 30 Earth-year seasonal cycle which *may* have permitted the development of methane ice caps that expand and recede like the water ice caps on Earth (and the water/carbon dioxide ice caps on Mars). Water ice is also present on Titan, beneath the methane surface features, and possibly extends up into the atmosphere in the form of ice mountains. Titan's mantle is, in turn, largely composed of water ice that gives way to a rocky core perhaps 600 miles beneath the surface. The absence of a magnetic field indicates that Titan has no significant amount of ferrous metallic minerals in its core.

The presence of nitrogen, a hydrocarbon atmosphere and water indicate that Titan's surface is very much like that of the Earth four billion years ago before life evolved on the latter body. It has been suggested that this similarity to the prebiotic 'soup' that covered the Earth in those bygone days could presage a similar chain of events on Titan.

TITAN
Diameter: 3200 miles (5150 km)
Distance from Saturn: 759,100 miles (1,221,600 km)
Mass: 6.1818×10^{23} lb (1.36×10^{23} kg)
Rotational period (Titanian day): 15.9 Earth days (383 hours)
Sidereal period (Titanian year): 15.9 Earth days
Inclination to ecliptic plane: .3°
Mean surface temperature: $-288°$ F
Major atmospheric components: Nitrogen (94%)
Other atmospheric components: Methane, Helium, Ethane, Acetylene, Propane, Diacetylene, Methylacetylene, Hydrogen cyanide, Cyanoacetylene, Cyanogen, Carbon dioxide, Carbon monoxide

Below: Saturn's shrouded moon, the gargantuan Titan. We have no map of Titan because its surface is hidden beneath a thick hydrocarbon atmosphere. The southern hemisphere appears lighter than the northern, and a well defined darker band can be seen near the equator. *Right:* Layers of haze cover Titan in this image taken by Voyager 1 on 12 November 1980 at a range of 13,700 miles. The colors are false to show the details of the haze. The divisions in the haze occur at 124, 233 and 310 miles above the moon's limb.

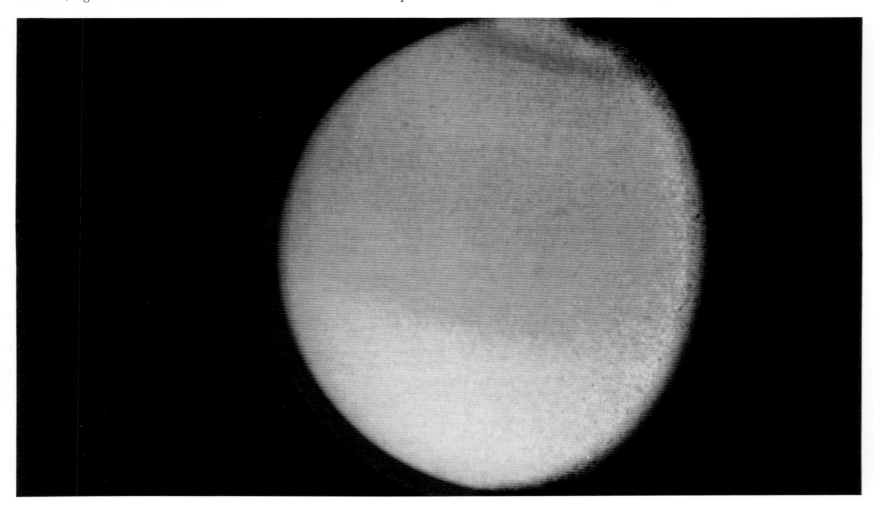

A dark, rocky moon, Hyperion is less completely ice-covered than its larger brothers closer to Saturn, although water-ice is prevalent over much of its crater-pocked surface. Though it has several craters with diameters in excess of 30 miles, Hyperion's most distinguishing feature is its irregular shape.

Elliptical shapes are common among smaller moons throughout the Solar System, but it is uncommon to find one of Hyperion's size that is not more perfectly spherical. The mystery is deepened by the fact that the long axis is not oriented toward Saturn, which tends to indicate that Hyperion may have been the victim of a collision with another body— such as a large meteorite—at some time in its relatively recent geologic history.

In Greek mythology, Hyperion's namesake was one of the Titans, a son of Uranus and Gaea, and father of Helios, Selene and Eos (the Sun, the Moon and the dawn). Hyperion was often referred to by the Greek poets as the Sun god and as such was often identified with Apollo.

Discovered in 1671 by Giovanni Cassini (1625-1712), Iapetus is the third largest of Saturn's moons in terms of size. On those terms it is, in fact, a near twin of Rhea, but is a good deal less dense. As such it probably has a higher proportion of ice in relation to rock in its composition.

The most intriguing thing about Iapetus is that its entire leading hemisphere is as black as asphalt while its trailing hemisphere contains a more familiar crater-pocked ice and rock landscape. The nature and source of this vast dark area is unknown, but some crater floors on the trailing hemisphere appear to be equally dark and this tends to suggest that the black material is extruded from beneath an otherwise icy surface.

The fact that this dark area is apparently unblemished by icy, light colored meteorite craters indicates that the material—whatever it is— probably is renewed regularly. One is reminded of the molten sulfur flows that are constantly resurfacing Jupiter's moon Io, or the lava flows in the Earth's Hawaiian Islands.

Like his brother, the mythological Hyperion, the Iapetus of Greek mythology was a Titan. Son of Uranus and Gaea, he was the father of Atlas, Epimetheus, Menoetius and Prometheus. According to Greek legend, Iapetus was imprisoned by Zeus in Tartarus after the rebellion of the Titans against the gods.

The outermost of Saturn's known moons, Phoebe was discovered in 1898 by American astronomer William Henry Pickering (1858-1938). Phoebe has several features that distinguish it from all the other moons of Saturn: non-synchronous rotation, a retrograde orbit—and the plane of that orbit, which is tilted 150 degrees from Saturn's equatorial plane.

This is *10 times* the inclination exhibited by the orbit of Iapetus, and all the other moons—from tiny Atlas to gigantic Titan—orbit within *two* degrees of Saturn's equatorial plane.

Because of these unusual characteristics and because of Phoebe's irregular shape, it has been suggested that this moon may be either an asteroid or a comet nucleus that has been trapped into orbit by Saturn's gravity.

The fact that Phoebe seems to be more rocky than icy would tend to mitigate against the comet nucleus theory.

In Greek mythology, Phoebe was a title given to Artemis in her role as goddess of the Moon. It is parallel to Phoebus, the title given to Apollo in his character of Sun god.

Below: **In this NASA painting by Ron Miller, Saturn is shown as it might appear when viewed from the surface of Rhea. Rhea is an icy wasteland and is completely without an atmosphere; therefore, Rhea's mother planet may well be seen very clearly from the moon's surface. The second largest of Saturn's moons, Rhea is still only half the size of Titan.**

Far Right: **This view of Iapetus, which is lit from above, shows the heavily cratered northern hemisphere toward the bright trailing side of the moon.**

The north pole is near the large central peak crater partly seen in the shadow at the top of the photo. Voyager 2 took this photo from 1.1 million miles away on 22 August 1981, the day that it made its closest approach to this distant moon.

HYPERION
Diameter: 249 × 155 × 149 miles (400 × 250 × 240 km)
Distance from Saturn: 921,500 miles (1,483,000 km)
Mass: 5×10^{19} lb (1.1×10^{20} kg)
Rotational period (Hyperionian day): 21.28 Earth days (510.7 hours)
Sidereal period (Hyperionian year): 21.28 Earth days
Inclination to ecliptic plane: .6°
Largest surface feature: Scarp system 186 miles (300 km) long

IAPETUS
Diameter: 905 miles (1460 km)
Distance from Saturn: 2,212,100 miles (3,560,000 km)
Mass: 8.77×10^{20} lb (1.93×10^{21} kg)
Rotational period (Iapetan day): 79.33 Earth days (1904 hours)
Sidereal period (Iapetan year): 79.33 Earth days
Inclination to ecliptic plane: 14.7°
Largest surface feature: The Cassini Regio, an entire hemisphere uniformly jet black

PHOEBE
Diameter: 137 miles (220 km)
Distance from Saturn: 8,046,800 miles (12,950,000 km)
Rotational period (Phoeben day): 9 Earth hours
Sidereal period (Phoeben year): 550.3 Earth days
Inclination to ecliptic plane: 150°

Iapetus (Mercator Projection)

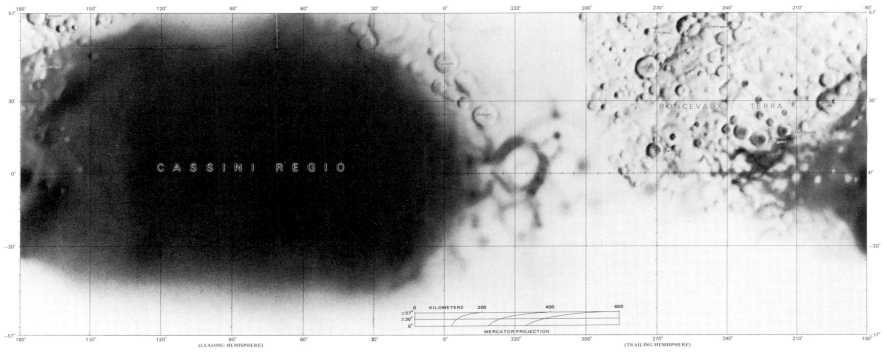

Iapetus (North Polar Projection)

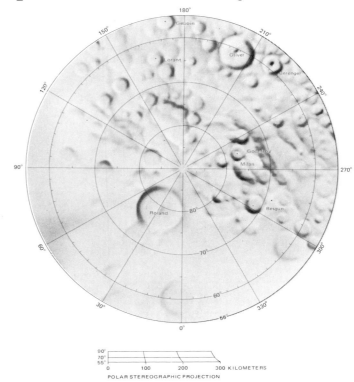

URANUS

The first outer Solar System planet to be correctly identified as such in historical times, Uranus was identified in 1781 by the German-born English astronomer William Herschel while he was working at Bath. The planet is named for the earliest supreme god of Greek mythology. The personification of the sky, mythical Uranus was both son and consort to the goddess Gaea and father of all the Cyclopes and Titans.

Uranus has an axial inclination of 98 degrees. Discovered in 1829, this is a phenomenon that is unique in the Solar System. With such an axial inclination, Uranus is seen as rotating 'on its side' at a near right angle to the inclination of the Earth or Sun. The poles of Uranus, rather than its equatorial regions, are pointing alternately at the Sun.

Uranus is a gaseous planet like Jupiter, Saturn and Neptune, with a distinct blue-green appearance, probably due to a concentration of methane in its upper *atmosphere*. In terms of size, it is smaller than Jupiter and Saturn, while being very close to the size of Neptune. Its solid core is composed of metals and silicate rock with a diameter of roughly 270,000 miles. Its core is, in turn, covered by an icy *mantle* of methane ammonia and water ice 6000 miles deep.

As with the other gaseous planets, the predominant elements in the Uranian atmosphere are hydrogen and helium, although the Voyager 2 observations in 1986 indicated that the atmosphere was only 15 percent helium, versus 40 percent, as originally postulated. Other atmospheric constituents include methane, acetylene and other hydrocarbons.

The clouds that form in this atmosphere are moved by prevailing winds that blow in the same direction as the planet rotates, just as they do on Jupiter, Saturn and Earth. The lowest temperature (-366 degrees Fahrenheit) is recorded at the boundary between *troposphere* and *stratosphere*. Surprisingly, both the poles show similar temperatures whether or not they are sunlit. The coldest latitudes seem to be those between 15 and 40 degrees. In the upper atmosphere, temperatures increase to −190 degrees Fahrenheit, while in the interior, temperatures are extremely hot—as are the interiors of Jupiter and Saturn.

Prior to the flyby of Voyager 2 in January 1986, Uranus was thought not to have a magnetic field, but this assumption proved false. The magnetic field of Uranus is tilted at a 60 degree angle to the planet's rotational axis (compared to 12 degrees on Earth). The magnetic field has roughly the same intensity as the Earth's, but whereas the Earth's magnetic field is generated by a molten metallic core, the one surrounding Uranus seems to be generated by the electrically conductive, super pressurized ocean of ammonia and water that exists beneath the atmosphere.

Uranus, like Jupiter and Saturn, has a system of *rings*, of which the first nine were discovered by Earth-based observers in 1977. In 1986 Voyager 2 observed these in detail and identified two more. This ring system is much more complex than that of Jupiter, but less so than Saturn's spectacular system. The system around Uranus seems to be

Right: This view of Uranus was recorded by Voyager 2 on 25 January 1986, as the spacecraft left the planet and set forth on its cruise to Neptune. The blue-green color, which can be seen by ground-based astronomers, is the result of methane in the Uranian atmosphere. *Below:* A false color image of the nine rings of Uranus.

relatively young and probably did not form at the same time as the planet. The particles that make up the rings may be the remnants of a moon that was broken by a high velocity impact or torn apart by gravitational effects of Uranus.

The widest ring known before Voyager 2 was the outermost ring, Epsilon—an irregular ring measuring 14 to 60 miles across. In 1986 Voyager's cameras helped identify a new innermost ring, designated 1986 U2R, that is 1550 miles wide. The narrowest complete rings are less than a mile wide, while faint, possibly incomplete, rings have been identified which are 160 feet across. The rings are composed of large blocks of ice with small dust particles scattered throughout the system. The outer edge of the system, the outer edge of the Epsilon ring, is sharply defined and is located 15,800 miles from the Uranus cloud tops. At this point the Epsilon Ring is just 500 feet thick, and surprisingly devoid of fragments with diameters below one foot.

URANUS
Diameter: 32,116 miles (51,800 km)
Distance from Sun: 1,862,480,000 miles (3,004,000,000 km) at aphelion
1,695,700,000 miles (2,735,000,000 km) at perihelion
Mass: 3.953×10^{25} lb (8.698×10^{25} kg)
Rotational period (Uranian day): 17.3 Earth hours (retrograde)
Sidereal period (Uranian year): 30.685 Earth days (84 Earth years)
Eccentricity: 0.047
Inclination of rotational axis: 97.9°
Inclination to ecliptic plane (Earth=0): .77°
Albedo (100% reflection of light=1): .34 to .5
Mean temperature: −350° F
Maximum temperature: −190° F
Minimum temperature: −366° F
Largest feature: Not visible
Major atmospheric components: Hydrogen (85%)
Helium (15%)
Other atmospheric components: Ammonia
Sulfur
Methane
Acetylene
other hydrocarbons

THE URANIAN MOONS

Prior to the observations by Voyager 2, Uranus was known to have just five moons. Photographs returned by the spacecraft increased the number of known moons to 15, with all 10 of the newly-discovered moons located *within* the orbital paths of the original five. One of the new moons, 1985 U1, was discovered by Voyager's cameras in late 1985, and the rest were discovered in the photos taken during the January 1986 Voyager flyby of the Uranian system. With the exception of 1985 U1 and 1986 U7—the largest and smallest of the 'Voyager' moons—all of the newly discovered members of the group are very uniform in size, with diameters ranging between 31 and 37 miles.

The innermost of the moons are 1986 U7, located between the Delta Ring and the Epsilon Ring, and 1986 U8, on the opposite side of the Epsilon Ring. Thus straddling the Epsilon ring, these two small bodies probably act like the shepherd moons of Saturn, controlling and defining the position and shape of the ring.

Of the five large Uranian moons, Miranda is the smallest and innermost, being less than three times larger than 1985 U1. It was discovered in 1948 by the Netherlands-born American astronomer Gerard Kuiper

---

The Inner Group of Uranian Moons

1986U7
Diameter: 25 miles (40 km)
Distance from Uranus: 30,900 miles (49,700 km)
Rotational period: Unknown
Sidereal period: Unknown

1986U8
Diameter: 31 miles (50 km)
Distance from Uranus: 33,425 miles (53,800 km)
Rotational period: Unknown
Sidereal period: Unknown

1986U9
Diameter: 31 miles (50 km)
Distance from Uranus: 36,800 miles (59,200 km)
Rotational period: Unknown
Sidereal period: Unknown

1986U3
Diameter: 37 miles (60 km)
Distance from Uranus: 38,400 miles (61,800 km)
Rotational period: Unknown
Sidereal period: Unknown

1986U6
Diameter: 37 miles (60 km)
Distance from Uranus: 38,960 miles (62,700 km)
Rotational period: Unknown
Sidereal period: Unknown

1986U2
Diameter: 50 miles (80 km)
Distance from Uranus: 40,140 miles (64,600 km)
Rotational period: Unknown
Sidereal period: Unknown

1986U1
Diameter: 50 miles (80 km)
Distance from Uranus: 41,072 miles (66,100 km)
Rotational period: Unknown
Sidereal period: Unknown

1986U4
Diameter: 37 miles (60 km)
Distance from Uranus: 43,400 miles (69,900 km)
Rotational period: Unknown
Sidereal period: Unknown

1986U5
Diameter: 37 miles (60 km)
Distance from Uranus: 46,800 miles (75,300 km)
Rotational period: Unknown
Sidereal period: Unknown

1985U1
Diameter: 105 miles (170 km)
Distance from Uranus: 53,440 miles (86,000 km)
Rotational period: Unknown
Sidereal period: Unknown

Schematic Map of the Uranian Moon System

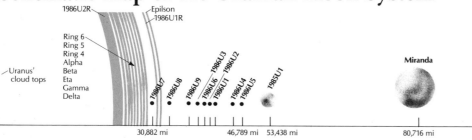
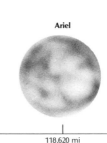
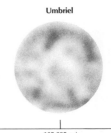

1986U2R
Epilson
1986U1R
Ring 6
Ring 5
Ring 4
Alpha
Beta
Eta
Gamma
Delta
Uranus' cloud tops

1986U7 1986U8 1986U9 1986U6 1986U3 1986U1 1986U2 1986U4 1986U5 1985U1

Miranda   Ariel   Umbriel

30,882 mi   46,789 mi 53,438 mi   80,716 mi   118,620 mi   165,285 mi

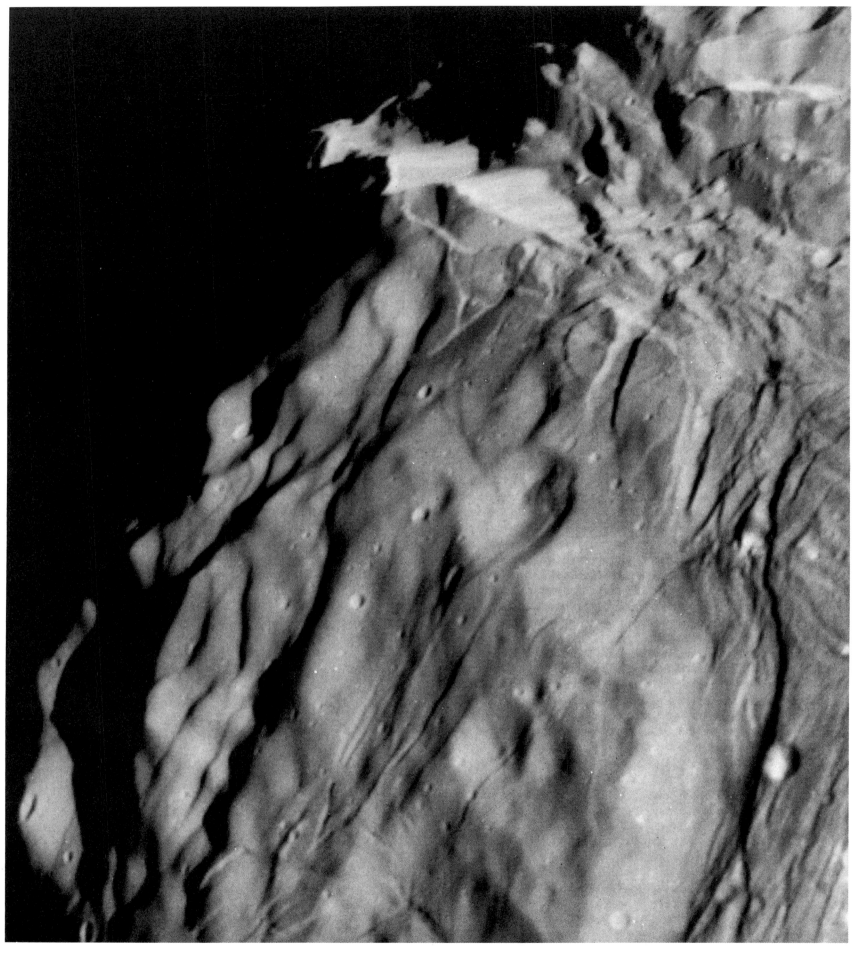

Above: A Voyager 2 view of Miranda over the Inverness Corona toward Argier Rupes with crater Alonso on the upper right. The Inverness Corona, first known as 'the Chevron,' is a series of pressure faults.

The nickname was used informally when the feature was first observed in January 1986. By year's end, the more conventional name had been bestowed.

Titania

Oberon

271,104 mi

362,508 mi

(1905-1973), and is named for the daughter of Prospero in Shakespeare's *The Tempest*.

Miranda's composition is about half water ice, with the balance being divided between silicate rock and methane-related organic compounds. On its surface there are huge fault canyons 12 miles deep and evidence of intense geologic activity. It has been much more geologically active than the other Uranian moons.

Given Miranda's surface temperature, −335 degrees Fahrenheit, much of the moon's geologic activity must be the result of the tidal effect of the gravitational pull of Uranus which has 'mobilized' a flow of icy material at a low temperature from within Miranda.

Discovered in 1851 by the English amateur astronomer William Lassell (1799-1880), Ariel is named for a spirit, the servant of Prospero, in *The Tempest* by William Shakespeare. Ariel's composition is about 50 percent water ice, 30 percent silicate rock and 20 percent methane ice. The major surface characteristics on Ariel are swaths of what appear to be fresh frost.

It is largely devoid of impact craters with diameters in excess of 30 miles and has the brightest surface of any of the Uranian moons. Ariel also appears to have undergone a period of intense geologic activity, which has produced many fault canyons and has resulted in many outflows of water ice from the interior. Where the longer canyons intersect, the surfaces are smooth, indicating that the valley floors are covered with huge glaciers.

Discovered in 1851 by William Lassell (1799-1880) at the same time that he identified Ariel, Umbriel is named for the dusky sprite in Alexander Pope's *The Rape of the Lock*.

While the surfaces of all the Uranian moons are darkened by the presence of methane ice, Umbriel is the darkest. Even its impact craters, which should theoretically show lighter-colored water ice in their bottoms, are dark. Nevertheless, Umbriel is thought to be composed mostly of water ice, with the balance made up of silicate rock and methane ice. As such, Umbriel is like the other Uranian moons, but it just carries most of its methane ice on its surface. Overall, it is the least geologically active of the Uranian moons.

The largest of the Uranian moons, Titania was discovered in 1787 by William Herschel (1738-1822), six years after he discovered Uranus itself. Not to be confused with Titan, Saturn's largest moon, Titania is named for the fairy queen of medieval folklore who was Oberon's wife.

Like its companions in the Uranian moon system, Titania is half composed of water ice, and like Ariel and Oberon, its surface is mostly water ice. The major feature on this icy surface is a huge canyon that dwarfs the scale of the Grand Canyon on Earth and is in a class with the Valles Marineris on Mars and the Ithaca Chasma on Saturn's Tethys.

Like the other Uranian moons, Titania is about 30 percent silicate rock and 20 percent methane-related organic compounds. It has been theorized that Titania may have a small co-orbital moon. If so, it would be the first co-orbital to be identified outside Saturn's system and it would be the eleventh moon for Uranus.

The outermost of the Uranian moons, Oberon was discovered by William Herschel at the same time that he discovered Titania, and six years after his discovery of their mother planet. Oberon is named for the fairy king of medieval folklore who was the husband of Titania. The name is derived from the Old French *Auberon* and is akin to the Old High German *Alberich*, which is thought to mean 'white, ghostlike apparition.'

Like the other Uranian moons, Oberon is composed of roughly 50 percent water ice, 30 percent silicate rock, and 20 percent methane-related carbon/nitrogen compounds. Unlike those of the others, however, Oberon's ancient, heavily-cratered surface shows very little evidence of internal geological activity. Being the second largest and most massive of the Uranian moons, as well as the farthest from the mother planet, Oberon is the moon least influenced by the tidal effects of the gravity of Uranus.

MIRANDA
Diameter: 217 miles (150 km)
Distance from Uranus: 43,600 miles (80,000 km)
Rotational period (Mirandan day): 1.41 Earth days
Sidereal period (Mirandan year): 1.41 Earth days
Inclination to ecliptic plane: 0°
Mean surface temperature: −335° F

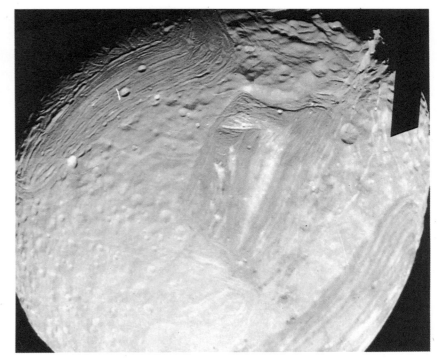

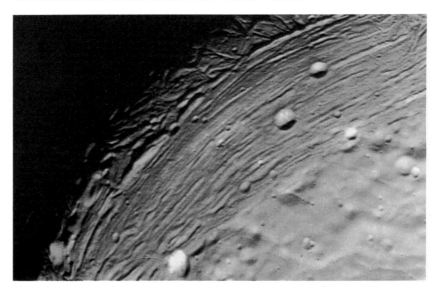

Above: **A mosaic image of Miranda showing, (left to right) Elsinore Corona, Inverness Corona and Arden Corona. The nick at the top of the photo represents missing information.** *Below:* **A view northwest over Elsinore Corona.**

Miranda
(South Polar Projection)

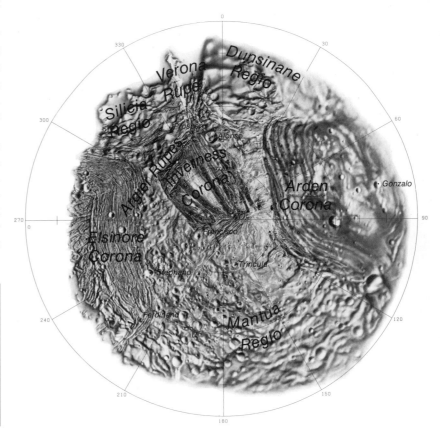

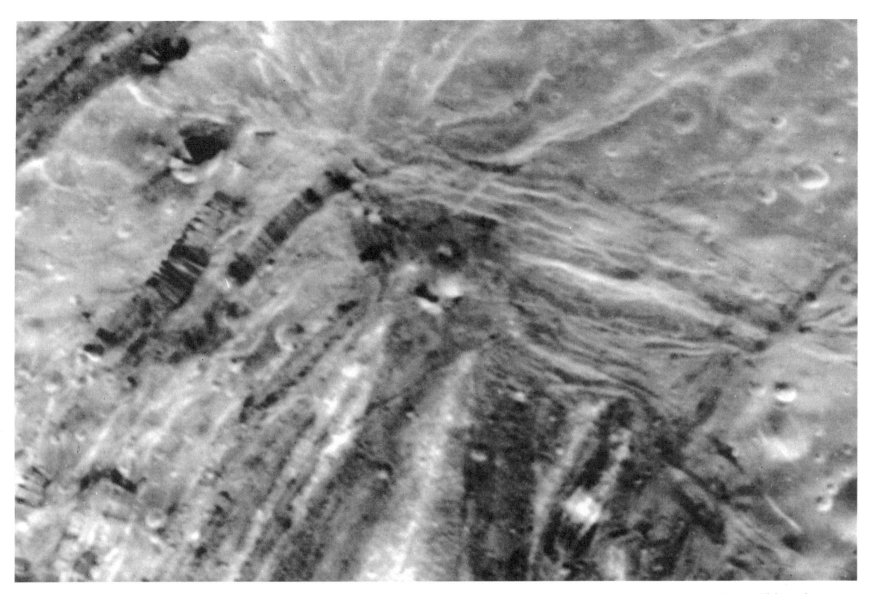

Above: A view of Inverness Corona and Mantua Regio. *Below:* This spectacular Voyager 2 photo shows the point on Miranda's surface at which Elsinore Corona (left) and Inverness Corona (right) nearly intersect. Like Inverness Corona, Elsinore Corona was originally known by its nickname—the Racetrack.

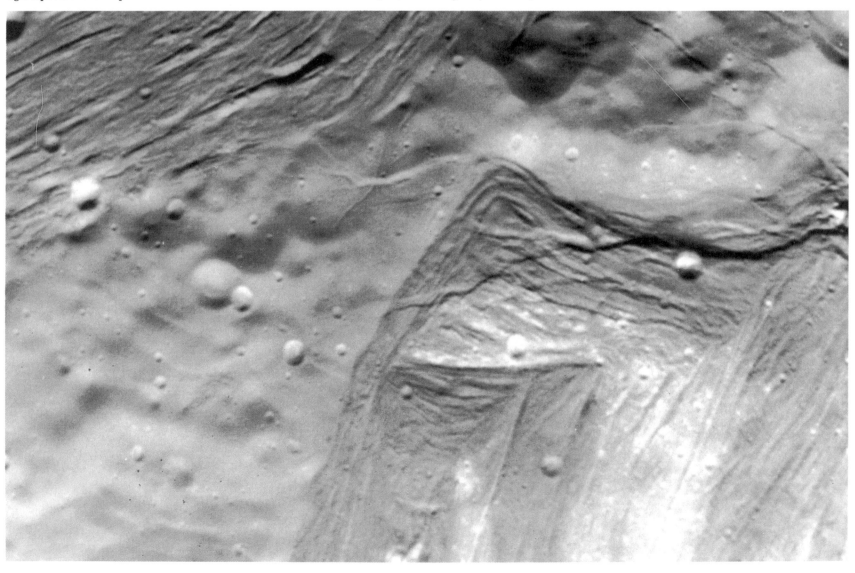

Ariel
(South Polar Projection)

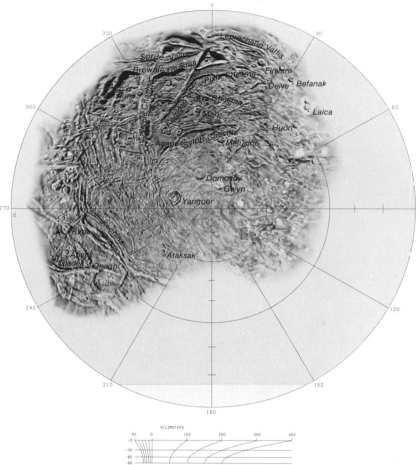

Umbriel
(South Polar Projection)

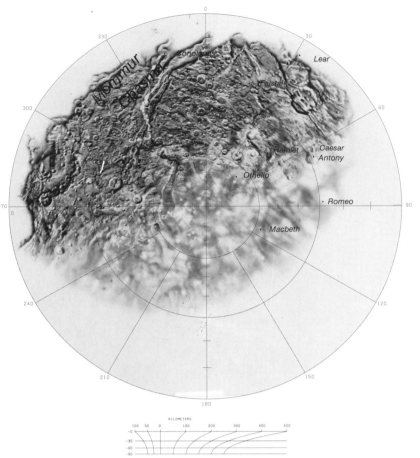

The southern hemispheric map *(at top)* of the bright moon Ariel coordinates well with the photo *(above)* of the same area. Recognizable on the lower left of the photo is Kachina Chasma, and at the top center of the photograph we find the complex of geographical features that include Pixie Chasma and Brownie Chasma.

In this photo *(above)*, in relation to the map of Umbriel *at top*, the craters Skynd, Vuver and Wunda can be seen on the upper perimeter of the moon's left crescent. Providing a sharp contrast to the moon's overall dusky methane coating, the light patch visible above the craters appears to be water ice.

ARIEL
Diameter: 720 miles (1160 km)
Distance from Uranus: 118,350 miles (190,900 km)
Rotational period (Arielian day): 2.52 Earth days
Sidereal period (Arielian year): 2.52 Earth days
Inclination to ecliptic plane: 0°

UMBRIEL
Diameter: 740 miles (1190 km)
Distance from Uranus: 165,280 miles (266,000 km)
Rotational period (Umbrielan day): 4.14 Earth days
Sidereal period (Umbrielan year): 4.14 Earth days
Inclination to ecliptic plane: 0°

Titania
(South Polar Projection)

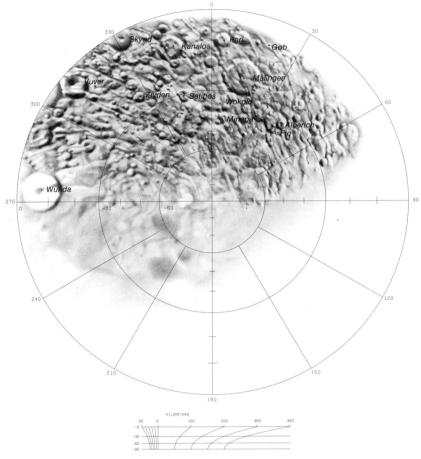

In coordinating the map *(at top)* with the photo *(above)* of Titania, Messina Chasma, Belmont Chasma and Rousillon Rupes can be seen as they arc down from the moon's upper crescent. Messina Chasma is a huge rift canyon, and the large crater Gertrude can be seen at the left edge of the crescent.

TITANIA
Diameter: 1000 miles (1610 km)
Distance from Uranus: 271,100 miles (436,300 km)
Rotational period (Titanian day): 8.71 Earth days
Sidereal period (Titanian year): 8.71 Earth days
Inclination to ecliptic plane: 0°

Oberon
(South Polar Projection)

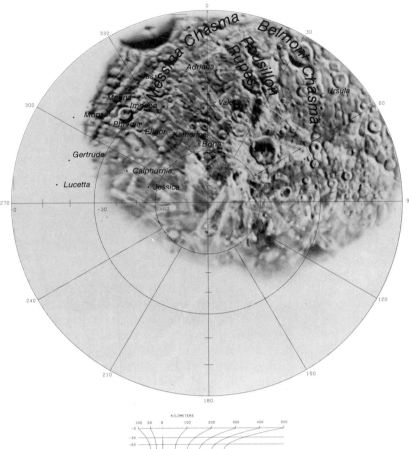

This photo of Oberon *(above)* clearly correlates with the map *at top*. Half-hidden in shadow along the upper crescent are (from left to right) Mommur Chasma and craters Coriolanus, Falstaff and Lear. Beyond the shadow lies a vast uncharted region. Oberon is the outermost Uranian moon.

OBERON
Diameter: 960 miles (1550 km)
Distance from Uranus: 362,500 miles (583,400 km)
Rotational period (Oberonian day): 13.46 Earth days
Sidereal period (Oberonian year): 13.46 Earth days
Inclination to ecliptic plane: 0°

NEPTUNE

The eighth planet in the Solar System, Neptune was first observed by Galileo Galilei (1564-1642) in December 1612 and January 1613 while the great Italian astronomer was conducting his observations of Jupiter. Galileo mistakenly recorded it as a fixed star, despite his having observed its motion relative to other stars.

The existence of an eighth planet was predicted in 1845 by Urbain Jean Joseph LeVerrier (1811-1877) in France and John Crouch Adams (1819-1892) in England, based on their analysis of anomalies in the orbit of Uranus. The following year Heinrich Ludwig D'Arrest (1822-1875) and Johann Galle physically observed it, and identified it as a planet for the first time.

Named for the Roman god of the sea, this blue-green giant is a near twin of Uranus in terms of its size and the chemical composition of its atmosphere. Unlike Uranus but like Jupiter, however, Neptune *radiates more heat than it absorbs*, and it also has a greater density and mass than the slightly larger Uranus. Like Jupiter and Uranus, Neptune may eventually be shown to have a faint *ring system*, as has been suggested by occultation data.

Physically, Neptune is characterized by a dark band at its equator and lighter colored *temperate zones* in its northern and southern hemispheres. The dark band is perhaps evidence of the shadows of planetary rings, or perhaps simply the absence in the equatorial region of the methane crystal haze and/or water ice crystal haze that drifts above the cloud tops in Neptune's colder temperate zones. Beneath this haze are clouds of ammonia; beneath these is a hydrogen atmosphere. Neptune probably has a rocky core roughly the size of the planet Earth that is covered to a depth of perhaps 5000 miles by an icy ocean of partly frozen water and liquid ammonia.

NEPTUNE'S MOON SYSTEM

Prior to the American Voyager 2 spacecraft encounter with Neptune in September 1989, the planet was known to possess two moons, although 1981 observations at the University of Arizona led to the prediction of at least one other moon.

The two Neptunian moons confirmed prior to 1989 are among the most peculiar in the Solar System. Triton, discovered less than a month after Neptune, is a huge object with the only retrograde orbit known in the Solar System; while Nereid, discovered more than a century after Triton, has the most elliptical orbit of any known moon in the Solar System.

Triton was discovered by English brewer and amateur astronomer William Lassell (1799-1880), just 17 days after the discovery of Neptune itself. Triton, like its parent planet, is named for a god of the sea—in this case, the merman son of the Greek god Poseidon and goddess Amphitrite.

Unique among all the known moons in the Solar System, Triton revolves around its mother planet in the direction opposite to Neptune's rotation. Its orbit is so close to Neptune, and is gradually getting so much closer, that one day Neptune's gravity might pull it apart and scatter it into a Saturn-like ring. (However, if this does happen it will not be for several million years.) Triton's surface, unlike that of Neptune, is rocky rather than gaseous, and this rocky surface is probably covered by methane frost and, perhaps, a faint methane atmosphere.

Nereid was discovered in 1949 by the Dutch-American astronomer Gerard Peter Kuiper (1905-1973) in an elliptical orbit far beyond the orbit of Triton. Named for the Nereids—sea nymph daughters of the Greek god Nereus—Nereid is much tinier than its brother Triton. Little is known about Nereid other than the fact that its orbit is extremely elliptical and what its size is relative to that of Triton.

TRITON
Diameter: 3700 miles (6000 km)
Distance from Neptune: 219,300 miles (353,000 km)
Mass: 6.229×10^{22} lb (1.370×10^{23} kg)
Rotational period (Tritonian day): 5.87 Earth days
Sidereal period (Tritonian year): 5.87 Earth days
Inclination to ecliptic plane: 159.9°

NEREID
Diameter: 300 miles (500 km)
Distance from Neptune: 3,454,800 miles (5,560,000 km)
Rotational period (Nereidan day): 359.9 Earth days
Sidereal period (Nereidan year): 359.9 Earth days
Inclination to ecliptic plane: 27.2°

NEPTUNE
Diameter: 30,758 miles (49,500 km)
Distance from Sun: 2,812,940,000 miles (4,537,000,000 km) at aphelion
2,762,720,000 miles (4,456,000,000 km) at perihelion
Mass: 4.672×10^{25} lb (1.028×10^{26} kg)
Rotational period (Neptunian day): 15.8 Earth hours
Sidereal period (Neptunian year): 60.2 Earth days (165 Earth years)
Eccentricity: 0.009
Inclination of rotational axis: 29.56°
Inclination to ecliptic plane (Earth = 0): 1.77°
Albedo (100% reflection of light = 1): .34 to .5
Mean temperature: −343° F
Major atmospheric components: Hydrogen
Helium
Methane
Other atmospheric components: Ammonia
Argon

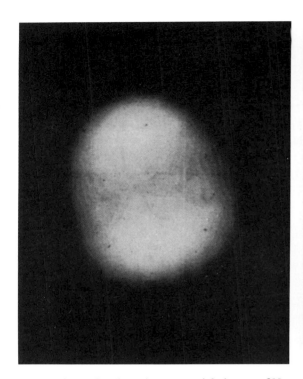 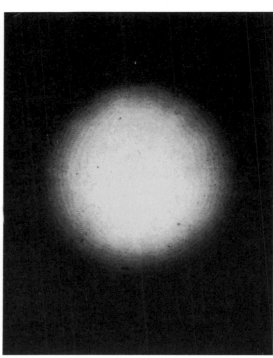 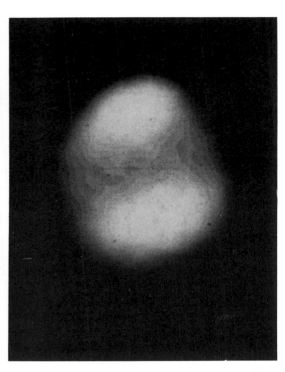

Above, left to right: These time sequential pictures of Neptune were taken at 9:40, 10:19 and 1:14 universal time on 5 May 1979. The pictures were recorded through an infrared methane absorption band filter. High clouds of ice crystals in the northern and southern hemispheres produce the two bright areas, while the absence of the haze layer in the equatorial regions reveals a deeper layer of methane gas which shows here as darker areas. During the period covered by these images the bright features may be seen to move towards the eastern limb of the planet. These pictures were taken with a charge-coupled device (CCD) on the Catalina Observatory 154-cm telescope by HJ Reitsema, BA Smith and SM Larson of the University of Arizona. *Below:* A NASA artist's illustration of Neptune and its largest moon, Triton. Nearly the twin of Uranus, Neptune departs from its brother planet in that it partakes of the Jovian quality of radiating more energy than it receives.

PLUTO

During the mid to late nineteenth century astronomers studying the revolutions of Uranus and Neptune detected slight anomalies that could be explained only by the gravitational effect of another body farther out in the Solar System. Around the turn of the century Percival Lowell (1855-1916) took up a systematic search of the heavens, looking for what he called 'Planet X.' When Lowell died in 1916, others continued the search, including William Pickering (1858-1938) of Harvard, who called the yet-undiscovered object 'Planet O.' In 1915, and again in 1919, Pluto was actually *photographed but not noticed* because it was much fainter than it had been predicted to be. By this time, the organized search for Planet X was largely abandoned. In the meantime, Pickering altered his theory regarding the hypothetical location of Planet 'O,' and for the first time predicted that the perihelion of its orbit might actually bring it briefly closer to the Sun than Neptune. It was a radical idea that turned out to be accurate for Pluto.

In 1929 the Lowell Observatory at Flagstaff, Arizona, resumed the search begun by its founder, using a 13-inch telescope and a wide-field survey camera. This proved to be the right approach, and on 18 February 1930 the young astronomer Clyde Tombaugh (1906-) identified a new planet in some photographs he had taken the previous month. The discovery was announced a month later on the 149th anniversary of the discovery of Uranus, and the new planet was called Pluto after the Roman god of the dead and the ruler of the underworld. The name was considered appropriate because of the planet's enormous distance from the Sun's warmth, and also because the first two letters were Percival Lowell's initials.

In the first years after it was discovered, physical data about Pluto was virtually impossible to obtain. In 1950, however, Gerard Kuiper at the Palomar Observatory estimated its diameter at 3658 miles, making it the second smallest planet in the Solar System. In 1965 it was observed in occultation with a 15th magnitude star, confirming that its diameter could not exceed 4200 miles. Thus it was that the 3658 estimate held until the 1970s.

In 1976 methane ice was discovered to exist on Pluto's surface. Until then the planet's faintness had been attributed to its being composed of dark rock. Since ice would tend to reflect light more so than dark rock, it would follow that if it *were* 3658 miles in diameter *and* covered with methane ice, it would be brighter than it is. Therefore, it was decided that Pluto was smaller than originally suspected, leading us to conclude that its diameter is less than the 2160 mile diameter of the Earth's Moon, and probably as small as 1375 miles. This would make it the smallest of

the nine planets and smaller than *seven* of the planetary moons. As estimates of Pluto's size continue to be revised downward, it becomes less and less likely that it has the mass to exert the gravitational force on Neptune's orbit that was originally predicted. If true, this would mean that Pluto is *not* 'Planet X,' and that 'Planet X' still exists and is yet to be discovered.

It has also been suggested that Pluto is perhaps the largest of a theorized belt of trans-Neptunian asteroids. However, that notion fails to take into account that Pluto is two and a half times the diameter of Ceres, the largest known asteroid, and nearly seven times larger than the average of the 18 largest known asteroids. Among the arguments that *can* be made for its not being a planet, or at least for its not being a 'normal' planet, are the peculiar aspects of its behavior. As we have noted, it has an extremely elliptical orbit. This orbit ranges from an aphelion of 49 AU, to a perihelion of 29.5 AU. The latter is actually closer to the Sun than the perihelion of Neptune's much more circular orbit, as Pickering had predicted. It has been pointed out that this highly elliptical orbit is more characteristic of asteroids, such as 944 Hidalgo and 2060 Chiron.

A second aspect of Pluto's behavior that sets it apart from other planets is its steep inclination to the ecliptic plane. The orbits of all the planets are within two-and-one-half degrees of this same plane, except Mercury, which is inclined at seven degrees, and Pluto itself, which is inclined at an acute 17 degrees, making it very unusual among its peers.

A theory concerning the physical nature of Pluto holds that at one time it was actually one of the moons of Neptune. It is further theorized that Pluto was somehow thrown out of its Neptunian orbit by some calamitous interaction with Neptune's moon Triton—perhaps even a collision. One of the Solar System's largest moons, Triton is more than

PLUTO
Diameter: 1375 miles (2200 km)
Distance from Sun: 4,572,500,000 miles (7,375,000,000 km) at aphelion
2,743,500,000 miles (4,424,000,000 km) at perihelion
Mass: 3×10^{23} lb (6.6×10^{23} kg)
Rotational period (Plutonian day): 6.3 Earth days (retrograde)
Sidereal period (Plutonian year): 90,465 Earth days
Eccentricity: 0.250
Inclination of rotational axis: 50°
Inclination to ecliptic plane (Earth = 0): 17.2°
Albedo (100% reflection of light = 1): .5
Mean surface temperature: −382.27° F
Maximum surface temperature: −350° F
Minimum surface temperature: −390° F
Major atmospheric component: Methane

CHARON
Diameter: Possibly 744 miles (1200 km)
Distance from Pluto: 12,000 miles (19,400 km)
Rotational period (Charonian day): 6.3 Earth days
Sidereal period (Charonian year): 6.3 Earth days
Inclination to ecliptic plane: Unknown
Mean surface temperature: −382° F

twice the size of Pluto and, as such, might have had the gravitational force to slam a competing object out of Neptunian orbit if it ventured close enough. Both Triton and Neptune's other known moon, Nereid, have unusual orbits that might possibly be relics of such a colossal event.

While its behavior partially defines it, and certainly sets it apart from other planets, less is known about Pluto's physical characteristics than is known about any other planet. Since no spacecraft will visit it in the twentieth century, we are left with only educated guesses about Pluto. We know that it is extremely cold, with noontime summer temperatures rarely creeping above −350 degrees Fahrenheit. Its rocky surface is known to also contain methane, probably in the form of ice or frost. Water ice may also be present, though this is not likely, and Pluto's mass suggests a rocky core. Pluto has generally been thought to have no atmosphere because its relatively small mass wouldn't give it sufficient gravity to retain an atmosphere, and it is too cold for even such a substance as methane to easily exist in its gaseous state. However, Scott Sawyer of the University of Texas has discovered what may be a tenuous methane vapor atmosphere on Pluto.

The discovery of the Plutonian moon Charon came about indirectly in 1978. While James Christy at the US Naval Observatory in Flagstaff, Arizona was attempting to measure Pluto's size, he thought he'd noticed that it was not spherical. Further observations led him to the conclusion that the elongation he had observed was due to the presence of a satellite very close to Pluto. Further calculations indicated that this newly discovered body was as close as 10,563 miles from Pluto.

Pluto's moon, named Charon—after the mythological son of Erebus and Nox who was appointed by the gods to ferry the souls of the dead across the river Styx—is closer in size to its mother planet than any other moon in the Solar System. Estimates of its diameter range from 497 to

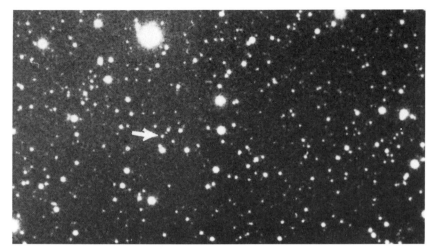

Above: One of the photos Clyde Tombaugh took of Constellation Gemini on 23 January 1930. The next month when he was reviewing all the photos he had taken, Tombaugh noticed that one of the pricks of light had moved—he had discovered Pluto! *Below:* An artist's conception of the mysterious Pluto (left) and its comparatively oversized moon, Charon—with the sun just a point of brilliant light in the enormous distance.

744 miles, the later being roughly half the diameter of Pluto. Its mass has been estimated at between five and ten percent that of Pluto.

Charon revolves around Pluto every 153 hours, exactly matching Pluto's period, meaning that the same hemisphere of Charon faces the same hemisphere of Pluto at all times. (From Earth, we can observe only one side of the Moon's surface, but the Earth rotates against the revolution of the Moon, so that the Moon is visible regularly from most of the regions of the Earth's surface.)

METEORITES

Known as *meteoroids* when outside a planet's atmosphere, as *meteors* when falling through the Earth's atmosphere, and as *meteorites* when they are found intact or when referring to their craters, these relatively small bodies exist throughout the Solar System and frequently impact other bodies in the Solar System. Despite their small size, meteorites are an extremely important component of the Solar System because their impact craters have contributed extensively to the surface texture of nearly every planet, moon and asteroid.

The major meteorite cratering took place in the few billion years that followed the formation of the Solar System 4.6 billion years ago, but the effects remain. Most planets and moons have thousands of four billion year old meteorite impact craters, many of incredible size. On the Earth's Moon there are Copernicus and Tycho, and the incredible eroded craters such as those that formed Mare Crisium, and Mare Orientale. Jupiter's Callisto was battered by so many meteorites that virtually no other type of surface can be seen, while on Saturn's Mimas, the crater Herschel spans a third of that moon's diameter.

Not only have meteorites created the features by which we recognize various bodies in the Solar System, they provide us with the means to determine the sequence of events in a body's history. For example, craters that have been disturbed by faulting, erosion or subsequent impact craters can be identified as relatively ancient, while those that are superimposed on other features can be dated as more recent. The relative number of craters found on or near another type of geologic feature can serve to date that feature. For example, the Mare Imbrium on the Earth's Moon is a huge, ancient crater that was formed very soon after the Moon itself. This basin was, in turn, filled by an outflowing of molten rock 3.2 billion years ago, and the number of *new* craters in this smoother basin, compared to the number of craters on older terrain, helps to date the epoch when the Solar System received most of its meteorite cratering.

The most intense period of cratering took place in the Solar System's first half billion years and, though it has tapered off, it has never stopped. On Earth most, but not all, of the effects of cratering have been eradicated by erosion. Only on Jupiter's Io, which is constantly being resurfaced by frenetic volcanic activity, is there a visible surface unscarred by meteorite craters.

With most of the extremely large meteorites expended in the first half billion years, the Solar System's moons and planets have been subjected to a constant bombardment of smaller particles for four billion years. On planets and moons without atmospheres the meteorites simply strike the surface full force. In the case of those with atmospheres, however, all but the very largest burn up in the atmosphere, briefly becoming fiery-tailed meteors or *shooting stars*—the very bright ones being called *fireballs*.

In the Earth's atmosphere, meteoroids become visible as meteors at an altitude of 60 miles. The fiery streaks are due to compression, rather than friction, as is occasionally suggested. Since the meteoroids enter the Earth's atmosphere at speeds of up to 45,000 mph, the air ahead of them is compressed like the air in the cylinder of a diesel engine and the heat is transferred to the moving body, turning it into a meteor or shooting star.

There are thousands of meteoroids entering the Earth's atmosphere every year, but their average weight is less than one ounce, and even the brightest fireballs weigh less than five pounds and are burned up without ever reaching the Earth's surface. More than 2000 meteorites have been discovered on the surface, however, and eight have been identified as weighing more than 15 tons. The largest, the Hoba West, discovered near Grootfontein in Southwest Africa, weighed 70 tons. The second largest, Ahnighito, was found by Admiral Peary at Cape York, Greenland and weighted 34 tons.

One of the largest, and certainly one of the most well preserved, meteorite craters on Earth is located in northeastern Arizona. Known as Barringer Crater, the crater is similar to those on Mercury or the Moon. An impressive sight when viewed firsthand, it is 3900 feet across and 600 feet deep, hardly a large crater by Solar System standards.

Meteorites on Earth are classified geologically as *Aerolites* (stone), *Siderites* (stony iron), *Siderolites* (iron) and *Tektites* (volcanic glass)—although the extraterrestrial origin of Tektites is now in doubt. All of the largest meteorites, such as the Hoba West and Ahnighito, are Siderolites, while the largest Aerolite on record (found in China in 1976)

weighed only 3894 pounds. Siderolites are the most common meteorites and Tektites are the rarest. While other types of meteorites are found throughout the Earth and have been falling to the surface continuously for 4.6 billion years, only four major Tektite showers are theorized to have occurred in history. These were in Europe and North America during the *Tertiary Period* and in Australia and Africa during the *Pleistocene Period*.

Meteorites provide enigmatic views of the geology of the Solar System because they are frequently composed of rock types unlike anything that exists on Earth. It is thought that some meteorites may have had their origin in other planets or within the Asteroid Belt.

Search teams in Antarctica have recovered a number of meteorites. The photos *at top and in the middle* show two views of a meteorite thought to be of Martian origin.

The meteorite *shown directly above* weighs nearly 40 pounds. It was discovered in 1978 at about the same time another search team found a rare carbonaceous chondrite meteorite.

Right: The comet Ikeya-seki streaks across the sky at sunrise.

COMETS

The most ethereal of the objects in the Solar System, comets are essentially 'snowballs' of carbon dioxide, methane or water ice that have extremely *elliptical* orbits and which exhibit spectacular *tails* when heated by the Sun. Comets travel around the Sun in fixed elliptical orbits that have perihelions less than those of the inner terrestrial planets and aphelions that can be as great as, or greater than, those of the outermost planets. The period of time that it takes for a comet to make a complete revolution around the Sun may range from a few years to many centuries. The comets Encke and Giacobini-Zinner, for example, are observed with periods of 3.3 and 6.5 years respectively, while Halley's Comet has an observed period of 76.3 years. Some comets have periods of truly extraordinary durations. The comet Kohoutek, which was discovered in 1973, will not make another turn around the Sun until the year 76,973, and the Great Comet of 1864 will not reappear for 2.8 million years!

Because of their small size, comets cannot be seen from Earth until the Sun heats up their enormous tail. Thus they have, in years past, seemed to appear suddenly and almost from nowhere. In Roman times they were considered 'bad omens,' and in the Middle Ages their appear-

Above: **A false color image of Comet Halley's coma, obtained with a 6-inch telescope and photometer on 13 December 1985. The image was obtained through a yellow (optical) filter, but is color coded to show the rate of increase of brightness. (Data obtained by Kevin Krisciunas at Mauna Kea, Hawaii. Image processing by Colin Aspin, Joint Astronomy Centre, Hilo, Hawaii.)**

ance was always considered to be some sort of 'sign.' The arrival overhead of Halley's Comet in 1066, however, was certainly not a 'bad omen' for William the Conqueror at the Battle of Hastings.

In 1682 Edmond Halley (1656-1742), England's second Astronomer Royal, successfully and scientifically calculated the period of the Great Comet of 1682 at 76.3 years. He did not live to see it reappear in 1758, but it did reappear as he predicted it would, and it has borne his name—and has been the most famous of comets ever since. Since Halley's time we have understood comets as scientifically predictable natural phenomena rather than as 'omens' or 'signs.' Nevertheless, the 1910 appearance of Halley's Comet led to numerous predictions of catastrophe, and even of the end of the world. It is uncertain what sort of mumbo jumbo might be read into the fact that Halley's Comet was very difficult to see from Earth with the naked eye in 1986.

A comet, as we've noted, is basically an icy 'snowball.' This 'snowball,' usually containing a solid core, is the permanent part of the comet and is known as its *nucleus*. The cometary nucleus is usually quite small. Halley's Comet, for example, has an *irregular nucleus* that is only about nine miles long and five miles wide. The nucleus, in turn, is surrounded by a hydrogen cloud.

As the nucleus nears the orbit of Mars on its journey inward from the distant reaches of the Solar System, interaction with the solar warmth causes it to develop a fuzzy halo, or *coma*. (The word coma, as used here, is the Latin word for 'hair,' rather than the Greek word for 'deep sleep.') As the nucleus and coma reach the orbit of the Earth, a tail begins to develop as the Solar Wind blows material away from the nucleus. Upon

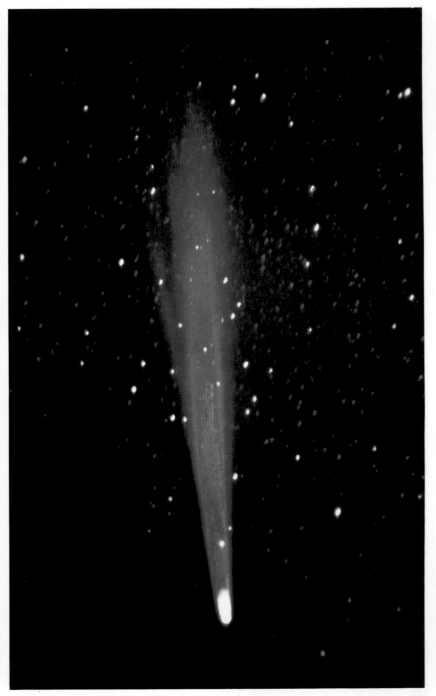

Counterclockwise from upper left: **A model of a cometary nucleus; a composite image of the icy nucleus of Halley's Comet photographed by the European Space Agency spacecraft Giotto in 1986—north is at the top of the photo and the Sun is located off to the left (note the dust jets escaping from the nucleus in the innermost frame, and the gas envelope surrounding the nucleus); and a spectacular image of Halley's Comet, photographed during its celebrated 1910 visit to the near-Earth region of the Solar System. The most-well known of comets, it was the center of enormous media attention in 1910 and 1986. The dimensions of its nucleus are approximately 9 by 5 by 5 miles.**

the formation of the tail, the coma is known as the comet's *head*. Tails may be composed of particulate impurities released from the nucleus, in which case they will appear curved. Tails may also be composed of ionized gases, in which case they will be straight.

Cometary tails grow longer and brighter the closer they approach to the Sun. Some may be almost invisible, and some, such as that of Halley's in 1910, may span half the visible sky! Donati's Comet, which appeared in 1858, had two gas tails and a particulate dust tail that reached a length of nearly 50 million miles.

The Great Comet of 1811, which had a coma with a diameter of 1.2 million miles, had a tail nearly 100 million miles in length. The longest tail on record, however, was that of the Great Comet of 1843, which reached from near the Sun to well beyond Mars, a distance of over 200 million miles!

Some comets may get no closer to the Sun than the orbit of Jupiter or Mars, but some, such as 1979-Ki, get so close that they collide with the Sun and are destroyed. There is no confirmed instance of a comet colliding with the Earth, but in 1908 an object glowing brighter than the Sun, and suspected to have been a comet, crashed into the Tunguska region of Siberia doing massive damage.

After a comet rounds the Sun and starts its journey back to the outer Solar System, the tail, still Solar wind-blown ions or particles, is observed to precede the nucleus rather than to trail it. As the comet moves away from the Sun, the tail grows smaller and finally vanishes. The coma then shrinks and disappears, and the barely visible icy nucleus recedes into the far reaches of the Solar System.

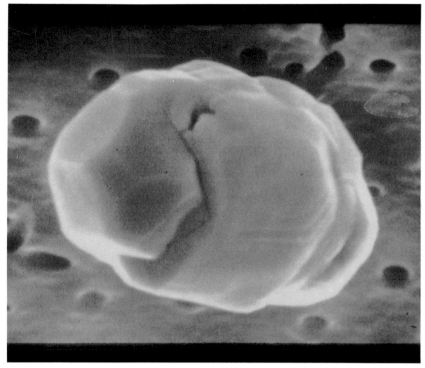

Above: **An electron micrograph of a suspected cometary dust particle.** *Below:* **This Giotto photo of Halley's Comet shows the dented, oblong shaped nucleus, with dust jets escaping from the sunlit side of the comet. This nucleus' mass is 80–100 million tons.**

PART TWO

THE LOCAL REGION OF OUR GALAXY

Only a few sensory experiences are considered universally and innately beautiful. Among them are the following sights: fields of flowers in bloom, rainbows, waterfalls, young children's smiling faces, the sparkle of precious gems, and the view of the night sky filled with stars.

Over the centuries the stars have served us for reckoning time, as navigational beacons, and as a basis for myths. At best the unaided eye can detect a couple of thousand stars at any moment. Ancient nomads, astrologers, and story tellers saw patterns in the arrangement of stars in the sky and delineated the constellations. Some individual stars were given names. Only recently have we begun to understand what the stars are, how far away they are, and how they live and die.

As recently as the sixteenth century the stars were considered to be situated just beyond the orbit of the planet Saturn in an Earth-centered cosmos. The Polish cleric Nicholas Copernicus (1473-1543) demonstrated that the motions of the planets against the stars could be more simply explained if the Sun were in the center of our system. He asked rhetorically, 'Who would place this lamp of a most beautiful temple in a better place?'

Astronomers call the distance between the Earth and the Sun the Astronomical Unit. It amounts to 149.6 million kilometers (92.9 million miles). The *relative* sizes of the planetary orbits have been known since the time of Johannes Kepler (1571-1630), but it was less than a century ago that the value of the Astronomical Unit was known to better than one percent. With modern radar techniques it is possible to calibrate the distance scale in the solar system to one part in 10 million. The proof of this is the accuracy with which we can direct artificial satellites throughout the solar system.

How much more space there is between the stars than between the planets! If we assume that the brightest stars in the sky are predominantly nearby and the fainter stars are further away, we would guess that

Sirius (the brightest star other than the Sun) is very close. Yet its apparent brightness is less than one ten billionth that of the Sun's. Since light intensity diminishes proportional to the square of the distance, Sirius would be at least 100,000 times more distant than the Sun.

We must differentiate between a star's apparent brightness and its intrinsic brightness. If all the stars were placed at the same distance from us, they would exhibit a very wide range of apparent brightnesses. One can verify this readily by looking at an open star cluster in a small telescope, as the size of a cluster is small compared to its distance, yet the apparent brightnesses show a great range.

The first star catalogues of the ancient Greeks divided the stars into five brightness classes. The brightest stars were said to be 'of the first magnitude.' The faintest stars visible to the unaided eye were classed as fifth magnitude. There are many more faint stars than bright stars. We now define the magnitude scale such that five magnitudes corresponds to exactly a factor of 100 in luminosity, and we allow for magnitudes outside the range of 1 to 5. (Sirius, at an apparent visual magnitude of -1.46, is exactly 100 times brighter than a star of magnitude 3.54.)

What we estimate by eye or with an astronomical light meter is the apparent magnitude of a star (how many photons per second we receive). The faintest star visible in a six-inch telescope under excellent conditions is about 14th magnitude. The faintest objects that can be detected with the world's largest telescopes are about magnitude 27.

It is also useful to convert these values to some standard distance, so that we can compare the intrinsic brightnesses of stars. By agreement that distance is 10 parsecs. The absolute magnitude of the Sun (ie, the apparent magnitude it would have if it were 10 parsecs away) is 4.8. The

At right: Sirius, the Dog Star in Canis Major. Though 8.6 light years distant, to Earth dwellers it is the brightest star besides our Sun. At an apparent magnitude of -1.5, its closest rival is Canopus, of apparent magnitude -0.8. Apparent magnitude is a function of the star's actual brightness and its distance from us. See the text, above.

bright white star Vega has an absolute magnitude of 0.5. It puts out more than 50 times as many photons per second as the Sun.

Is a particular star an intrinsically faint one that happens to be very close, or is it a very luminous one that is very far away? With nothing but the apparent brightness of the star, you cannot tell.

At the end of the seventeenth century astronomers began measuring the positions of the stars with ever increasing accuracy. By the turn of the twentieth century a million stars were catalogued in this way. Some were singled out for special attention, and their positions were measured with extreme care.

It had already been shown in the early eighteenth century that some stars were drifting with respect to the others. The fixed stars were not exactly fixed. If one could wait long enough the constellations would all change shape. These changes of star positions are called proper motions. Because of the immense distances of the stars and their actual velocities across the line of sight, these angular changes are necessarily small. They are measured in seconds of arc per year (or per century). On average the stars with the largest proper motions will be nearby and those with immeasurable proper motions will be predominantly distant. But for an individual star, one does not know solely on the basis of its proper motion if it is moving through space at a fast clip while being situated at a great distance, or if it is a slower moving star that is nearby. Also, its space motion could be directed almost exactly at or away from the Sun, in which case the proper motion would be very nearly zero. Analogously, if a toy plane with little lights on it flies by at night at a distance of 100 yards, going several yards per second, can you tell the difference between that and a full size plane going a couple of hundred mph at a much greater distance if all you can see are pinpoints of light?

Now do an experiment. Hold up one finger in front of your face. Open one eye at a time while looking at a distant background. Your finger will appear to jump back and forth as you open each eye alternately. As you move your hand further from your face, the amount your finger appears to jump back and forth will decrease. The distance between your eyes is necessarily constant and the triangle formed by that baseline and the distance to your finger becomes skinnier and skinnier. If you are blinking an object back and forth which is at a distance of 57 times the separation of your eyes, the total angular shift will be one degree. If the triangle is 3438 times the size of the baseline, the parallax angle is one arc minute. If the triangle is 206,265 times the size of the baseline, the parallax is one arc second.

Given the great distances of the stars compared to the size of the Earth's orbit, the angular shifts of the nearby stars (with respect to the distant stars) are very small. The largest stellar parallax known is less than one arc second. This means that the nearest stars are more than 200,000 Astronomical Units away. (The position of the Earth at one time of the year is the view of one 'eye' and six months later we get the view from the 'other eye.')

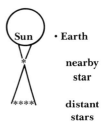

In practice things are more complicated. The position of a star will be the combination of many superimposed motions. We shall consider only two. If the star has a large proper motion and a small annual parallax the position of the star will change as follows:

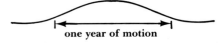

one year of motion

If a star has a smaller proper motion and a larger parallax the combination of the two would give:

one year
of motion

This is like watching a single horse on a merry-go-round, which happens to be situated on a flatcar of a moving train. The combined motion

makes a long wavy line or a curly-Q, depending on the speed of the train compared to the rate of the circular motion.

Stars were chosen for parallax measurement on the basis of their apparent brightness or high proper motion values. Thomas Henderson measured the parallax of Alpha Centauri (the third brightest star in the sky) in 1832 (but he did not reduce his data till several years later, by which time he could not claim priority for this astronomical first). Wilhelm Bessel measured the parallax of the double star 61 Cygni, which he selected on the basis of its large proper motion (5.22 arc seconds per year). Wilhelm Struve was the third astronomer in the 1830s to measure a parallax, his being a determination of the distance to the bright star Vega.

Some bright stars, like Deneb (Alpha Cygni), turned out to have very small or immeasurable parallaxes because they are instrinsically bright, but are distant stars. Many faint red stars with large proper motions were shown to be nearby.

In the early part of the nineteenth century the German optician Fraunhofer aimed a spectroscope at the Sun and noticed that among the band of colors were many dark lines. In 1859 Kirchhoff and Bunsen determined that the dark lines were due to the chemical elements, and could be used much like fingerprints for the identification of the composition of the Sun's atmosphere. With the advent of photographic methods, astronomers began classifying the spectra of stars. The scheme still used today was derived at Harvard at the turn of the twentieth century and hinges on the strength of the hydrogen lines in the spectra. Stars of spectral type A have the strongest hydrogen lines, and B stars have weaker hydrogen lines. Not all the letters of the alphabet are still used, and the spectral types were rearranged in order of decreasing temperature of the stars, giving O, B, A, F, G, K, M. Subdivisions of spectral types were defined (eg, G0, G1, G2, etc). The Sun (6000 degrees K) is of spectral type G2. Vega (10,000 degrees K) is an A0 star. Betelgeuse (at 2500 degrees K) is M2.

Stellar spectra also differ because of the sizes of the stars. Supergiant stars have very narrow spectral lines, because they rotate very slowly. B dwarf stars rotate rapidly and have wider spectral lines. The luminosity classes are as follows: supergiants (100 times the size of the Sun), bright giants, giants (10 times the size of the Sun), subgiants, dwarf stars (also known as Main Sequence stars), then subdwarfs, and finally white dwarfs (about one-fiftieth the Sun's size). The range of intrinsic brightness is 10 billion (25 magnitudes).

The spectral lines give us evidence of the abundance of elements and molecules in the stellar atmospheres. Most stars have approximately the same composition, but the strengths of the spectral lines hinge very much on the temperatures. Only trace amounts of metals like calcium, magnesium and iron exist in the Sun's atmosphere, but because of its particular temperature and the structure of these atoms, the spectral lines due to metals rival those due to hydrogen (which is by far the most abundant atom). Hotter stars show few metallic lines but strong hydrogen and helium lines. Cooler stars show molecular lines, like titanium oxide, zirconium oxide, or molecular carbon.

The spectral lines also allow us to measure the velocities of the stars along the line of sight (called radial velocities). If there is a component of the star's motion directed toward the observer, the spectral lines are shifted toward shorter wavelengths (the blue shifts). If the velocity component is directed away from the observer, the spectral lines are shifted toward longer wavelengths (the red shifts). Given the Earth's motion about the Sun at 18.6 mi/sec (30 km/sec), this must be subtracted out for a study of the motion of the Sun with respect to the nearby stars.

Imagine that all the stars were fixed in space and only the Sun were moving. In the direction of the Sun's motion the stars would all have spectra with spectral lines blue shifted by an amount corresponding to the Sun's velocity. In the opposite direction of the sky one would measure the stars to have spectral lines red shifted by the same amount. The stars situated on the 'equator' 90 degrees from these 'poles' would have zero relative velocity along the line of sight, but would all have measurable proper motions, whose values would correspond to the speed of the Sun and the distances between the Sun and those individual stars.

The real local ensemble of stars is more complicated than this, but the effect just mentioned can be demonstrated. There is a point in the sky where the stars are on the average coming toward us. On the opposite place in the sky the stars are, on the average, moving away from us. The proper motions at the 'poles' are randomly distributed and average zero, while at the 'equator' between the 'poles' the proper motions are a maximum and are preferentially directed away from the place stars are streaming toward us. Thus we have evidence that the Sun is indeed moving through the local portion of the galaxy, and at a rate of 9.6 mi/sec (15.4 km/sec) toward the eastern part of the constellation Hercules. At this rate it will cover about 15 parsecs in one million years.

Since space is three dimensional (at least), one can break down the Sun's motion into three perpendicular components: 1) directed toward the Galactic Center, 2) in the direction of the rotation of the galaxy, and 3) perpendicular to the galactic plane. The Sun (plus the solar system) is moving 4.3 mi/sec (7 km/sec) perpendicular to the galactic plane. It oscillates up and through the plane with a period of about 60 million years, reaching a height of about 80 parsecs above and below the plane. With the galaxy rotating once every 220 million years or so, this makes for a very slow merry-go-round ride.

Following Sirius and Canopus, the brightest star is Alpha Centauri, which turns out to be a triple star system. It consists of a G2 dwarf star (almost identical to the Sun), and a K0 dwarf star, separated by 18 arc seconds on the sky, with a third companion of spectral type M2 about 2.2 degrees away. Because this third star has the largest parallax known, it is known as Proxima Centauri.

Another interesting star was discovered by the American astronomer EE Barnard. Barnard's star has the largest proper motion known, more than 10 arc seconds per year. In less than 200 years it moves the diameter of the full Moon against the background of stars. It has a very large space velocity, 86 mi/sec (139 km/sec).

Sirius and Procyon (Alpha Canis Minoris) are both near enough to have their trigonometric parallaxes measured. In each case, however, once their proper motions and parallaxes are taken into account, they still have variable positions. The nineteenth century astronomer Bessel attributed their erratic motions to unseen companions. Indeed, in 1862 a companion to Sirius was found, an 8th magnitude white star, previously undetected because it was swamped by the excessive brightness of the other star. In 1896 Procyon's companion was found to be an 11th magnitude white star. Both faint companions are white dwarfs.

Not all analyses of star positions bear such fruit. Barnard's star has undergone considerable study, and the evidence seemed to point toward the existence of one or two Jupiter-sized planets. Other nearby stars show evidence of non-stellar companions. However, these deductions hinge on trusting the residuals of star positions measured in the ten thousandths of a second of arc, or of radial velocity changes measured in the tens of *meters* per second. At present we have no indisputable evidence for any extra-solar planets, but technology is on the verge of making this important breakthrough.

Below: **Altair in Aquila has a true magnitude 10 times our Sun's—yet at 16.6 light years distance, its apparent magnitude is .77. Compare with Sirius (see previous pages). Barnard's star is the second closest to Earth, yet has an apparent magnitude of 9.5.**

The table on pages 132-133 contains data on stars approximately closer than 17 light years (5.2 parsecs). There are some 1300 identified stars in more than 1000 systems nearer than 20 parsecs, yet these numbers considerably underestimate the true values.

If we divide the nearby stars by spectral types and distances, we find that the surveys are complete to only about 10th magnitude (the faintest star that can be seen in 7×50 binoculars). We know the true number density of the brighter stars, but not the faintest stars (those with absolute magnitudes fainter than about 13). Of the stars nearer than 17 light years with known spectral types, 78 percent are orange or red dwarfs (K and M stars), and 10 percent are white dwarfs. All these stars are intrinsically faint. Since many were found on the basis of their large proper motions, we have undoubtedly missed some of the stars with smaller velocities. It can be estimated that 50 percent of the stars nearer than 10 parsecs have not yet been found. They will be mostly red dwarfs or white dwarfs. Some will be 'failed stars' (with less than 0.08 solar masses), also known as brown dwarfs.

More than half of the stars are part of multiple star systems (doubles, triples, etc). Another way of saying this is as follows. Pick five stars at random and look at them under high magnification. Two will turn out to be double (comprising four stars). That would make two doubles and three singles—a total of seven stars in five systems, and four of the seven stars are found in multiple systems.

Multiple stars are particularly important for determinations of stellar masses. Using an equation called Kepler's Third Law we can calculate the *sum* of the masses of a binary star system given the absolute orbit size and the period of revolution of the stars. Some binaries have orbital periods of years, some decades or longer. Say a binary star has a combined mass of three solar masses, and one of the stars is a G2 star like the Sun. Then its companion has a mass of two solar masses.

Some stars were discovered to be double because they eclipse each other. Their light output is not constant, depending on how much one star is covering up the other. These binaries are typically too close to be separated into two individual pinpoints of light.

Some stars are found to be double on the basis of their spectra, which consist of two superimposed sets of lines that shift back and forth as the stars, giving rise to each spectrum, orbit each other. These are called spectroscopic binaries, which are also too close to be resolved as separate stars.

Once we have classified stellar spectra and measured the parallaxes of these stars, we can correlate the intrinsic brightnesses of the stars with their temperatures, a correlation first noted by the Danish astronomer Hertzsprung and the American astronomer HN Russell. (See the graph atop page 133 for data on the nearest stars.) The diagonal band is called the Main Sequence, and stars 'on' it are burning hydrogen in their

cores. Stars in the lower left hand corner of the diagram are remnants of evolved massive stars, while stars that would be above the Main Sequence in the diagram (none nearer than 17 light years) would be giants and supergiants.

Astronomers also measure the apparent brightness and colors of the stars. Understandably, the colors are very well correlated with the spectral types. By classifying the spectrum of a star too distant to have its parallax directly measured (greater than 30 or 50 parsecs), and measuring its apparent brightness and color, we can use data on nearby stars of similar spectral type and color to estimate the other star's absolute magnitude. Its distance can then be calculated. For an individual star, this may only be good to ± 30 percent, but for an entire star cluster we can achieve accuracies better than 10 percent.

Another important method of measuring stellar distances is called the moving cluster method. As mentioned in the Introduction, five of the seven stars in the Big Dipper are part of a sparse cluster of stars that formed about 100 million years ago. The stars move through space almost parallel, and because of a perspective effect, like train tracks converging at the horizon, the proper motions appear to intersect at a point on the sky some angular distance from the cluster. Using this angle, the proper motions, and the radial velocity data, the distance to the cluster can be determined. For the Ursa Major cluster the distance is about 25 parsecs.

The most fundamental distance calibrator other than the Astronomical Unit and nearby stellar parallaxes is the distance to the Hyades cluster, using a variety of methods, including the moving cluster method. The Hyades cluster covers much of the constellation Taurus (not including the bright star Aldebaran), and consists of several hundred stars. Its distance is found to be 45.7 ± 0.8 parsecs. The corresponding trigonometric parallax would be 0.0219 ± 0.0004 arc seconds, which exhibits an accuracy unattainable with the direct parallax method.

Once the nearby star clusters have had their distances accurately measured, the distances of the more remote star clusters can be determined by measuring the relative brightness of stars of identical spectral types (by comparing the brightness of the Main Sequence of one cluster with that of another). Some of these clusters are found to have stars whose light output is variable. Certain types of pulsating variable stars have absolute magnitudes which can be calibrated in such a way that they can be used as 'standard candles'—if the calibration of some at a known distance can be made, the distance to similar variables in other clusters or in the general field can be obtained.

The astronomy of the local region of the galaxy is one of fundamental distance and luminosity calibration. There is very little gas and dust to be detected, and we are left with only stars of various forms. But it is the measurements on these stars that allow us to build a fundamental and solid first rung on the cosmological distance ladder. On this basis we may confidently proceed to the galaxy as a whole.

At right: A spectrum-luminosity diagram for stars nearer than 17 light years. Most of the stars (plotted as circles) are found on the Main Sequence. The position of the Sun is marked with an X. White dwarf stars are plotted as open squares. O and B stars, none of which are found closer than 17 light years, would be found on an extension of the Main Sequence to the upper left. Giants and supergiants would be found off the top of the diagram.

Stars Nearer than 17 Light Years
(5.2 Parsecs)*

Star name		Spectral type	Proper motion	Radial velocity (km/sec)	Apparent visual magnitude	Absolute visual magnitude	Parallax	Distance (light years)
Sun		G2			−26.72	4.85		(1 AU)
Alpha Centauri	A	G2	3.68	− 22	−0.01	4.35	0.743	4.4
	B	K0			1.33	5.69		
(Proxima Cen)	C	M5	3.85	− 16	11.05	15.45	0.761	4.3
Barnard's star	A	M5	10.34	−108	9.54	13.25	0.552	5.9
Wolf 359	B*	M8	4.70	+ 13	13.53	16.68	0.426	7.7
BD +36° 2147	A	M2	4.78	− 84	7.50	10.49	0.397	8.2
	B				>10.5	13.5		
Sirius	A	A1	1.33	− 8	−1.46	1.42	0.377	8.6
	B	DA			8.68	11.56		
Luyten 726-8	A	M5.5	3.36	+ 29	12.45	15.27	0.367	8.9
(UV Ceti)	B	M5.5		+ 32	12.95	15.8		
Ross 154		M4.5	0.72	− 4	10.6	13.3	0.345	9.4
Ross 248		M6	1.60	− 81	12.29	14.80	0.318	10.3
Luyten 789-6		M7	3.26	− 60	12.18	14.60	0.305	10.7
Epsilon Eridani		K2	0.98	+ 16	3.73	6.13	0.302	10.8
Ross 128		M5	1.38	− 13	11.10	13.50	0.301	10.8
61 Cygni	A	K5	5.22	− 64	5.22	7.58	0.296	11.0
	B	K7			6.03	8.39		
Epsilon Indi	C*	K5	4.70	− 40	4.68	7.00	0.291	11.2
Procyon	A	F5	1.25	− 3	0.37	2.64	0.285	11.4
	B	DF			10.7	13.0		
Struve 2398	A	M4	2.29	0	8.90	11.15	0.282	11.6
	B	M5	2.27	+ 10	9.69	11.94		
BD +43° 44	A	M1	2.90	+ 13	8.07	10.32	0.282	11.6
	B	M6		+ 20	11.04	13.29		
CD −36° 15693		M2	6.90	+ 10	7.36	9.59	0.279	11.7
Tau Ceti		G8	1.92	− 16	3.50	5.72	0.277	11.9
BD +5° 1668	A	M5	3.77	+ 26	9.82	11.98	0.270	12.1
CD −39° 14192	B*	M0	3.46	+ 21	6.67	8.75	0.260	12.5
Kapteyn's star		M0	8.72	+245	8.81	10.85	0.256	12.7
Krüger 60	A	M3	0.86	− 26	9.85	11.87	0.253	12.9

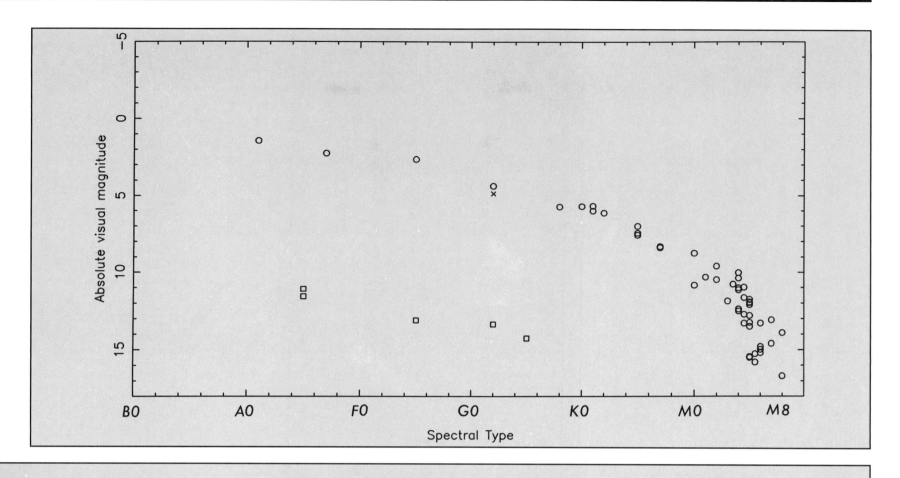

Star name		Spectral type	Proper motion	Radial velocity (km/sec)	Apparent visual magnitude	Absolute visual magnitude	Parallax	Distance (light years)
	B	M4.5			11.3	13.3		
Ross 614	A	M7	1.00	+ 24	11.07	13.08	0.252	12.9
	B				~14.6	~16.6		
BD − 12° 4523		M5	1.18	− 13	10.12	12.10	0.249	13.1
van Maanen's star		DG	2.99	+ 54	12.37	14.26	0.239	13.6
Wolf 424	A	M6	1.76	− 5	13.16	14.98	0.231	14.1
	B	M6			13.4	15.2		
Giclas 158 − 27		M	2.06		13.8	15.5	0.226	14.4
CD − 37° 15492		M4	6.11	+ 23	8.63	10.39	0.225	14.5
BD + 50° 1725		K7	1.45	− 26	6.59	8.32	0.222	14.7
CD − 46 11540		M4	1.06		9.36	11.03	0.216	15.1
CD − 49° 13515		M1	0.81	+ 8	8.67	10.32	0.214	15.2
CD − 44° 11909		M5	1.16		11.2	12.8	0.213	15.3
Luyten 1159-16		M8	2.09		12.27	13.91	0.213	15.3
BD + 68° 946	A	M3.5	1.31	− 22	9.15	10.79	0.213	15.3
	B				>14	>16		
BD − 15° 6290		M5	1.14	+ 9	10.17	11.77	0.209	15.6
L145-141		D	2.69		11.44	13.01	0.206	15.8
40 Eridani	A	K1	4.08	− 42	4.43	5.99	0.205	15.9
	B	DA	4.07	− 21	9.53	11.09		
	C	M4.5		− 45	11.17	12.73		
BD + 20° 2465	A	M4.5	0.49	+ 11	9.43	10.98	0.204	16.0
	B*							
BD + 15° 2620		M4	2.30	+ 15	8.50	10.02	0.201	16.2
Altair		A7	0.66	− 26	0.76	2.24	0.198	16.5
AC + 79° 3888		M4	0.89	− 119	10.92	12.38	0.196	16.6
70 Ophiuchi	A	K1	1.12	− 7	4.22	5.67	0.195	16.7
	B	K5			6.00	7.45		
BD + 43° 4305	A	M4.5	0.83	− 2	10.2	11.65	0.195	16.7
	B	DG2?			11.9	13.35		
Stein 2051	A	M4	2.36		11.09	12.51	0.192	17.0
	B	D		12.44	13.86			

*Data presented here was obtained from *The Catalogue of Nearby Stars* by W Gliese (Karlsruhe: Verlag G Braun), 1969, except for data on the star Giclas 158-27, which was found in Peter van de Kamp's article 'The nearby stars,' *Annual Review of Astronomy and Astrophysics*, 1971.

Distance in parsecs is reciprocal of parallax in arc seconds. Spectral type D indicates white dwarf (eg, DG is a white dwarf with the color of a G star). Very faint or unseen companions are marked by an asterisk. Unless otherwise specified, proper motion, radial velocity, and parallax of component(s) are taken to be the same as that of the primary star of the given system.

PART THREE

THE MILKY WAY GALAXY

A casual perusal of the night sky reveals a diffuse band of light that extends 360 degrees around the sky, passing through such constellations as Sagittarius, Cygnus, Cassiopeia, Perseus, and Orion. The width and intensity of this band of light ('the Milky Way') is not constant, and in some places, such as Cygnus, there are dark patches, attributable to an absence of light due to a lack of light sources, or the dimming of light by some material in front of the sources of light.

The observational investigation of the structure of our home galaxy was begun in the late eighteenth century by the German-born English astronomer William Herschel. Using a 20-foot focal length telescope and magnification giving a field of view of one-fourth of a degree, he counted the number of stars in 3400 fields distributed around the sky. Herschel showed that we appeared to be situated in a flattened arrangement of stars whose larger dimension he estimated to be 850 times the distance to Sirius, and whose smaller dimension was 155 Sirius distances. The band of the Milky Way was easily attributable to our being situated in the middle of a flattened star cluster.

During the nineteenth century most professional astronomers measured positions of stars or calculated the orbits of comets, asteroids, and planetary satellites. Galactic astronomy was on hold until the advent of improved photographic methods, which received a boost about 1880 with the invention of dry photographic plates, which were much more sensitive than the previously used wet collodion emulsions.

In 1890 only several dozen stellar parallaxes were known and some proper motions for stars as faint as 7th magnitude, but hardly any data was available for stars fainter than 9th magnitude. In 1906 the Dutch astronomer JC Kapteyn mapped out his plan of Selected Areas, which defined 206 selected 'gauge fields' distributed over the entire sky, and proposed them for detailed study. (One of the most intensively studied fields is Selected Area 57, which covers the North Galactic Pole of our galaxy.)

At right: The Constellation Orion. Contained within Orion are M 42—the Great Nebula in Orion, distinguishable by its pinkish color—and M 43—the Lesser Nebula in Orion—(see also the 'closeup' photo of these on pages 152–53), as well as the star Rigel, the sixth brightest as seen from Earth. (Photo by Lee Coombs) *Above:* A star cluster in Sagittarius. (Photo courtesy of US Naval Observatory.)

By 1922 Kapteyn and his colleagues had produced a model of the galaxy which was remarkably similar to that of Herschel, though larger. It appeared to be a flattened ellipsoid, like a fat pancake, with a diameter of 12,000 parsecs and a thickness of 1500 parsecs. The Sun was situated very near its center.

By this time another, radically different, model had been proposed, which was based on the brightness of variable stars called Cepheids. In 1908 Henrietta Leavitt at Harvard had discovered that certain variable stars in the Small Magellanic Cloud (a companion to our galaxy) exhibited a correlation between the apparent magnitudes and the periods of variation. Since the range of distances of the stars in the Small Magellanic Cloud is small compared to the distance to the Cloud, this implied a relationship between the intrinsic brightnesses (absolute magnitudes) of the variables and their periods. The period-luminosity law was nailed down with observations of more nearby Cepheids, whose distances could be determined by other methods. This enabled Cepheids to be used as 'standard candles' for the determination of distances to far away clusters, assuming, of course, that all Cepheids of a given period were alike.

The American astronomer Harlow Shapley exploited the period-luminosity law for the calculation of the distances of globular clusters that contained Cepheids. He noted that most globular clusters were situated in a particular region of the sky, toward the constellation Sagittarius. Shapley assumed that the centroid of the globular cluster system coincided with the center of our galaxy. He estimated that the diameter of the galaxy was 300,000 light years (92 kiloparsecs).

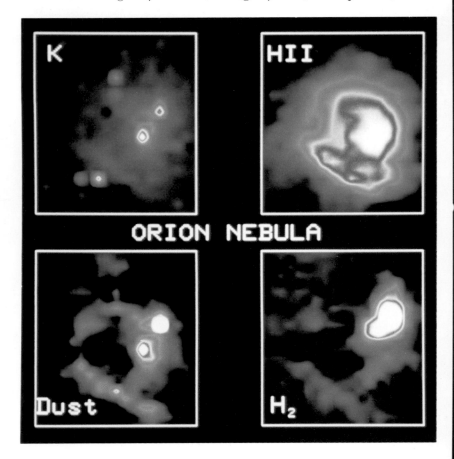

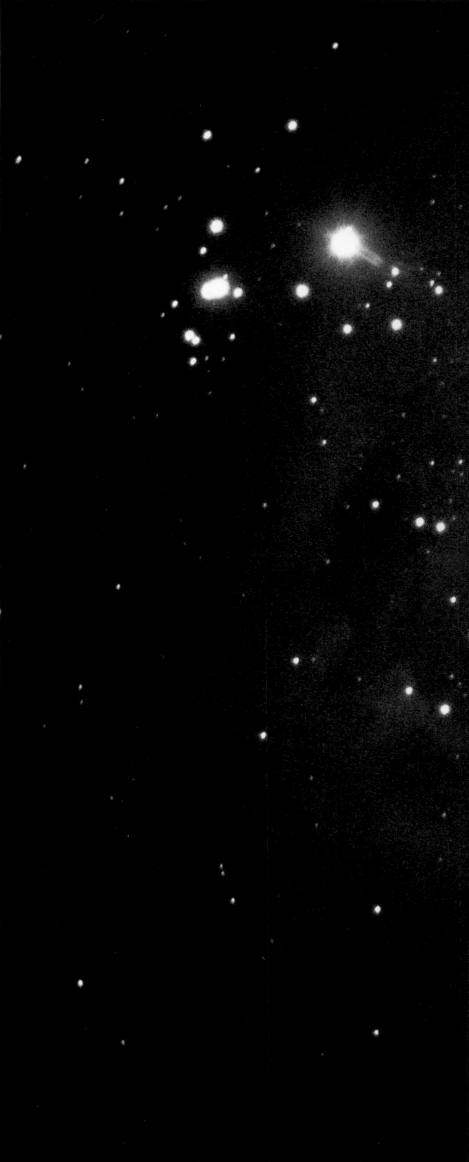

Above: The Orion Nebula (M 42), as mapped with the United Kingdom Infrared Telescope at Mauna Kea in 1986 at a resolution of about 20 arc seconds. (Data by Ian Gatley and colleagues. Image processing by Bernard McNally.)

Upper left (Labelled 'K'): The K-band filter is a broad band filter centered at a wavelength of 2.2 microns. This image shows the distribution of stars, the great majority of which are invisible at optical wavelengths because they are hidden by dust. At near infrared wavelengths the dust can be penetrated.

Upper right (Labelled 'H II'): This shows the distribution of ionized hydrogen atoms. Taken through a narrow band filter centered at 2.166 microns, the wavelength of an atomic hydrogen line called the Brackett gamma line.

Lower left (labelled 'dust'): Taken through a narrow band filter at a wavelength of 3.3 microns, this shows the infrared light which is believed to be emitted by small organic dust grains—or large molecules—when they are bathed in soft ultraviolet light from the hot, young stars in the Orion cluster.

Lower right (Labelled 'H₂'): This shows the distribution of shocked molecular hydrogen gas. Taken through a narrow band filter at a wavelength of 2.122 microns.

At right: The Dumbbell Nebula (M 27), in Vulpecula. M 27 is approximately 850 light years distant. (Photo by Bill Iburg) *Overleaf:* The Lagoon Nebula (M 8). (See also pages 138–39.) The red glow is caused by interaction of the nebular hydrogen cloud with light emanating from stars lying behind, and within, the cloud. Most nebulae are within 30 degrees north or south of the galactic plane. (Photo by Lee Coombs)

Until 1930 astronomers generally brushed aside the notion that there was a generally diffused absorbing medium in space. However, they worried a lot about errors in their distance calculations induced by making such an assumption. As the Englishman AS Eddington pointed out, this is like a man who refuses to sleep in a supposedly haunted room and says, 'I do not *believe* in ghosts, but I am *afraid* of them.'

Observations of spiral nebulae showed dark lanes of material. Is the great rift in Cygnus one of these? Certain objects like the Coalsack seemed devoid of stars, but were more likely areas where opaque dust was hiding the stars further away.

In 1930 the American astronomer RJ Trumpler at Lick Observatory demonstrated that interstellar dust must be there. He compared the distances to star clusters derived on the basis of the brightness of their stars with the distances based on the angular diameters of the clusters and found that the fainter clusters had more and more discordant distances based on the two different methods of calculation. He attributed this to an absorbing medium that dimmed light by 0.67 magnitudes per 1000 parsecs of path length.

It was also observed that some stars have absorption lines in their spectra which are due to clouds of gas along the line of sight. And faint

Above: M 5, the globular star cluster in the constellation Serpens. This object is 27,000 light years from Earth, and has an integrated magnitude of 6.2. Discovered in 1702, it is said to have a diameter of 130 light years. (Photo by Lee Coombs)

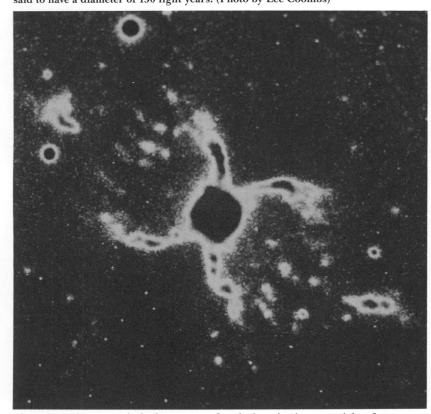

Above: He2-104—a star in its late stages of evolution ejecting material to form a two-lobed 'bubble' type outflow. This is a false color image of atomic hydrogen gas (the Balmer alpha line at 6563 Ångströms, in the optical wavelength region of the spectrum). (Courtesy of Hugo Schwarz/Colin Aspin ESO/UKIRT, March 1988)
At right: The Crab Nebula (M 1) in Taurus. This is the remnant of a supernova that was observed from Earth in 1054 AD—a stellar cataclysm that was so intensely bright, it was visible to the unaided eye in daylight. (Photo by Lee Coombs)

stars of a particular spectral type (eg, distant B or A stars) had different colors than nearby stars of the same spectral type. Not only was there interstellar gas and dust in the galaxy, but the dust reddened the light as well as diminished its intensity.

Once the absorbing effect of dust is taken into account, the implied size of Shapley's Big Galaxy is much reduced. We presently estimate that the diameter of the galaxy is 25 kiloparsecs (80,000 light years), with a thickness of one kpc (3,000 light years). Very young stars and interstellar dust are confined to a layer only 100 parsecs thick. The Sun is 8.8 ± 0.7 kpc from the Galactic Center, which is at the heart of the central bulge, five kpc in diameter.

Since the inner planets move around the Sun faster than the outer planets, it was proposed in the 1920s that we search for evidence of the differential rotation of the galaxy, assuming it to have a distant, massive nucleus. The reader will recall that stars of spectral type O and B are the brightest and hottest stars. They can be observed at great distances. The mathematical theory of differential galactic rotation stipulated that the stars will be systematically coming towards us or receding from us as a function of their longitude along the galactic plane. If we divide such stars (O and B stars, and Cepheids) into distance groups, we find that the more distant stars show the expected radial velocity variations as a

The celestial band called the 'Milky Way' is a product of our line-of-sight along the galaxy's horizontal plane and the concomitant visual massing of stars and interstellar dust. Here, we see the Milky Way in the constellation Scutum, *above*, and in the constellation Sagittarius *at right*. (Photos by Lee Coombs)

142

Our home galaxy contains many visible wonders which can be viewed through binoculars, with a small telescope, or by means of long exposure photography. There are an estimated 160 concentrated globular clusters in our galaxy, each containing 10^5 to 10^7 stars. Our galaxy contains an estimated 18,000 galactic star clusters. We have catalogued thousands of double stars and tens of thousands of variable stars. Planetary nebulae and diffuse nebulae (star formation regions) are also found in abundance. Supernova remnants, such as the Crab Nebula in Taurus, are to be found as well, though not in large numbers.

New insights into the nature of the constitution of the galaxy have been obtained at a variety of wavelengths. Optical astronomy reveals stars not much different from the Sun and the various objects in our solar system. Ultraviolet astronomy helps us unravel the mysteries of hot stars and their active outer atmospheres. Infrared astronomy allows us to study cool stars, to investigate the composition of planetary atmospheres, and to probe regions of star formation obscured by opaque dust. Millimeter and submillimeter astronomy allow us to study the chemistry in giant molecular clouds. Radio astronomy allows us to map out atomic hydrogen, determine the rotation curves of galaxies, and to measure radiation in interstellar plasmas. X-ray and gamma-ray astronomy from satellites give us evidence of very energetic processes taking place near black holes or in the cores of 'active galactic nuclei.'

A few examples will suffice. When a star forms from the collapse of a cloud of dust and gas, the embryonic star is often surrounded by a disk of material, which channels the flow of two jets of high-velocity gas, one out of each side of the disk. These are call 'bipolar outflow sources.'

Above: **The Trifid Nebula (M 20), in Sagittarius: the tri-part, 'trifid' appearance is due to dark dust lanes. This object, approximately 2000 light years distant, has a diameter of 30 light years and an integrated magnitude of nine. (Photo by Lee Coombs)** *At right:* **The Lagoon Nebula and the Trifid Nebula (M 8 and M 20) as imaged with an eight-inch, f/1.5 Schmidt at an exposure time of six minutes. (See also pages 138–39 and 148–49.) (Photo by Bill Iburg)** *Overleaf:* **The Great and Lesser Nebulae in Orion (M 42 and M 43). See also page 135. (Photo by Lee Coombs)**

Images of such objects, obtained at optical and near infrared wavelengths, are to be found in this chapter.

Using a method called 'speckle interferometry' it is possible to sum together many short exposures of a bright star, freezing out variations of the transmission in the Earth's atmosphere. This allows us directly to measure the diameters of reasonably nearby supergiant stars like Betelgeuse and map out the spots on its surface.

From optical spectroscopy we conclude that some stars exhibit violent processes in their outer atmospheres. Some of these stars have large regions of star spots, and as the stars rotate we alternately see regions which are cooler (with many spots) and hotter (with few spots). As a result, these stars are found to be variable in their light output. Data on

spotted stars is routinely gathered by amateur astronomers using small telescopes and accurate light meters, and the data is used by professional astronomers. The regions of activity on some Main Sequence stars can be mapped using a spectroscopic method called 'Doppler imaging.' While we usually think of the stars as mere points of light, modern observational methods have allowed us to map out features smaller than 0.001 arc second—a remarkable achievement!

Below: **The Milky Way, with nebula M 16 in Serpens (at photo right), and the Omega Nebula (M 17). (Photo by Lee Coombs)** *At right—above and below:* **Optical and infrared images of M 17. (Photo courtesy of National Optical Astronomy Observatories)** *Overleaf:* **The double cluster NGC 869 and 884, 7000 light years away, in Perseus. NGC 869 is one of the youngest clusters known, at 10 million years. (Photo by Bill Iburg)**

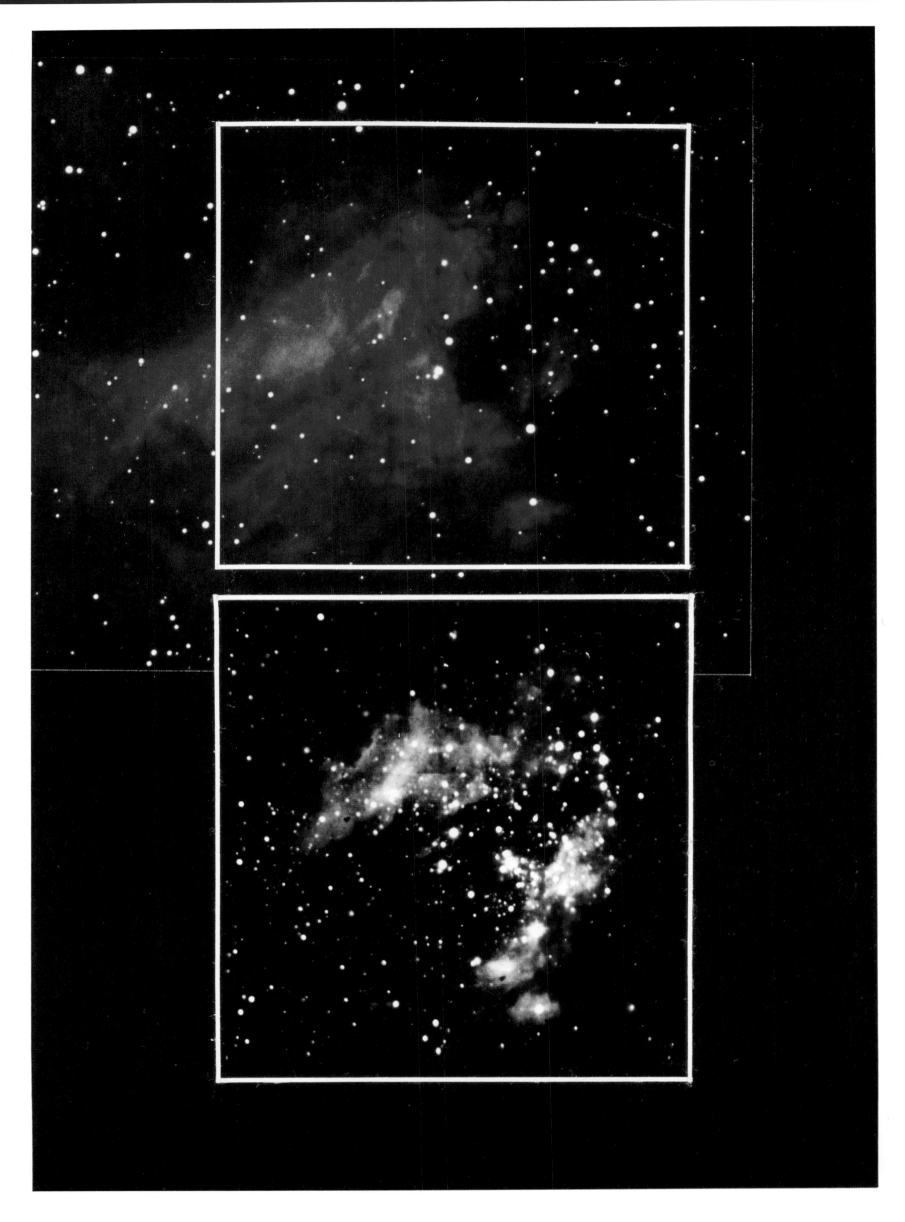

Since our Galactic Center is 100 times closer than any other object like it, it has been the subject of intense study, particularly at infrared wavelengths. (Visual light from the Galactic Center is dimmed by 30 magnitudes, but infrared light can penetrate the dust in the galactic plane.) We find that about one to four million solar masses of material is concentrated in the inner parsec of the galaxy, either in a very concentrated star cluster, or in a massive black hole. Whatever object(s) is(are) there, a strong wind is given off, which blows away the surrounding gas with a velocity of 466 mi/sec (750 km/sec), leaving a reasonably gas-free, doughnut-shaped ring of dust and gas with an inside diameter of 3.4 parsecs (11 light years), which is rotating with a velocity of 56 mi/sec (90 km/sec). A compact source (less than 20 Astronomical Units in size) of radio waves is found one arc second away from the object designated as the center of the galaxy. One problem with the notion of a massive black hole is that it requires only a 100 solar mass black hole to provide the observed amount of gamma-ray radiation.

We are now reasonably confident that we know how our galaxy is shaped, how big it is, and what it is made of (except the halo of dark matter). From what we *can* see, there is much that is impressive.

For Further Reading

Bok, Bart, 'The Milky Way Galaxy,' *Scientific American*, March, 1981, pp 92-120.

Mihalas, Dimitri, and Binney, James, *Galactic Astronomy: Structure and Kinematics* (San Francisco: WH Freeman), 1981.

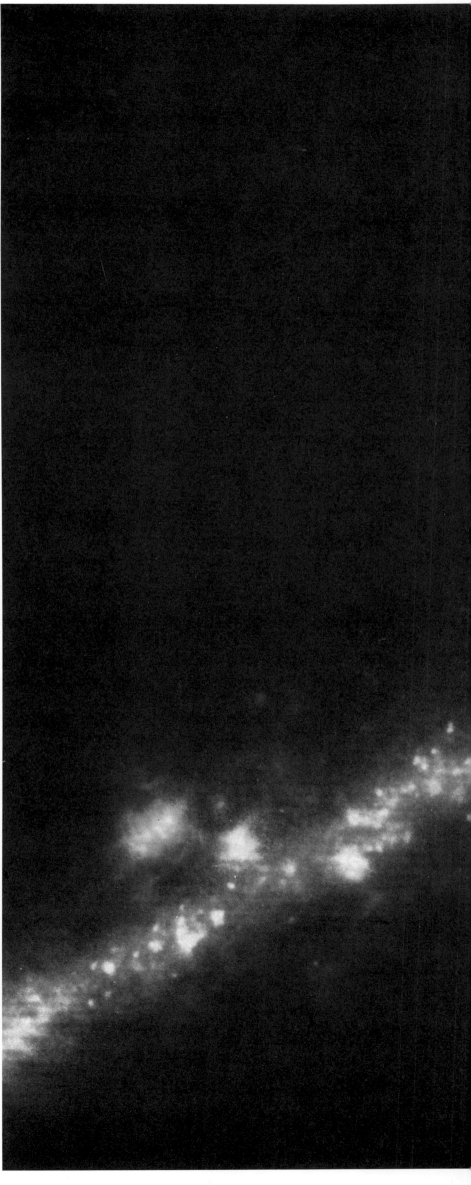

Above: **The Milky Way in Cygnus. (Photo by Lee Coombs)** *At right:* **An infrared photograph of the central Milky Way. This photo was taken by the (NASA) Jet Propulsion Laboratory's Infrared Astronomical Satellite (IRAS). The bulge in this band is our Galactic Center, approximately 33,000 light years from our solar system. Even at this immense distance, our Galactic Center is 100 times closer to us than any of the (seemingly countless) other objects like it in the universe. It takes close to 225 million years for our Solar System to revolve around this center. Please see the text, this page.**

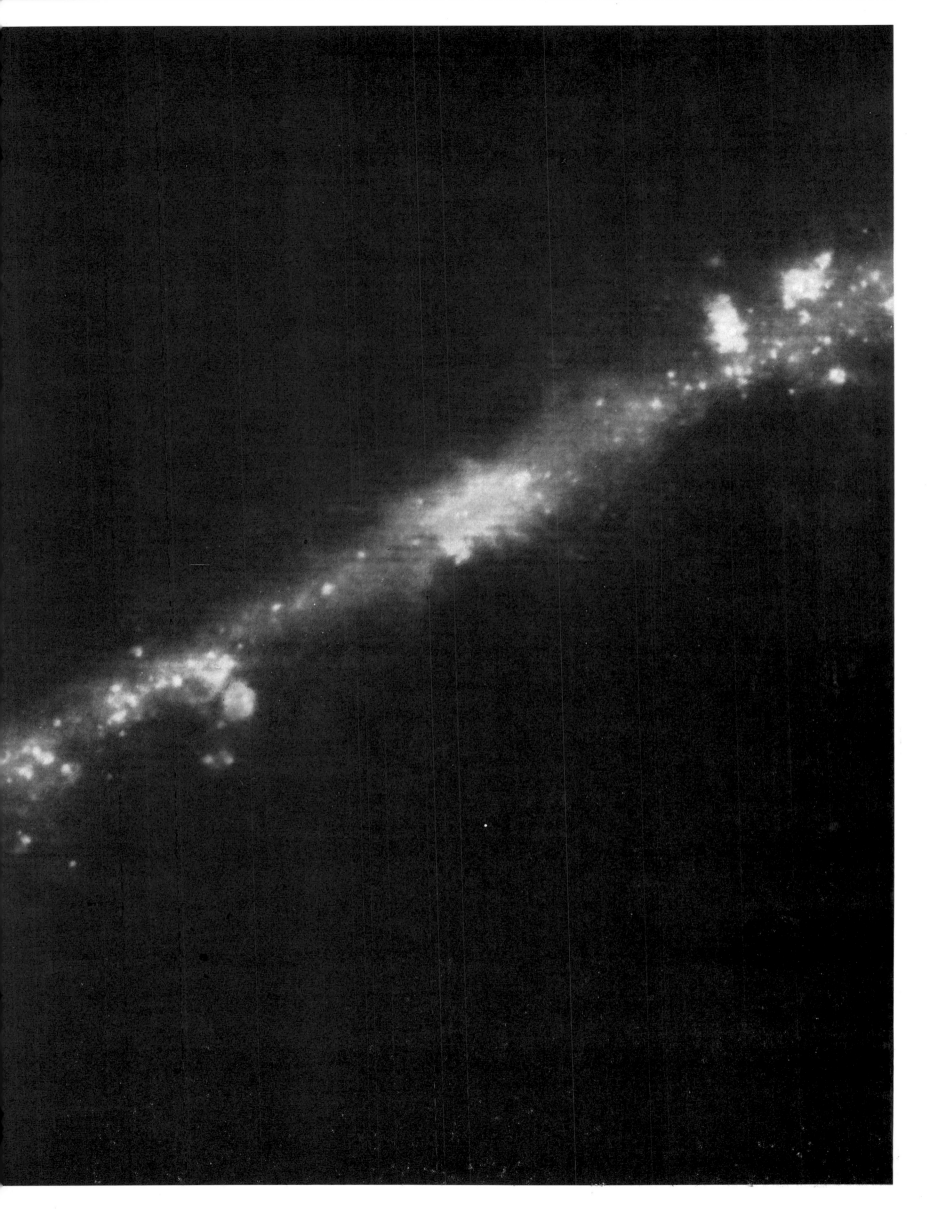

H 1.65	K 2.2	L 3.5
L′ 3.8	M 4.8	N 10.2
	Q 20	

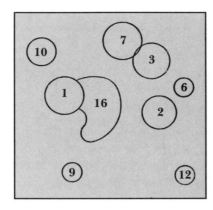

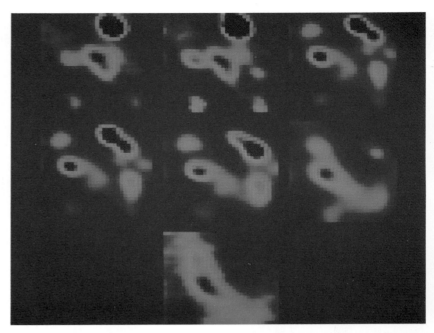

Above and *right:* Maps of the nuclear region of our galaxy at wavelengths of 1.65, 2.2, 3.5, 3.8, 4.8, 10.2, and 20 microns. Each map is only 16 arc seconds on a side (0.75 parsecs at the distance of the Galactic Center). These images were obtained at the NASA Infrared Telescope Facility, Mauna Kea, Hawaii, by D Lester, D Thompson, D DePoy, and J Hamilton.

Below: An infrared image at a wavelength of 2.2 microns of the central 30 parsecs (100 light years) of our galaxy. Obtained with a 50-inch (1.3 meter) telescope at Kitt Peak, Arizona. (Courtesy National Optical Astronomy Observatories.)

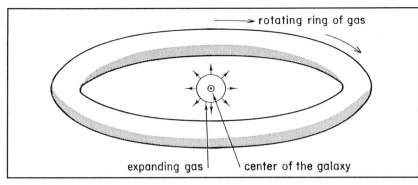

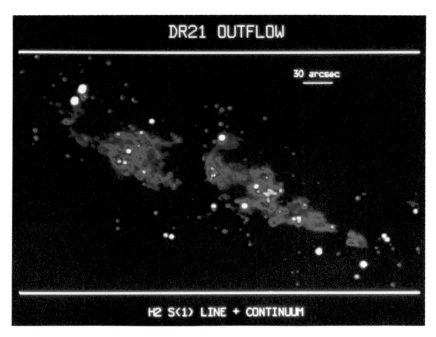

Above: A schematic diagram of the structure of the central 2 parsecs of our galaxy.
Below: A view of shocked molecular hydrogen gas surrounding the nucleus of our galaxy. The plot is color coded by velocity. Red areas are gas moving away from us. Blue areas are gas moving towards us. This shows that a lumpy ring of gas is rotating around the galactic nucleus. (Courtesy Ian Gatley and colleagues, United Kingdom Infrared Telescope, Mauna Kea, Hawaii.)
At right: Shocked molecular hydrogen gas in the bipolar outflow source DR 21, observed at an infrared wavelength of 2.122 microns with the United Kingdom Infrared Telescope and a 3596-channel infrared camera. (Courtesy of Ron Garden and Adrian Russell)

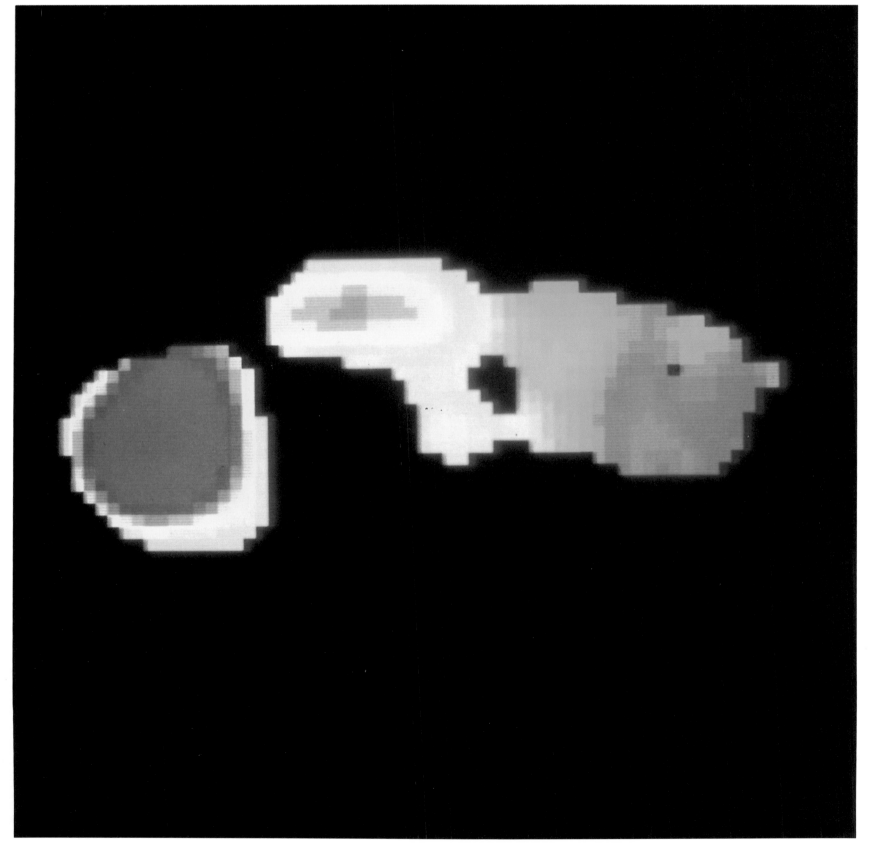

PART FOUR

NEARBY GALAXIES

Extragalactic astronomy is a twentieth century pursuit, but has roots stretching back at least two centuries. The successful French comet hunter Charles Messier compiled the first lists of 'nebulous' (ie, cloudy-looking) celestial objects in order to be able to differentiate new comets from fuzzy patches of light that looked like comets but were permanently situated at certain celestial coordinates. While Messier discovered many comets with his small refracting telescope, his fame today rests on his published list of nebulae, 109 in number (though three of them—numbers 40, 91 and 102—do not exist). The Andromeda Nebula, visible to the unaided eye, is number 31 in Messier's catalogue, or M 31. Some Messier objects obviously were clusters, but others defied explanation at that time.

William Herschel spent 20 years looking for new nebulae with a 20-foot focal length reflecting telescope, raising the number of known nebulae to 2500. This was due to Herschel's systematic search technique and the greater light gathering power of his telescope. (The bigger the diameter—and hence the surface area—of the objective of a telescope, the greater its ability to reveal faint objects and also detailed structure in these objects. The latter characteristic is called 'resolving power.')

Following William Herschel, his son John extended the number of known nebulae by mapping the southern skies from South Africa with a 20-foot focal length telescope of 18.25-inch aperture.

The largest telescope built by William Herschel had a focal length of 40 feet and a diameter of 48 inches. Like all his telescopes, it had a polished metal mirror. (Today's reflectors have mirrors of glass or ceramic, with a thin, evaporated film of metallic alloy.) By contrast, the largest refracting telescope of Herschel's era had a diameter of only 9.6 inches. Herschel's telescope had 25 times the light gathering power and, theoretically, five times the resolving power. Many of Messier's fainter objects were revealed to be made of stars, and the thought naturally

Above: M 66 in Leo, magnitude 9.2, is a type Sb spiral galaxy similar to ours. (Photo courtesy of the US Naval Observatory) *At right:* The Whirlpool Galaxy (M 51), a type Sc loose spiral, with its irregular companion galaxy NGC 5195 at the end of one of its 'arms.' M 51 is 15 million light years from Earth. (Photo by Lee Coombs)

arose: Could all nebulae be resolved into stars, if only one had a large enough telescope?

A wealthy Irishman, the Third Earl of Rosse, completed a massive 72-inch diameter reflector in 1845. With this telescope he and his colleagues observed the first known spiral nebula, M 51, also known as the Whirlpool Nebula. While they could make out bright and dark spiral lanes, individual stars could not be discerned.

If we look at the spectrum of a distant, compact conglomeration of many stars, it will be the blended together spectra of all those stars combined. One would expect to see the familiar absorption lines of normal stellar spectra. After the advent of astronomical spectroscopy, one of the first major surprises came in 1864 when William Huggins aimed his spectroscope-equipped telescope at a nebula in Draco and saw instead a single bright green line. At once he knew he was observing luminous gas instead of the sum of the light of many stars. This proved that all nebulae were not necessarily made of stars. (Today we recognize these gaseous objects as planetary nebulae, diffuse nebulae, reflection nebulae and supernova remnants.)

In 1885 a nova was seen in the Andromeda Nebula, a new star that became brighter than 7th magnitude. If it was like the supernova observed in 1572 by Tycho Brahe, which became as bright as the planet Venus (some 11 magnitudes brighter than the star in Andromeda), it followed that the Andromeda Nebula was 200 times more distant. We now know that Tycho's supernova was three to five kiloparsecs away, and M 31 is 675 kiloparsecs away. But this is getting ahead of the story.

The most significant compilation of nebulae was published by JLE Dreyer, who had spent four years observing with Lord Rosse's 72-inch reflector. In 1888 he published *The New General Catalogue*, containing 7840 objects—all those listed by Messier, the Herschels, his own discovered with Lord Rosse's telescope and those found by others. In 1895 Dreyer published a supplement called *The Index Catalogue of Nebulae*, containing 1529 objects, some discovered photographically. A century later we still refer to most bright galaxies by their NGC or IC numbers, though, of course, many objects in these catalogues are not galaxies. (The globular cluster M 13 in Hercules is NGC 7205, and the Ring Nebula in Lyra—M 57—is also known as NGC 6720.)

At the turn of the twentieth century James Keeler showed, from long exposure photographs with the 36-inch Crossley reflector at the Lick Observatory, that many of the nebulae exhibited spiral structure. some were just elliptical blurs. Yet it was not until 1925 that Edwin Hubble clinched the extragalactic nature of these nebulae. Using the 100-inch reflector at Mount Wilson, Hubble was able to resolve M 31 and M 33 into stars. Some of these stars were found to be Cepheid variables. Hubble estimated these two nebulae to be 285,000 parsecs away. Just prior to this the Estonian astronomer Ernst Opik had shown, using a spectroscopically-determined light curve of M 31, that its distance must be 480,000 parsecs, if its mass and luminosity were comparable to the values for our galaxy. The discrepancy was due to errors in the assigned absolute magnitudes of the Cepheids. (Only in the 1950s did astrono-

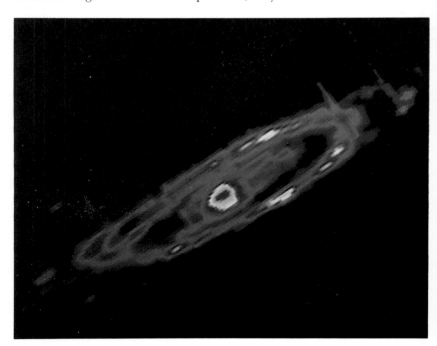

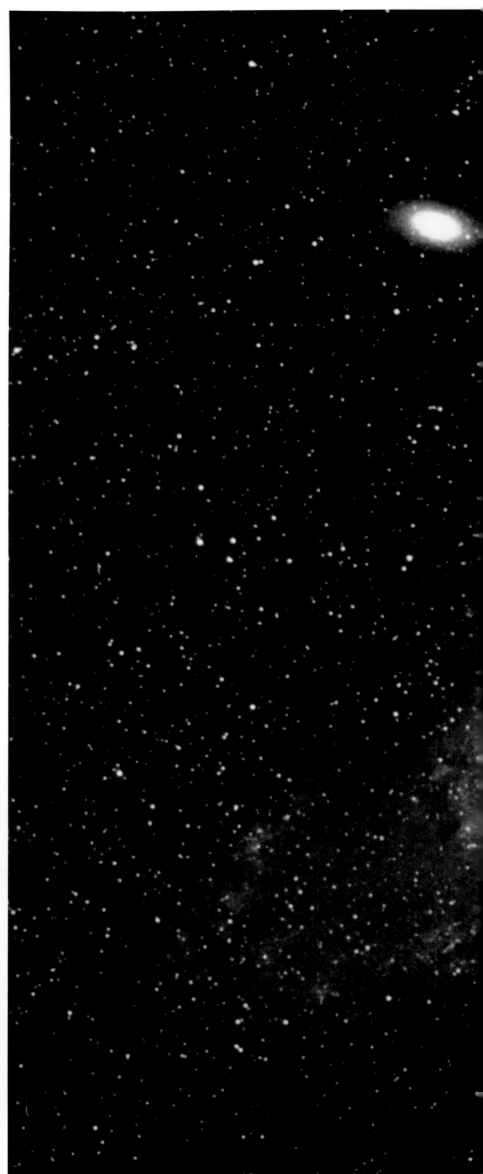

At right: **The Great Galaxy in Andromeda (M 31) and elliptical companions M 32 (left) and NGC 205. This type Sb galaxy, similar to our own (see also M 66), is our largest neighboring galaxy.** *Above:* **M 31 as imaged by IRAS (see page 158).** *Overleaf:* **Spiral M 81 (left) in Ursa Major, and dust-shrouded galaxy M 82. (Photo by Lee Coombs)**

mers realize that there are two groups of Cepheids. The Cepheids found in spiral arms are brighter by 1.4 magnitudes for a given period than Cepheids with the same period in globular clusters.)

While Hubble is considered the founder of modern extragalactic research, he was motivated in his most important work by the discoveries of VM Slipher of Lowell Observatory, who had measured the radial velocities of some spiral nebulae and reported in 1914 that M 31 was *approaching* us at 186 mi/sec (300 km/sec), while two other nebulae were receding at 684 mi/sec (1100 km/sec). These were unheard of velocities in galactic astronomy, and further cemented the special character of spiral nebulae.

Slipher had at his (occasional) disposal only a 24-inch refractor, with which he obtained his spectra. (Some exposures took more than one night!) Hubble, exploiting the great light gathering power of the 100-inch, obtained many radial velocities of spiral nebulae in the 1920s, and in 1929 set forth his famous velocity-distance relation: the more distant galaxies were receding from us at a speed proportional to the distance. The proportionality constant we call Hubble's constant, which is in the range of 31 to 62 mi/sec/Mpc (50 to 100 km/sec/Mpc). Thus, galaxies 100 Mpc distant are receding from us at 3107 to 6214 mi/sec (5000 to 10,000 km/sec). Only a few of the very nearest galaxies have blue shifted spectral lines. This can happen in a generally expanding universe because on small scales—such as in our own galaxy—local gravitational attraction can overwhelm the general expansion.

It was Hubble who first classified the galaxies by appearance as follows: ellipticals (E0 to E7, with E0 being perfectly round and E7 being most flattened); S0 galaxies (flattened, with a central bulge, but without noticeable spiral structure); regular spirals, ranked according to our ability to resolve spiral structure (Sc being most open, Sb being

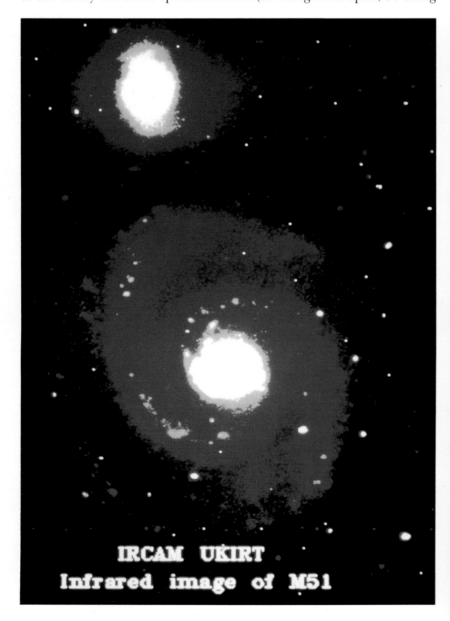

IRCAM UKIRT
Infrared image of M51

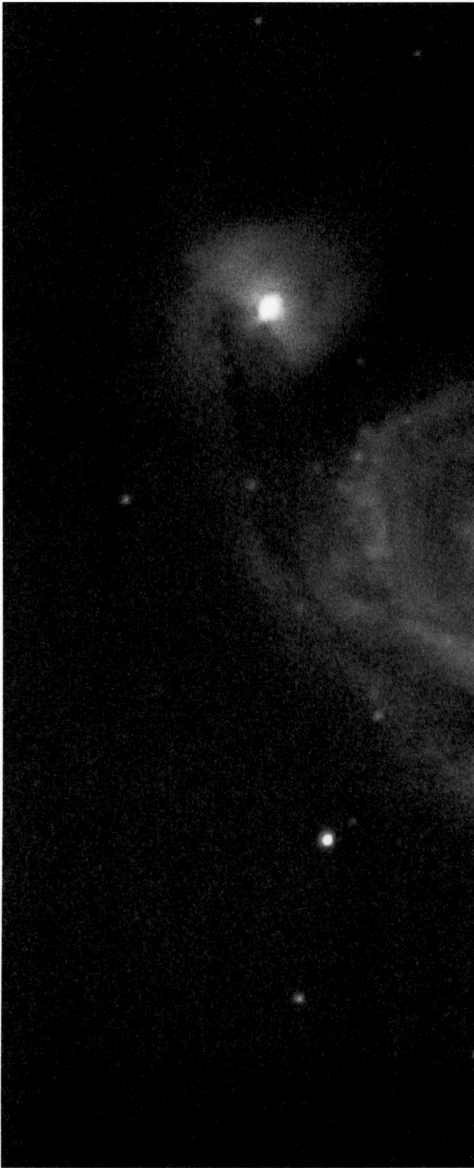

Above: M 51, the Whirlpool Galaxy in Canes Venatici, at a resolution of 1.2 arc seconds. This image was obtained with the United Kingdom Infrared Telescope, Mauna Kea, Hawaii, by Gillian Wright, Mark Casali, and Dolores Walther using a 3596 channel infrared camera and a broad band filter centered at a wavelength of 2.2 microns. What is shown is primarily the distribution of red giant stars.

At right: The Whirlpool Galaxy (M 51) (see pages 162–163), and NGC 5195, as imaged with a 14-inch telescope. M 51 is 37 million light years from us. (Photo by Bill Iburg)

tighter and Sa being tightest); barred spirals (SBa, SBb, and Sbc); and irregulars. Our galaxy is classed as intermediate between Sb and Sc, or Sbc.

Seyfert galaxies, first identified by the American astronomer Carl Seyfert in 1943, are another important type. They are usually spirals of very high luminosity and have intensely bright, star-like nuclei. Other galaxies with active galactic nuclei are named after the Armenian astronomer Markarian, who published a list of 600 such objects in 1968. While normal spiral galaxies show absorption lines in their spectra, active galaxies exhibit very broad emission lines, attributable to discrete clouds of gas moving at velocities which are large compared to the escape velocity of the galaxies. The spectra of active galaxies resemble those of quasars.

We speak of radio galaxies and X-ray galaxies, if such objects emit a lot of radio or X-ray light, respectively. We also speak of interacting

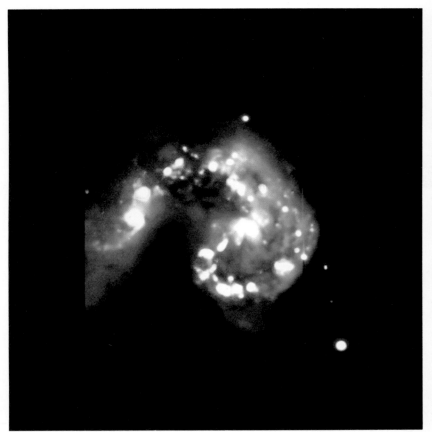

Above: Optical and infrared images of the colliding galaxies NGC 4038 and 4039. (Courtesy National Optical Astronomy Observatories.)
At right: The 'Blackeye Galaxy' (M 64) in Coma Berenices—a spiral of approximate magnitude 8.5. Its distinct dark dust lane gives it its name. (Photo by Bill Iburg)

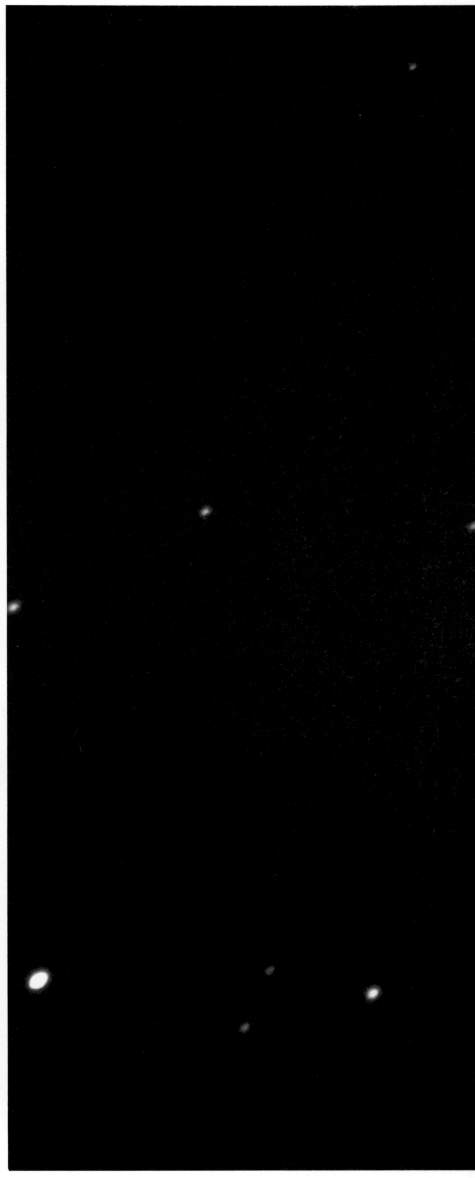

170

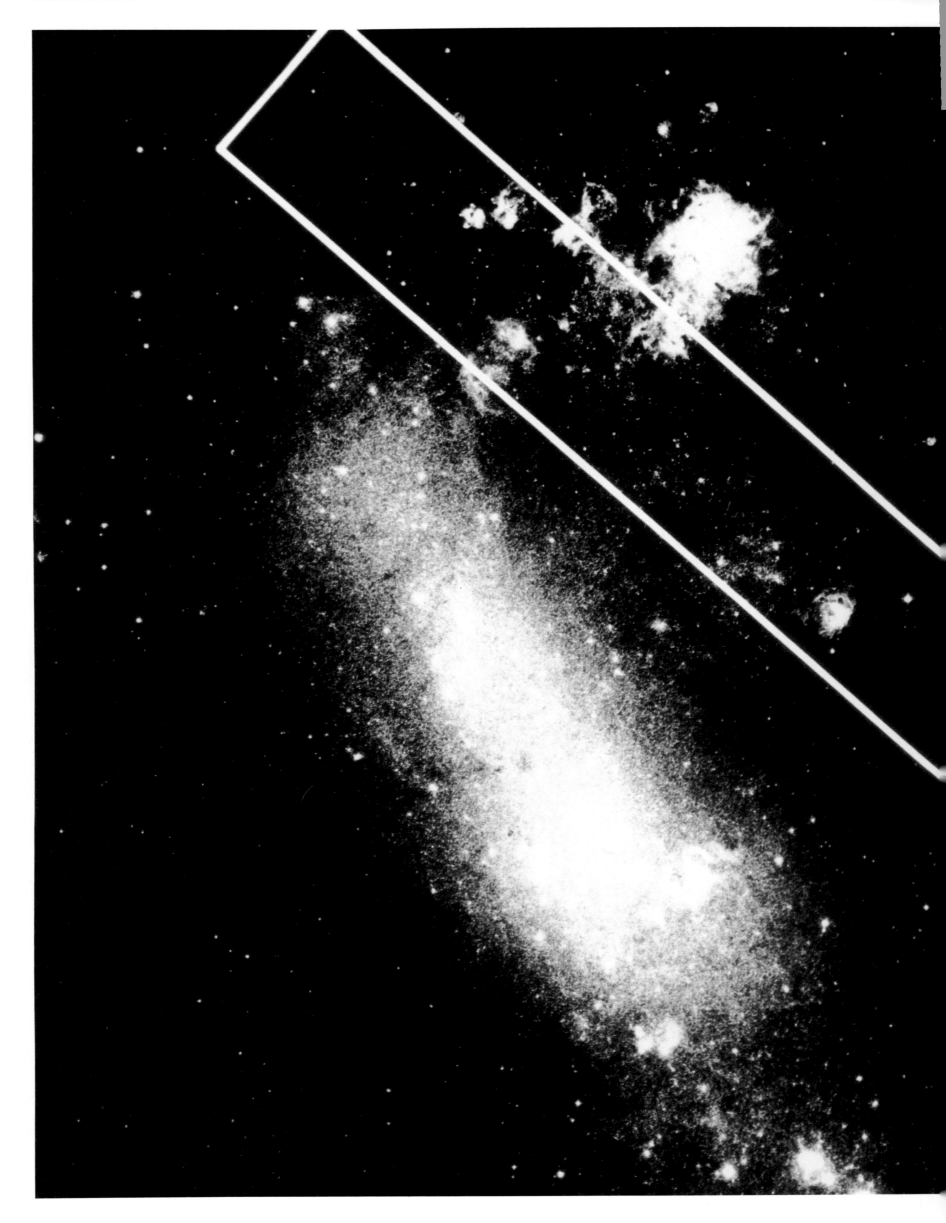

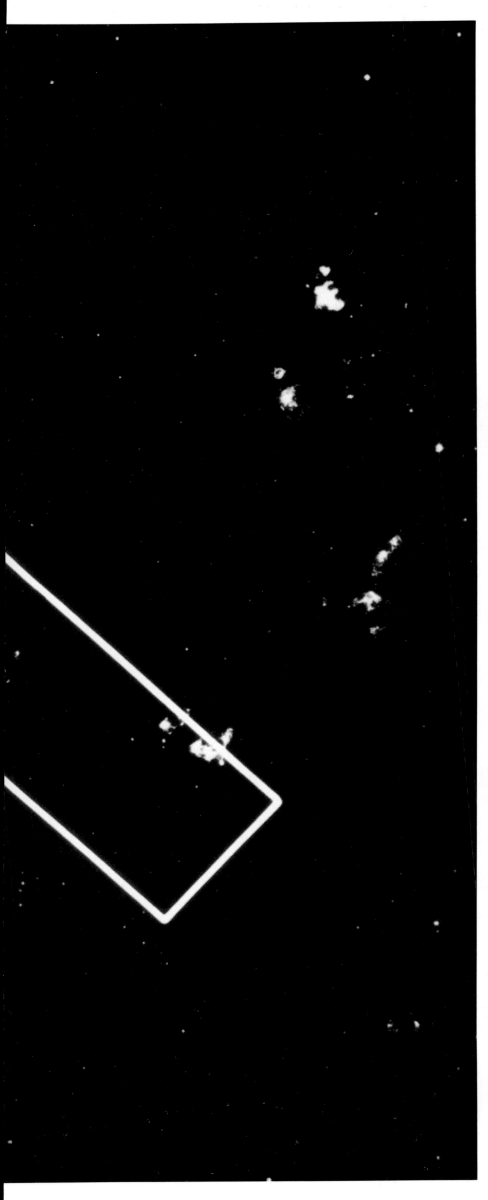

galaxies if two or more galaxies are close enough to be pulling each other apart. Galaxies which have merged are often strong radio sources.

While the building blocks of stars are atoms, and the building blocks of galaxies are stars, the building blocks of the universe are galaxies and clusters of galaxies. The scaling of stars and galaxies is very different, however. If stars in a galaxy are scaled down to the size of people, the nearest neighbors are 60,000 miles apart. If galaxies are scaled down to the size of people, then the distance between neighbors is about 300 feet. As Paul Hodge points out, 'The universe would seem like a somewhat expanding baseball game, with lots of open space between the players.'

Our galaxy has two satellite galaxies, which are visible from the southern hemisphere. They are named after the explorer Ferdinand Magellan. Both are irregular galaxies. A supernova burst forth in the large Magellanic Cloud on 24 February 1987, which brightened to apparent visual magnitude 3.0 by 20 May. It was the brightest supernova since Kepler's in 1604. (Of course, because the LMC is 170,000 light years away, this explosion really took place 170,000 years ago.) Astronomers are still studying this exciting object with the most advanced techniques, allowing theories about the final stages of life of massive stars to be refined. While Supernova 1978A was expected to produce a pulsar, at the time of this writing none has yet been found.

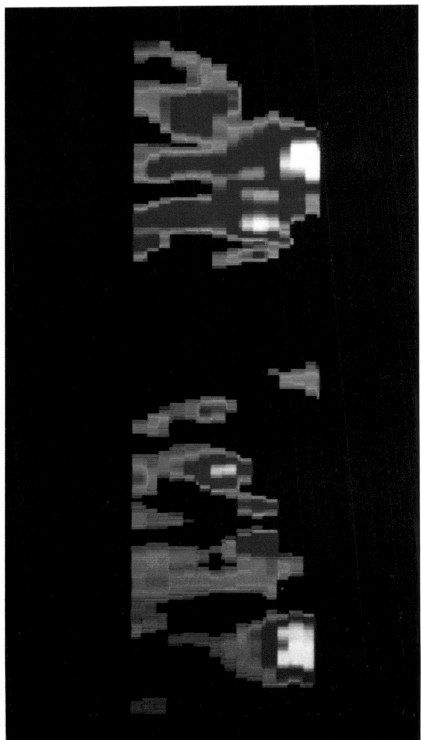

At left: A photo of the Large Magellanic Cloud, taken with the use of an optical telescope. The area indicated by the rectangular 'box' coincides with the area that is the subject of the photograph shown *above*. This infrared image was obtained by the Infrared Astronomical Satellite (see also pages 158 and 164).

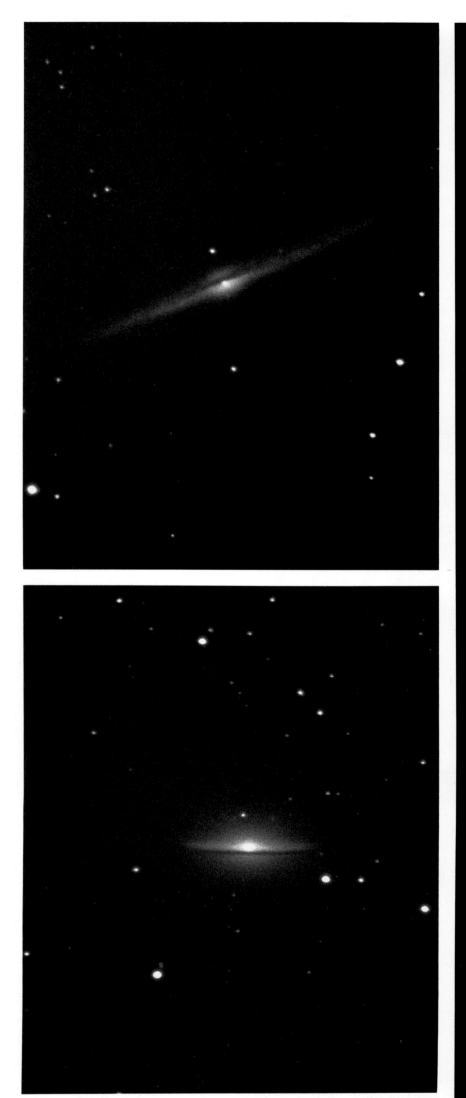

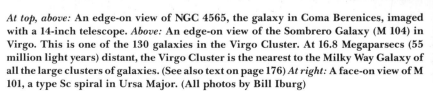

At top, above: An edge-on view of NGC 4565, the galaxy in Coma Berenices, imaged with a 14-inch telescope. *Above:* An edge-on view of the Sombrero Galaxy (M 104) in Virgo. This is one of the 130 galaxies in the Virgo Cluster. At 16.8 Megaparsecs (55 million light years) distant, the Virgo Cluster is the nearest to the Milky Way Galaxy of all the large clusters of galaxies. (See also text on page 176) *At right:* A face-on view of M 101, a type Sc spiral in Ursa Major. (All photos by Bill Iburg)

The Milky Way and the Magellanic Clouds are part of a conglomeration of galaxies called the Local Group. The accompanying table lists 30 members. The bright spirals M 31 and M33 are included, plus a number of elliptical and irregular galaxies. Only 10 percent of the Local Group are what could be considered large, bright galaxies; most of the rest are dwarf galaxies. Just as the galaxy makes few massive (bright) stars, so the universe makes few massive (bright) galaxies. But bright stars and

bright galaxies can be seen at great distances, giving us a much different impression of what the galaxy or universe is, based on what it *looks like* rather than what it is *made of*.

Some of the galaxies in the Local Group exhibit subclustering, as listed in the table below.

Clusters of galaxies are common, and isolated galaxies are rare. Out to a radius of 25 Mpc, beyond which the galaxy counts are less complete, we can identify 179 *groups* that contain 69 percent of the galaxies. An additional 20 percent of the galaxies are included in *associations* (a number of linked groups), while an additional 10 percent are included in linked associations, or *clouds*. Only one percent of galaxies are by themselves, outside of clouds.

The Local group is part of the Coma-Sculptor Cloud (*see facing page*), which contains 163 galaxies in 16 groups. It is falling towards the Virgo Cluster at a velocity of about 186 mi/sec (300 km/sec). The Virgo Cluster, at a distance of 16.8 Mpc, contains 130 galaxies and is associated with 104 other galaxies in 38 groups. Eleven galaxies in the constellation Virgo are bright enough to be found in Messier's catalogue (numbers 49, 58, 59, 60, 61, 84, 86, 87, 89, 90 and 104). One of these, the giant elliptical M87, is so massive (6×10^{12} solar masses) that it is believed to have swallowed other, smaller galaxies. This is known as galactic cannibalism.

In R Brent Tully and J Richard Fisher's *Nearby Galaxies Atlas* there are 2367 galaxies with radial velocities less than 1864 mi/sec (3000 km/sec), nearer than 40 Mpc if the Hubble constant is 17 mi/sec/Mpc (75 km/sec/Mpc). This includes all types of galaxies, giving us plenty of objects to investigate. And while such objects are faint enough to require the use of large telescopes for study, they bring us only one percent of the way from our galaxy to the visible edge of the universe.

For Further Reading

Hodge, Paul, 'The Local Group: Our Galactic Neighborhood,' *Mercury*, January-February, 1987, pp 2-15.

Hodge, Paul, *Galaxies* (Cambridge: Harvard University Press), 1986.

Smith, Robert, *The Expanding Unvierse: Astronomy's 'Great Debate,' 1900-1931* (Cambridge: Cambridge University Press), 1982.

Tully, R Brent, and Fisher, J Richard; *Nearby Galaxies Atlas* (Cambridge: Cambridge Unviersity Press), 1987.

Tully, R Brent, *Nearby Galaxies Catalog* (Cambridge: Cambridge University Press), 1987.

Above: The type Sa tightly-wound spiral galaxy NGC 7217 in Pegasus—one of several spirals in Pegasus, which is associated with the constellation Andromeda. Galaxy NGC 7217 has a magnitude of approximately 11.5. In the vastness of the intergalactic universe, the concept of 'localness' involves trillions of miles of distance—in instances of extreme closeness. (Photo courtesy of US Naval Observatory)

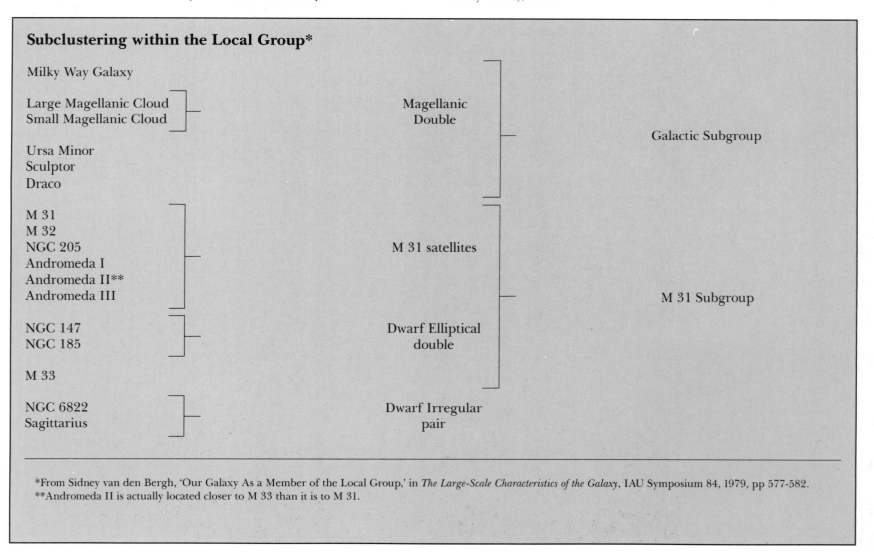

Subclustering within the Local Group*

Milky Way Galaxy

Large Magellanic Cloud
Small Magellanic Cloud — Magellanic Double

Ursa Minor
Sculptor
Draco

— Galactic Subgroup

M 31
M 32
NGC 205
Andromeda I
Andromeda II**
Andromeda III — M 31 satellites

NGC 147
NGC 185 — Dwarf Elliptical double

M 33

NGC 6822
Sagittarius — Dwarf Irregular pair

— M 31 Subgroup

*From Sidney van den Bergh, 'Our Galaxy As a Member of the Local Group,' in *The Large-Scale Characteristics of the Galaxy*, IAU Symposium 84, 1979, pp 577-582.
**Andromeda II is actually located closer to M 33 than it is to M 31.

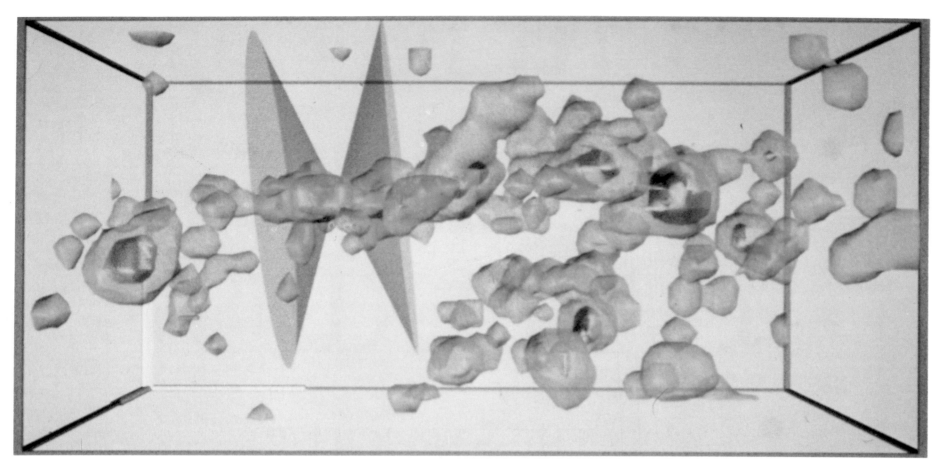

Above: The Coma-Sculptor Cloud of galaxies. The dimensions are $20 \times 16 \times 10$ Mega-parsecs, assuming a Hubble constant of 47 mi/sec/Mpc (75 km/sec/Mpc). The green contour is one galaxy/Mpc³. The view is edge on to the plane of the Local Supercluster.

The Milky Way galaxy is at the origin of the blue cones, which delineate the 'zone of avoidance' due to dust in our galactic plane (galactic latitudes -20 to $+20$ degrees). (Courtesy R Brent Tully, University of Hawaii.)

The Brightest Members of the Local Group*

Name	Type	Position R A	Dec	Distance (millions of light years)	Magnitude Apparent	Absolute
M31 (NGC 224)	Sb	00 40	+41	2.2	4.4	−21.6
Milky Way	Sbc	17 42	−28	0.03	—	−20.6
M33 (NGC 598)	Sc	01 31	+30	2.5	6.3	−19.1
Large Magellanic Cloud	Irr	05 24	−69	0.2	0.6	−18.4
Small Magellanic Cloud	Irr	00 51	−73	0.3	2.8	−17.0
IC 10	Irr	00 17	+59	4.0	11.7	−16.2
NGC 205	E5 pec	00 37	+41	2.2	8.6	−15.7
M32 (NGC 221)	E2	00 40	+40	2.2	9.0	−15.5
NGC 6822	Irr	19 42	−14	1.8	9.3	−15.1
WLM	Irr	23 59	−15	2.0	11.3	−15.0
IC 5152	Sd	21 59	−51	2.0	11.7	−14.6
NGC 185	E3 pec	00 36	+48	2.2	10.1	−14.6
IC 1613	Irr	01 02	+01	2.5	10.0	−14.5
NGC 147	E5	00 30	+48	2.2	10.4	−14.4
Leo A	Irr	09 56	+30	5.0	12.7	−13.5
Pegasus	Irr	23 26	+14	5.0	12.4	−13.4
Fornax	E3	02 37	−34	0.5	8.5	−12.9
GR8	Irr	12 56	+14	4.0	14.6	−11.0
DDO 210	Irr	20 44	−13	3.0	15.3	−11.0
Sagittarius	Irr	19 27	−17	4.0	15.6	−10.6
Sculptor	E3	00 57	−33	0.23	9.1	−10.6
Andromeda I	E3	00 43	+37	2.2	14.0	−10.6
Andromeda III	E5	00 32	+36	2.2	14.0	−10.6
Andromeda II	E2	01 13	+33	2.2	14.0	−10.6
Pisces (LGS 3)	Irr	01 01	+21	3.0	15.5	− 9.7
Leo I	E3	10 05	+12	0.6	11.8	− 9.6
Leo II	E0	11 10	+22	0.6	12.3	− 9.2
Ursa Minor	E5	15 08	+67	0.3	11.6	− 8.2
Draco	E3	17 19	+57	0.3	12.0	− 8.0
Carina	E4	06 40	−50	0.3	(>13.0)	(>− 5.5)

*From Paul Hodge, 'The Local Group: Our Galactic Neighborhood,' in *Mercury*, Jan-Feb 1987, pp 2-15.

PART FIVE

DISTANT GALAXIES

AND THE STRUCTURE OF THE UNIVERSE

As early as 1784 William Herschel noted the tendency of 'nebulae' to cluster. Describing the concentration of galaxies in Coma Berenices and Virgo, he reports: 'One of these nebulous beds is so rich, that, in passing through a section of it in the time of only 36 minutes, I detected no less than 31 nebulae, all distinctly visible upon a fine blue sky.' Just as close pairings of stars reveal actual physical doubles, one would rightly presume that the clustering of positions of nebulae in the sky is indicative of their clustering in three dimensional space.

With the photographic emulsions available at the turn of the twentieth century, James Keeler estimated that 120,000 nebulae were accessible to the 36-inch Crossley reflector at Lick Observatory. By the 1930s this estimate had been revised upward to four and one-half to five million. With a modern four meter telescope and advanced electronic imaging arrays, one can estimate that in the single magnitude range of 23 to 24 at a wavelength of 9000 Angstroms (at the far red end of the optical window) there are 10,000 galaxies per square degree, or more than 400 million over the whole sky. At still fainter magnitudes (about 27th magnitude in the blue part of the optical window), approximately 15 percent of the sky background is covered with galaxies, amounting to 150,000 per square degree, or six billion over the whole sky.

Extensive searches for galaxy clusters have been carried out since the 1950s after the completion of the National Geographic Society-Palomar Observatory Sky Survey, which gave us photographs of the entire sky north of declination − 33 degrees to a limiting magnitude of 21.1 in the blue and 20.0 in the red. George Abell examined the Palomar Sky Survey for 'rich' clusters of galaxies. To qualify as *rich* a cluster had to have 50 members no fainter than two magnitudes dimmer than the third brightest galaxy. Furthermore, a rich cluster was defined to be less

than 1.5 Mpc in size. Along the way he found some clusters that did not quite qualify (less than 50 members of the required brightness). His results were as follows:

# galaxies/cluster	# clusters found
30-49	1030 (not complete)
50-79	1224
80-129	383
130-199	68
200-299	6
> 300	1

Even among rich clusters there is a strong tendency for galaxies to cluster in groups of dozens rather than hundreds. But these clusters are easily tied together into higher level entities. One speaks of groups, associations, and clouds.

By estimating the distances to clusters on the basis of Hubble's Law and the red shifts, or from the apparent brightnesses of the galaxies (while estimating their absolute magnitudes), we can construct models of the three dimensional structure of the universe. One can define the structure on the basis of the *presence* or the *absence* of the luminous galaxies, for there are volumes that are largely devoid of galaxies.

In 1981 the first galaxy void was discovered—a region in the constellation Bootes at a distance of 190 Mpc that is 171 Mpc in diameter. Subsequent analysis has shown that *some* galaxies are to found in this

Above right: **An X-ray picture, taken by NASA's High Energy Astronomy Observatory 2, of an object discovered in 1979—it was then the most distant (10 billion light years) and brightest quasar observed to emit X-rays, although quasars have been found as distant as 15.5 billion light years. To the lower right is quasar 3C 723, which is visible to small telescopes. The X-ray image *at right* shows several distinct young stars.**

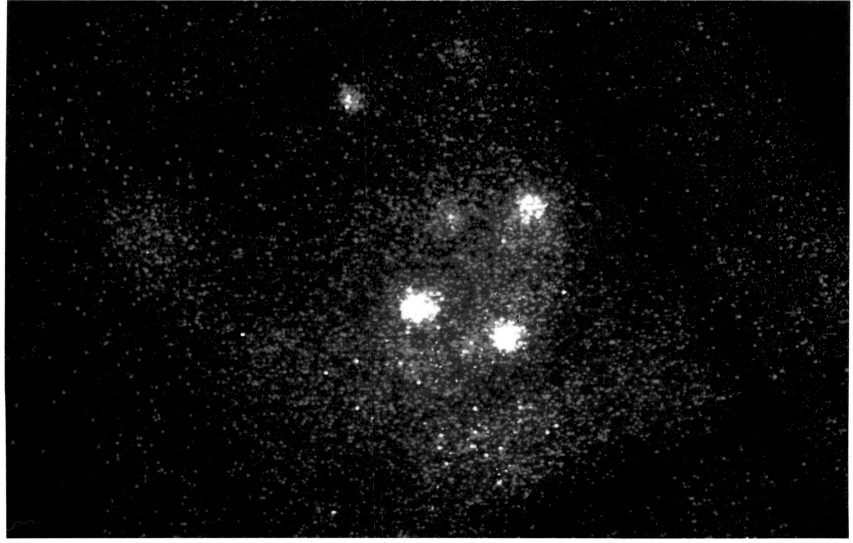

void, and that many other voids of comparable size exist within 350 Mpc. In fact, most of the galaxies in the local supercluster are to be found in nine 'clouds,' while most of the space between them is empty of luminous galaxies.

The galaxies show that the universe contains chains, sheets, filaments, and pancakes of galaxies. Conversely, one can define the structure of the universe in terms of the voids and say that the universe is made up of bubbles defined by relatively thin conglomerations of galaxies.

The largest known structure at the time of this writing is called the Pisces-Cetus Supercluster Complex, which is 360 by 200 by 80 Mpc in size and contains 10^{17} to 10^{18} solar masses of material (a million times our galaxy's mass). There can only be 10,000 such entities in the entire universe.

Cosmology is the study of the whole physical universe—its origin, present state, and eventual fate. Not surprisingly, it is a complex subject filled with unusual features. For example, if the radial velocity of an object is small compared to the speed of light, the fractional shift of the spectral lines of that object with respect to the laboratory wavelengths of individual lines is equal to the object's velocity divided by the speed of light. (An object receding at one percent of the speed of light has measured spectral lines that are one percent greater than the laboratory values.) But at higher velocities, closer to the speed of light, the situation is different. Objects with spectral lines shifted by 50 percent are reced-

ing at 38.5 percent of the speed of light. If the red shift is equal to 1.0, the velocity of recession is 60 percent of the speed of light. For red shifts of 4.5, the velocity of recession is 93.6 percent of the speed of light. Only an object with infinite red shift would be receding at the speed of light (which is a physical impossibility).

Another curious consequence of cosmological models involves the apparent sizes of galaxies. First consider a universe filled with galaxies of identical linear size (say, 20 kpc in diameter). As we look further out, the angular size of the galaxy diameters decreases steadily. This makes common sense. A mountain seen at a distance of 10 miles appears smaller than at a distance of one mile, and at 100 miles it appears smaller than at 10 miles. It turns out that the apparent sizes of galaxies decrease steadily with increasing distance (or red shift) if the actual density of the universe is very small compared to the critical density necessary to halt the general expansion. If the density of the universe is equal to the critical density, our test galaxies just mentioned would appear to get smaller and smaller, out to a distance corresponding to a red shift of 1.25, and beyond that they would start to get bigger! This is due to the effect of the curvature of space caused by the presence of matter.

It is a simple matter to relate the apparent magnitudes, absolute magnitudes, and distances for nearby stars. For more distant stars we must account for the effect of interstellar absorption. Providing we know the dimming effect of the dust in our galactic plane, we can directly relate the apparent magnitudes, absolute magnitudes, and distances of nearby galaxies. We use such 'standard candles' as Cepheid variable stars, the luminosities of whole globular clusters, or measurements of the brightnesses of supernovae. However, if galaxies are very

Below: **The Local Supercluster of galaxies. The dimensions are $50 \times 40 \times 35$ Mpc. The green contour is 0.5 galaxy/Mpc³. The Milky Way galaxy is on the left hand vertical surface, approximately in the middle. (Courtesy R Brent Tully, University of Hawaii.)**

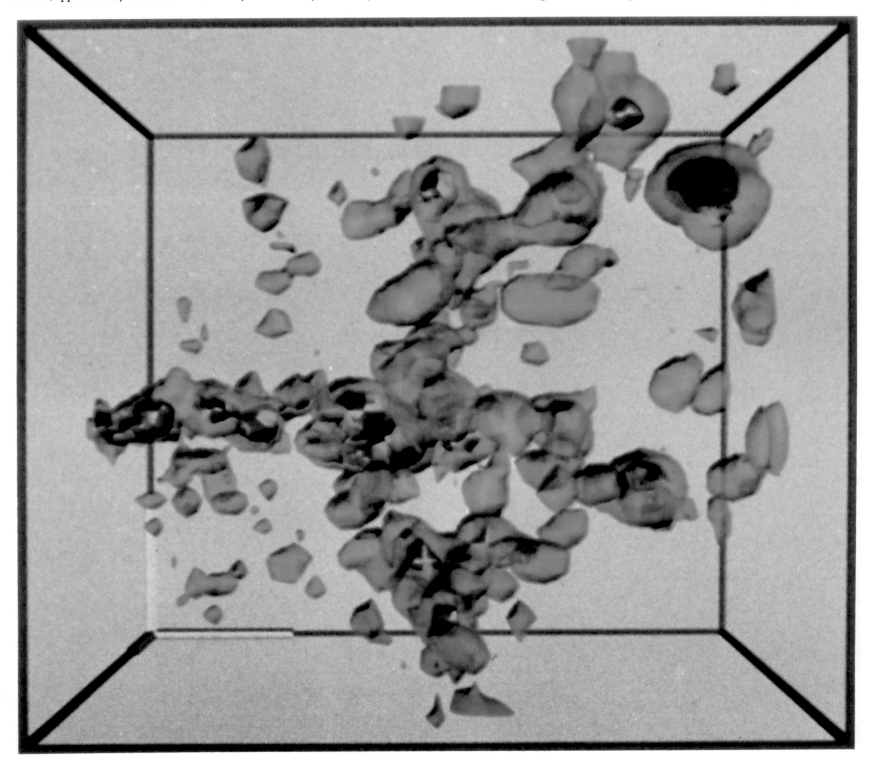

distant, their optical light is red shifted to the infrared, and what we measure at optical wavelengths is light that left the galaxy at ultraviolet wavelengths. Distance measurements based on apparent magnitudes must then include observations at a variety of different wavelengths, and must also include effects due to evolution of the objects (since we may be looking billions of years back into time).

In the case of supernovae, we can now distinguish two types. A Type I supernova, the more common type, is thought to be due to the *complete* explosion of a white dwarf star composed mostly of carbon and oxygen, which has a companion star so near that the mass of the companion flows onto the surface of the white dwarf. When the white dwarf's mass exceeds a critical limit (1.4 solar masses), the white dwarf explodes, leaving no remnant. The spectra of Type I supernovae show no hydrogen lines.

A Type II supernova is thought to be due to the explosion of a single star of mass 8 to 18 solar masses (generally of spectral type B). Such a star will leave behind either a neutron star or a black hole. Type II supernovae do show hydrogen in their spectra. They are about two magnitudes fainter at their brightest compared to Type I supernovae.

A large spiral galaxy such as ours should have a supernova every 20 to 100 years, but we have not seen one since 1604. Perhaps there were

Below: **A composite color image of objects as faint as 27th magnitude. Three separate images were obtained with the Cerro-Tololo Interamerican Observatory four meter reflector and three separate filters: 1) 3600-5200 Ångströms (blue filter); 2) 5800-7200 Ångströms (red filter); and 3) 7800-11000 Ångströms (very near infrared). The field is about 2.6 by 4.6 arc minutes. Most of the objects are galaxies at distances corresponding to red shifts of one to three. (Copyright © 1989 by JA Tyson.)**

some, but we did not notice them owing to the dimming effect of interstellar dust (which could be 50 magnitudes along the line of sight to a supernova in our galactic plane at a distance of many kiloparsecs). However, if we are looking perpendicular to our galactic plane, we can detect supernovae in galaxies hundreds of Megaparsecs away.

Beyond 1000 Mpc we observe very luminous galaxies and quasars. Following the development of radio astronomy after World War II, surveys were carried out at radio wavelengths in the 1950s. The most important of these was the revised third *Cambridge Catalogue*, published in 1962. (Objects from this list are known by their 3C numbers.) Astronomers sought optical counterparts of the radio sources. Some radio sources, such as Cygnus A, were found to be double. In many cases (Cygnus A being one) deep optical photographs revealed a faint galaxy between the radio lobes.

Optically derived red shifts of radio sources have been shown to be very large. Many of the 3C sources which are galaxies have red shifts of 0.6 to 1.8 (corresponding to recession velocities of 44 to 77 percent of the speed of light).

Some of the 3C sources are called quasars, or quasi-stellar objects, because at optical wavelengths they look like faint stars. (They have star-like nuclei typically less than one arc second in size.) Upon closer inspection many quasars are shown to have a fuzzy halo whose spectrum resembles that of an elliptical galaxy.

In 1963 Maarten Schmidt found that the quasar 3C 273 had a red shift of 15.8 percent of the speed of light, by far the largest red shift known at that time. If the red shift is interpreted to be indicative of its true radial velocity, and related to the distance using a Hubble constant

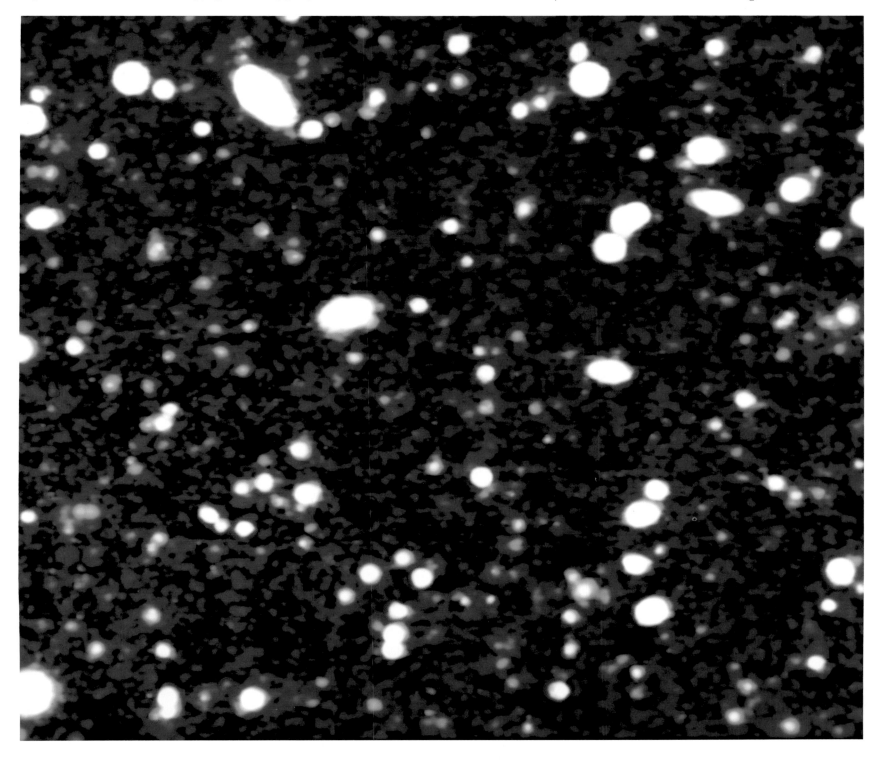

of 31 mi/sec/Mpc (50 km/sec/Mpc), 3C 273 would be at an effective distance of 865 Mpc. With an apparent magnitude of 12.8 to 12.4, its absolute magnitude would be -27.2 to -27.6, some eight magnitudes brighter than a Type I supernova at its brightest. If placed at a distance of 10 parsecs, 3C 273 would be brighter than the Sun!

Quasars are shown to be variable at radio and optical wavelengths on time scales as short as days. Thus, they must be as small as a few light-days in size, or comparable to the size of our solar system. They are regarded to be the extreme example of active galactic nuclei. In order to account for their extreme luminosities, it is generally believed that each quasar has a black hole of 10^8 to 10^9 solar masses that is accreting matter. Such a black hole has sufficient gravitational strength to 'swallow' any star or gas cloud that passes within three parsecs. As time goes on, it would necessarily increase in mass.

There are about a million quasars brighter than magnitude 21 distributed over the whole sky. The largest red shift of any object known at the time of this writing is a quasar with red shift 4.43. By the time you read this, more distant objects will probably have been discovered.

Recently, great progress has been made in the discovery of very distant galaxies. This is due to the development of modern electronic array detectors, which operate at optical and near-infrared wavelengths. The most distant galaxy known until 1987 had a red shift of 1.819. Then Simon Lilly of the University of Hawaii found that the radio galaxy 0902 + 34 has a red shift of 3.395. This is analogous to beating the world record in the long jump by 15 feet. Lilly's galaxy pushed us an extra one or two billion years into the past, but his record was of short duration. In 1988 Kenneth Chambers, George Miley, and Wil van Breugel found that the radio galaxy 4C 41.17 has a red shift of 3.8.

It should be pointed out that not all astronomers believe that the red shifts of quasars are necessarily due to the general expansion of the universe. Some quasars seem to be associated with galaxies which do not have correspondingly equal red shifts. The classic case is the galaxy NGC 4319—with a red shift of 1056 mi/sec (1700 km/sec)—which is connected by a luminous bridge to the quasar Markarian 205 (with a red shift of 21,000 km/sec). This subject is reviewed by Halton Arp in his book *Quasars, Redshifts and Controversies*. Unfortunately, there is as yet no sound physical explanation for discordant red shifts. Arp suggests that quasars are ejected by galaxies, but if this is true, why do we not see some nearby galaxies that have ejected quasars toward us, such that some quasars would have blue shifted spectral lines?

One piece of evidence in favor of the conventional interpretation of quasar red shifts involves the types of lines in their spectra. Usually, we measure the red shift of a quasar from the observed wavelengths of certain broad emission (bright) lines, such as the Lyman alpha line of neutral hydrogen, observed in the laboratory at 1216 Ångströms in the ultraviolet. At red shifts greater than 1.7 this line is observed in the optical window of the spectrum. Quasars with large red shifts show many (sometimes hundreds of) absorption lines at wavelengths shorter than the observed emission of the Lyman alpha line. These are attributed to the presence of many (ie, hundreds of) clouds of cooler hydrogen gas along the line of sight to the quasar at correspondingly smaller and smaller red shifts (ie, distances).

Another piece of evidence comes from the so-called gravitational lenses. Since gravity causes space to curve, the effect is that a light path can be bent by a gravitational field, as stipulated by General Relativity. During a total solar eclipse the *positions* of the stars near the limb of the eclipsed Sun are shifted in the direction opposite the center of the Sun. Similarly, if a galaxy containing some billions of solar masses were aligned along the line of sight to a quasar, it could lens multiple images of the quasar. While this phenomenon was predicted in 1937 by Fritz Zwicky, it was not observed until 1979. By 1988 some 17 gravitational lens candidates had been identified, but only five have stood up under careful analysis. For one of them, PG 1115 + 08 (the 'triple quasar'), there are multiple images of a 16th magnitude quasar of red shift 1.722. The lensing galaxy has a visual magnitude of about 22.5, and its color is consistent with it being at a distance corresponding to a red shift between 0.3 and 1. Since the quasar being lensed must be beyond the galaxy, the large observed red shift of the quasar images is evidence in favor of the notion that red shifts are 'cosmological.'

At the greatest observed red shifts (or distances) we are trying to detect galaxies which are more than 100 times fainter than the background night sky level on a moonless night, at an observatory far from any city lights. How can we hope to probe further out into the universe? One way is to observe with an orbiting telescope such as the Hubble

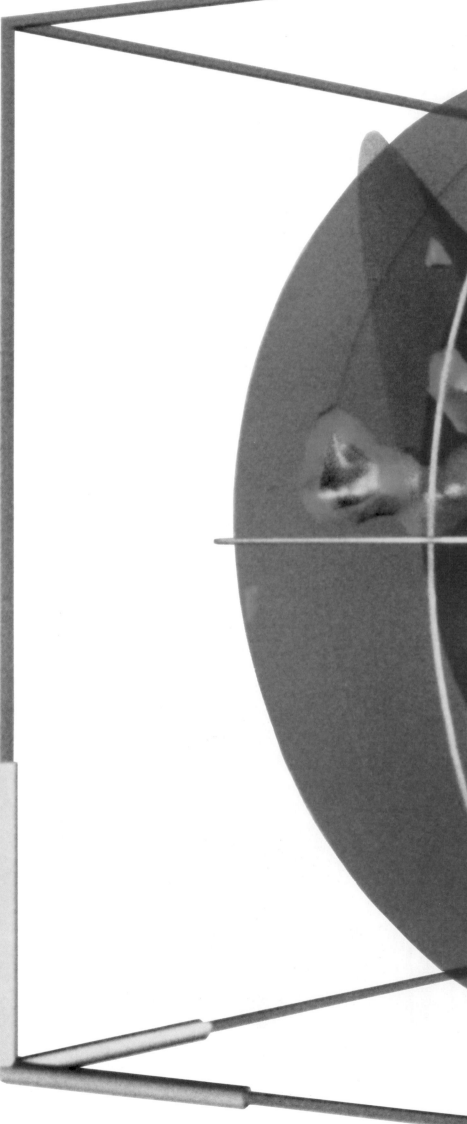

Below: The distribution of rich clusters of galaxies—the Pisces-Cetus Supercluster Complex. The diameter is 680 Mpc. The view is edge on to the plane of the Local Supercluster. (Courtesy R Brent Tully, University of Hawaii.)

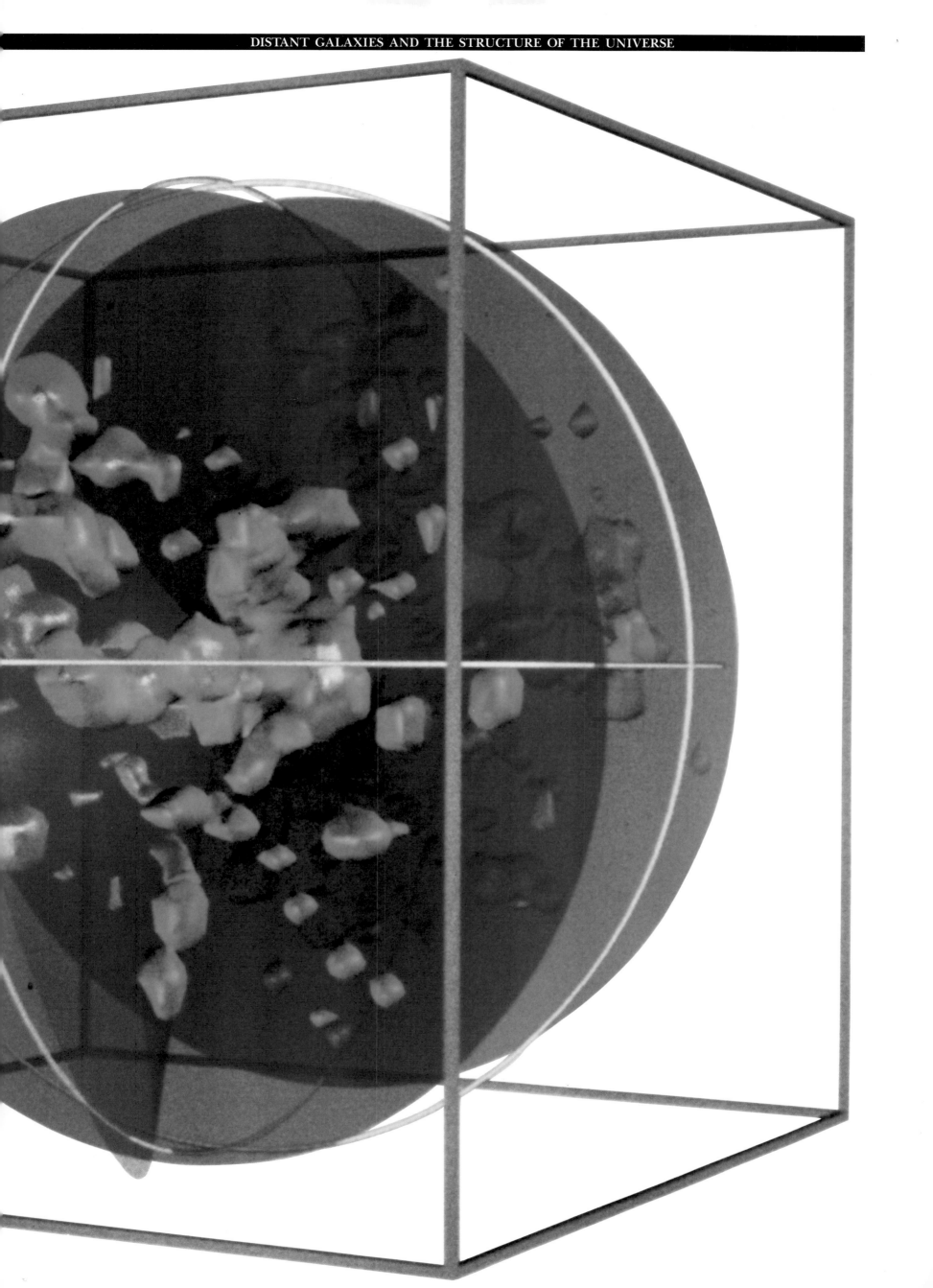

Space Telescope. The other is to observe the cosmic three degree background radiation at submillimeter and millimeter wavelengths. For if the universe originated in a Big Bang 10 to 20 billion years ago, we can see the remnant of the aftermath of the fireball at red shifts of 1500. What was once optical wavelength radiation is now visible at 450 microns to one millimeter. From millimeter wave observations carried out over the whole sky, the cosmic background radiation is uniform to one part in 10,000, with the derived temperature slightly hotter at one point in the sky and slightly colder at the opposite point on the sky. This is evidence of: 1) the uniformity of the universe on the largest scales; and 2) a motion of the Local Group of galaxies with respect to the rest of the universe. That motion is toward right ascension 10 hours 40 minutes, declination -13 degrees (just west of the constellation Crater in Eridanus) at a velocity of 354 mi/sec (570 km/sec).

Will the universe expand forever? That depends on the ratio of the actual density of the universe compared to that value necessary to halt the general expansion. On the basis of counts of actual galaxies we can state that a minimum of four percent of the critical density has been found.

However, we know from studies of the motion of galaxies in clusters that 15 times as much matter exists in clusters than we identify with luminous objects. The universe may indeed have enough mass to halt the general expansion, but then up to 96 percent of it would be 'dark matter.' What kind of dark matter? One hope was for 'massive neutrinos.'

The detection of neutrinos from the supernova of 1987 in the Large Magellanic Cloud allowed us to set an upper limit (the maximum allowable value, given the observations) for the neutrino's mass of 1/40,000 the mass of the electron. However, if the actual density of the universe equals the critical density, then neutrinos would have to be about 2.5 times heavier than the upper limit in order to make up all of the missing mass. So neutrinos are not the answer, though they may be part of it.

According to the inflationary scenario, discussed briefly in the Introduction, the actual density of the universe *equals* the critical density. Any slight difference before the epoch of inflation would have resulted in a universe many powers of 10 less dense or more dense than the critical density. Given that the known density is within a factor of 25 or less of the critical density, this is regarded by some as 'close agreement.'

Astronomical research has solved many riddles and, as expected in any science, has given us new questions and provided us with new challenges. Astronomy is the oldest of the sciences, but is more exciting today than ever.

THE EDWIN P HUBBLE SPACE TELESCOPE PROJECT

Probably the most important event in the history of astronomy is the deployment of the Edwin P Hubble Space Telescope. The idea behind the Space Telescope was simple: to place an extraordinarily sensitive telescope into orbit around the earth, high above the distorting effects of the Earth's atmosphere.

Placing a telescope in space has been a dream of astronomers for decades, dating back to before the advent of spaceflight. There, far above the distorting effects of the earth's atmosphere, astronomers would have an unimpaired view of the entire universe. The National Aeronautics and Space Administration is meeting this dream of astronomers through the Edwin P Hubble Space Telescope, a national observatory orbiting 320 nautical miles above the earth.

With the Hubble Space Telescope (HST) it will be possible to see *300 times* as much of the universe, and objects *seven times* more distant than

the most distant objects currently observable. This will vastly increase our knowledge and understanding of the universe and how it was formed. Indeed, if the universe was created 14 billion years ago (as some have postulated), and the Hubble Space Telescope has a range of 14 billion light years (which it theoretically does), we will be able to 'see' the creation of the universe in the light coming from objects 14 billion light years from Earth.

The Hubble Telescope is a 94.5-inch Ritchey-Chretien telescope, named in honor of American astronomer Edwin P Hubble, who made vital contributions to the understanding of galaxies and the universe through his work earlier this century.

While the mirror size and optical quality make the Hubble Telescope one of the largest and most precise astronomical instruments ever produced, its major advantage lies in the fact that it will be outside the earth's atmosphere.

The telescope's high vantage point will allow it to see farther and with greater clarity than any astronomical instrument ever built. Besides 'seeing' better it will detect more portions of the electromagnetic spectrum, such as ultraviolet light which is absorbed by the atmosphere before reaching the ground.

The heart of the Space Telescope is the Optical Telescope Assembly (OTA). The major segments of the OTA are the 94.5-inch primary mirror, a 12-inch secondary mirror, and the OTA's support structure.

The precision of the primary and secondary mirror is a major ingredient in the superb capability of the Space Telescope. If the mirror were scaled up to the size of the earth, none of the great mountain ranges would tower more than five inches above the lowest point. Light entering the Space Telescope is reflected off the primary mirror to the secondary mirror, 16 feet away. The secondary mirror sends the light through a hole in the center of the large mirror, back to the scientific instruments.

Providing all the essential systems to keep the Hubble Telescope operating in the hostile environment of space is the function of the Support Systems Module (SSM). The SSM also directs communications, commands, power, and fine pointing control for the telescope. Collectively, the SSM consists of the light shield on the front end of the telescope; the equipment section, with the main spacecraft electronics equipment; and the aft shroud, which contains the scientific instruments.

The Fine Guidance Sensors (FGS) feed roll, pitch and yaw information to the telescope's attitude control system. The pointing capability of the Hubble Telescope provided by the FGS is so precise it is often called a sixth scientific instrument. To point the telescope, the FGS must identify the position of specified stars. This pointing data can be used to calibrate space-distance relationships throughout the universe. The FGS will allow the telescope to point with a stability of 0.007 arc seconds, or roughly the equivalent of focusing on a dime in Los Angeles from a vantage point in San Francisco.

The Hubble Space Telescope carries five scientific instruments which are replaceable and serviceable in orbit. Four of the instruments, about the size of telephone booths, are located in the aft shroud, behind the primary mirror. They receive light directly from the secondary mirror. The fifth instrument, the Wide Field/Planetary Camera (WF/PC), is located on the circumference of the telescope and uses a pick-off mirror system.

The Faint Object Camera (FOC) does exactly what its name implies, observes faint objects. It does this by taking very low light levels and electronically intensifying the images. Objects as faint as 28th or 29th magnitude (the higher the magnitude, the fainter the object) should be observed by the FOC. By comparison, Earth-based telescopes can see to about 24th magnitude. Likely targets for the instrument are the search for extra-solar planets, variable brightness stars, and in its spectrographic mode, the center of galaxies suspected of concealing black holes.

The Faint Object Spectrograph (FOS) will measure the chemical composition of very faint objects. Visible light contains information used to determine the chemical elements which make up the light source. Special gratings and filters allow the FOS to make spectral exposures which not only reveal information about the makeup of a light source but also about its temperature, motion and physical characteristics. This instrument will study the spectra of objects in the ultra-

In 1984, Lockheed began assembly of the Edwin P Hubble Space Telescope in the world's largest 'clean room' *(right)*, at the company's Sunnyvale facility. (Photo courtesy of Lockheed Corporation)

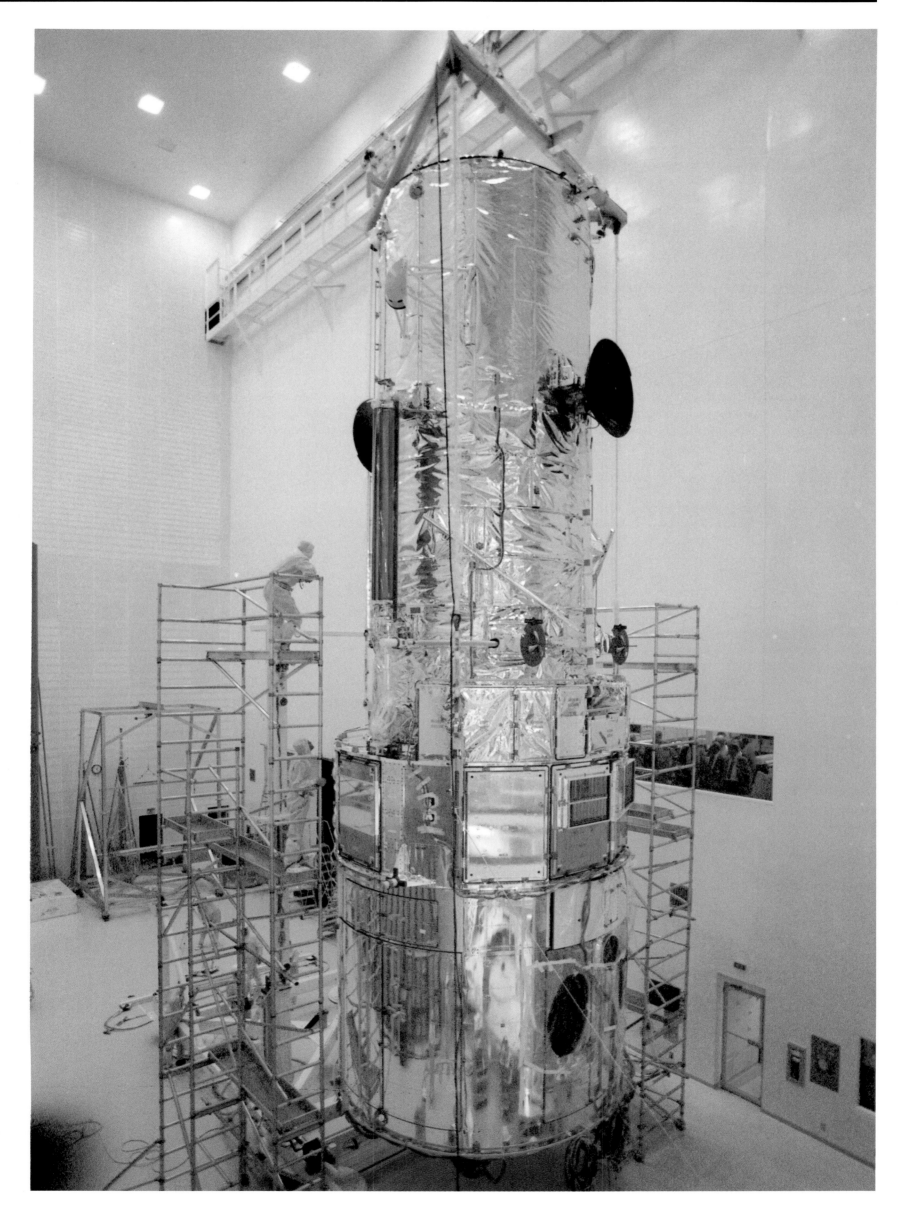

violet and visible wavelengths. Particular targets of interest are quasars, comets and galaxies.

While performing in much the same way as the FOS, the High Resolution Spectrograph (HRS) will observe only the ultraviolet portion of the spectrum. Ultraviolet light is filtered by the Earth's atmosphere and the only spectrographic measurements taken in this light have been from previous space observatories. The HRS will be used to investigate the physical make-up of exploding galaxies, interstellar gas clouds, and matter escaping from stars.

With no moving parts, the High-Speed Photometer HSP is the simplest of the five Space Telescope instruments. It will allow astronomers to take very exact measurements of the intensity of light coming from stellar objects. In addition, it will provide very precise measurements, down to the microsecond level, of time variations in the light. The amount of light received from an object is an important factor in determining its distance making the HSP useful in refining the scale of the Milky Way galaxy and other nearby galaxies.

Actually two separate cameras in one housing, the WF/PC should return some of the most spectacular visual images from the Hubble Space Telescope. In the Wide Field mode the instrument will view large areas of space and provide exquisite views of galaxies and star fields. In the Planetary mode, it will provide glimpses of the planets comparable to those obtained on close fly-by missions.

After being deployed from the Space Shuttle's cargo bay, the solar arrays and high-gain antennae will be deployed. The Shuttle will remain on station nearby while final checks are completed, and after a period of calibration and verification, astronomers at the Space Telescope Science Institute will begin their observations of the sky.

Provisions have been made for in-orbit repair and maintenance of the Space Telescope. Astronauts can remove old instruments and replace them with more advanced or different types of devices. Repairs to many of the systems or instruments can also be accomplished in orbit. The Telescope can be returned to earth for major refurbishment and alteration if necessary. The operating life of the Hubble Space Telescope may be 15 years or more with refurbishment and modernizing using the Space Shuttle.

The Office of Space Science and Application at NASA Headquarters is responsible for overall program management, financial and scheduling provisions, and the science policy development and direction. Marshall Space Flight Center in Huntsville, Alabama is responsible for the development and operation of the Space Telescope system as the 'lead' NASA Center. In Greenbelt, Maryland, the Goddard Space Flight Center is managing the scientific instruments, mission operations, and data management. It is also charged with monitoring the Space Telescope Science Institute.

The Space Telescope Science Institute is operated by AURA, the Association of Universities for Research in Astronomy. The Institute is located on the Homewood Campus of Johns Hopkins University in Baltimore, Maryland. It is the job of the Institute to determine the observational program of the Space Telescope while in orbit, insuring that the observatory will be used to its maximum advantage.

Lockheed Missiles & Space Company, Sunnyvale, California, is the systems integrator of the Space Telescope satellite. It is also responsible for the design, development and manufacture of the Support Systems Module. Perkin-Elmer Corporation, Danbury, Connecticut, manufactured the Optical Telescope Assembly.

Right: **An artist's rendition of the incredible Edwin P Hubble Space Telescope (HST) in orbit. With the Hubble, astronomers will be able to see 14 billion light years into the distant reaches of the universe. The Hubble will do more than just open new frontiers, it will allow mankind to see 300 times more of the universe than ever before. (Photo courtesy of Lockheed Corporation)**

For Further Reading

Arp, Halton, *Quasars, Redshifts, and Controversies* (Berkeley, California: Interstellar Media), 1987. An extensive review of this work was published in *Sky and Telescope*, January, 1988, pp 38-43.

Longair, Malcolm, *Theoretical Concepts in Physics* (Cambridge: Cambridge University Press), 1984, chapter 15.

Rowan-Robinson, Michael, *The Cosmological Distance Ladder: Distance and Time in the Universe* (New York: WH Freeman), 1985.

Turner, Edwin L, 'Gravitational Lenses,' *Scientific American*, July, 1988, pp 54-60.

Verschuur, Gerrit L, *The Invisible Universe Revealed: The Story of Radio Astronomy* (New York: Springer-Verlag), 1987.

GLOSSARY

Absolute Magnitude: The apparent magnitude an object would have if it were situated at a distance of 10 parsecs.

Albedo: A measure of an object's reflecting power; the ratio of reflected light to incoming light in which complete reflection would give an albedo of 1.0.

Ångström: A unit of length equal to 10^{-8} centimeter. Visible light ranges in wavelength from 3500 to 7000 Ångströms.

Antimatter: Particles with charge opposite to that of ordinary matter, such as an antiproton or antielectron (also known as a positron). When particles and their anti-particles meet, they are converted into high energy light waves.

Antoniadi Nomenclature: A universal system of designations devised by the Greek-born French astronomer Eugene (Eugenios) Antoniadi (1870-1944) for naming geologic features on solid surfaced celestial bodies other than the Earth or the Earth's Moon. Specifics of this system are included in this Glossary.

Aphelion: The point in an object's orbital path when it is farthest from the Sun. The opposite of Perihelion.

Apparent Magnitude: The measured brightness of a celestial object given its intrinsic brightness and its distance from the Earth. Venus is as bright as magnitude -4.4. The Sun's apparent visual magnitude is -26.7. The brightest star, Sirius, has apparent magnitude -1.4. The faintest stars visible with the unaided eye have apparent magnitude $+6$, while the faintest objects detectable with the largest telescopes have apparent magnitudes of $+27$.

Arc Minute: An angle equal to 1/60 of a degree.

Arc Second: An angle equal to 1/60 of an arc minute, or 1/3600 of a degree. Star positions can be measured to better than 0.01 arc second.

Asteroids: Hard, rocky bodies, usually only a few kilometers in diameter, such as those orbiting the Sun in between the orbits of Mars and Jupiter.

Astronomical Unit (AU): A unit of measurement used to calculate intra-Solar System distances. One AU is equal to the distance from the Earth to the Sun, or 93 million miles. There are 206,265 AUs in a parsec.

Big Bang: The fiery explosion that is thought to have given rise to the universe.

Black Hole: An object so dense that even light cannot escape from it.

Catena: Antoniadi nomenclature for a row of craters.

Chasma: Antoniadi nomenclature for a chasm or steep-sided canyon.

Comet: From the Greek meaning 'a star with hair.' A comet's nucleus is only a few kilometers in diameter and is a frozen mass of ices, rocks, and dust. If the comet is close to the Sun the ices will sublimate (forming gas), some of the rocks and dust will be liberated, the nucleus will become surrounded by a glowing coma, and the comet will have a tail.

Conjunction: The alignment of two celestial bodies as viewed from a fixed point, such as from the Earth.

Dorsum: Antoniadi nomenclature for ridge.

Eccentricity: Eccentricity describes how elongated is an elliptic orbit; for ellipses e<1. Eccentricity equals the distance between the foci divided by the major axis. An eccentricity of zero signifies a circle. For the planets, the mean distances and eccentricities are:

planet	mean distance	eccentricity
Mercury	0.387 AU	0.206
Venus	0.723 AU	0.007
Earth	1.000 AU	0.017
Mars	1.524 AU	0.093
Jupiter	5.203 AU	0.048
Saturn	9.539 AU	0.056
Uranus	19.182 AU	0.047
Neptune	30.058 AU	0.009
Pluto	39.439 AU	0.250

Ecliptic: The plane in which the Earth revolves around the Sun. All the planets except for Pluto (17 degrees) and Mercury (7 degrees) revolve around the Sun in planes that are within 3.4 degrees of ecliptic.

Electromagnetic Spectrum: Light waves of all different wavelengths. From the most energetic to the least energetic the order is: gamma rays, X-rays, ultraviolet light, visible light (blue through red), infrared light, submillimeter waves, microwaves, and radio waves.

Electron: A negatively charged particle with mass 1/1836 that of the proton.

Ellipse: A geometrical shape such that the sum of the distances from any point on it to two fixed points (called the foci) is constant. All the planets have more or less elliptical orbits; a circle is a type of ellipse, but an *elliptical orbit* describes a planetary path that is more eccentric than concentric.

Elliptical orbit: An orbit that is not *concentric*, or circular, but shaped like an *eccentric* ellipse. All of the planets, except Pluto, have orbits that are very nearly perfectly circular. Pluto has an 'elliptical orbit.' Comets have *very* elliptical orbits.

Force: One of four fundamental interactions between different kinds of matter:

1) Gravitation: An attractive force exerted by all bodies having mass on all other bodies having mass. The gravitational force between two bodies varies as the product of the masses, and inversely as the square of the distance. Gravity is effectively the only long range force.

2) Electromagnetism: A force that governs how electrons and protons interact with each other in atoms. It is an attractive force if two particles have opposite electric charges, but is a repulsive force if two particles have the same charge. Over the range it is effective (10^{-8} centimeters) it is 10^{36} times more powerful than the gravitational force.

3) The strong nuclear force has a range of only three times 10^{-13} centimeters, but it is 100 times stronger than the electromagnetic force. The strong force is responsible for the binding together of protons and neutrons in atomic nuclei.

4) The weak nuclear force has a range of 10^{-16} centimeters (a thousand times less than the strong force), and it is 10^{16} times less intense. The weak nuclear force governs the interactions of particles like electrons and neutrinos and is responsible for processes such as the decay of radioactive nuclei.

Fossa: Antoniadi nomenclature for a narrow, shallow groove or ditch.

Galaxy: One of about 100 billion concentrations of visible matter that make up the universe, each containing a billion (10^9) to a trillion (10^{12}) stars, interstellar dust, gas, planets, asteroids and comets. Galaxies range in size from 1000 parsecs to 100,000 parsecs across.

Globular Cluster: A spherically shaped star cluster, typically 10 parsecs in diameter and containing 100,000 stars. Globular clusters were formed very early in the history of the universe, perhaps 13.5 billion years ago. A large spiral galaxy, such as the Milky Way, contains about 150 globular clusters.

Hubble Constant: The rate of expansion of the universe as a function of distance. Presently estimated at 31-62 miles (50-100 km) per second per Megaparsec (mi/sec/Mpc).

Hubble's Law: Demonstrates that more and more distant galaxies are receding from us at greater and greater speeds.

Hubble Time: The implied age of the universe, as deduced from the present rate of expansion. Presently estimated at 10 to 20 billion years.

Hydrogen: The most abundant element in the universe. A hydrogen atom is made up of a proton and an 'orbiting' electron.

Kiloparsec: A unit of length equal to 1000 parsecs. Abbreviated kpc.

Labyrinthus: Antoniadi nomenclature for a labyrinth, or a complex of interrelated canyons.

Light Year: A unit of measurement that equals the distance that light travels in one year (in a vacuum) at a speed of 186,281.7 miles per second, or six trillion miles.

Magnetosphere: The theoretically spherical region surrounding a star or planet that is permeated by the magnetic field of that body.

Magnitude: The brightness of a star or other celestial body as viewed from Earth with the naked eye on a clear night. The scale ranges from Magnitude 1, the brightest, to Magnitude 6, the faintest.

Mare: A 'sea' as observed on Earth's Moon. It is actually a vast, open basalt plateau and not a 'sea' in the sense of the Earth's seas. The plural is 'maria.'

Megaparsec: A unit of length equal to 1 million parsecs. Abbreviated Mpc.

Mensa: Antoniadi nomenclature for a mesa or butte.

Meteor Shower: A stream of very small, sand-like particles which fall into the Earth's atmosphere, where they vaporize due to their great speed. These particles were once frozen into the icy nuclei of comets.

Milky Way: The large spiral galaxy in which we live. As we are situated in the plane of the galaxy, there is a visible concentration of its stars that makes up the 'band of the Milky Way' seen in the night sky.

Mons: Antoniadi nomenclature for a mountain, particularly but not limited to volcanic mountains.

Neutrino: The name means 'little neutral one.' A product of the decay of atomic nuclei. The mass of the neutrino is less than 1/40,000 that of an electron (possibly even zero). A very large number of neutrinos is also let loose in a supernova explosion.

Neutron: A fundamental building block of atomic nuclei. Has zero net electric charge. Slightly more massive than a proton. Free neutrons (outside of atomic nuclei) are unstable, and decay into protons, electrons and antineutrinos on a time scale (with a half life) of 10.1 minutes.

Neutron Star: A very dense remnant of a supernova explosion in which the electrons and protons have combined to form neutrons.

Nova: Literally, a new star, because a nova suddenly appears where no star, or only a very faint one, was visible before. Novae arise from the evolution of very close double stars. As one star swells to become a red giant, its outer atmosphere is more strongly attracted to the companion star. This gas is pulled around the companion, forming a disk of accreting material. Where the incoming stream hits the disk, a hot spot appears, which is more luminous than the light of either star. Because of this mechanism, nova outbursts can happen many times in the life of a close double star. (See also Supernova.)

Open Cluster: A group of relatively young stars (less than 100 million years old) found in the plane of a spiral galaxy. A typical open cluster has 100 stars and is about five parsecs in diameter.

Parallax, Stellar: The angular shift of a nearby star against the distant background of stars or galaxies, due to the Earth's orbit about the Sun. It is possible to measure parallaxes accurately for stars no further than about 30 parsecs (about 100 light years).

Parsec: Contraction of 'parallax of a second of arc.' The distance at which the radius of the Earth's orbit about the Sun subtends an angle of one arc second (1/3600 of a degree). If a star were at a distance of one parsec from our solar system, its trigonometric parallax would be 1 arc second. Stars at a distance of 10 parsecs have parallaxes of 0.1 arc second. One parsec is about 3.26 light years. 1000 parsecs = one kiloparsec (one kpc). 1,000,000 parsecs = one Megaparsec (one Mpc).

Patera: Antoniadi nomenclature for an irregular, usually volcanic crater or caldera.

Perihelion: The point in an object's orbital path when it is closest to the Sun. The opposite of Aphelion.

Photon: An energy packet (quantum) of light.

Planet: From the Greek, meaning 'wandering star.' One of the nine principal bodies that orbit the Sun or potentially, *any* star.

Planetary Nebula: A round, glowing region of ionized gas which was ejected by a star less than eight solar masses at the end of its normal lifetime. In a small telescope a planetary nebula looks a bit like the disk of a planet. A white dwarf star will be found at the center of a planetary nebula.

Planitia: Antoniadi nomenclature for a lowland plateau or basin.

Planum: Antoniadi nomenclature for an upland plateau.

Positron: A particle with the mass of the electron, but with positive charge.

Powers of Ten: A notation for very large and small numbers. For example, 1000 is 10 times 10 times 10, or 10^3. One thousandth, or 0.001 is 10^{-3}. A million is a 1 followed by six zeroes, or 10^6, and one millionth is 10^{-6}.

Proper Motion: The transverse motion of a star, as measured against the distant stars or galaxies. Proper motions are measured in seconds of arc per year (or per century).

Proton: A positively charged fundamental building block of atomic nuclei. The nucleus of a hydrogen atom is a single proton.

Protostellar: 'Pre-Star' (adjective). A term used in reference to the materials (hydrogen and helium) that *will become* a star, while they are still a 'pre-star' gas cloud.

Pulsar: A rapidly rotating neutron star, most easily observed as a pulsing source of radio waves. Some pulsars spin faster than 100 times a second.

Quark: A building block of neutrons and protons. Two 'up' quarks (of charge $+2/3$) and one 'down' quark (charge $-1/3$) make up a proton, while one 'up' quark and two 'down' quarks make up a neutron.

Quasar: A fuzzy starlike object believed to be similar to a distant active galactic nucleus. A quasar is probably powered by matter streaming into giant black hole. The largest measured red shifts of quasars are about 4.5, corresponding to velocites of recession of 93 percent the speed of light.

Radial Velocity: The line of sight motion of a celestial body, measured from its spectrum. If the distance between the object and the observer is increasing, the spectral lines are red shifted (towards longer wavelengths). If the distance is decreasing, we observe blue shifted lines (toward shorter wavelengths).

Resolving Power: The ability of a telescope to discern detailed structure in the appearance of a celestial object. This depends primarily on the ratio of the wavelength of light at which the observations are made to the effective diameter of the telescope. However, at optical, infrared and ultraviolet wavelengths turbulence in the Earth's atmosphere limits the resolution of an image to about 0.5 arc seconds, even when the telescope is large and is situated on a very tall mountain.

Sidereal Period: For objects in the Solar System, the duration of time taken for a body to make a complete orbit, or revolution, around the Sun. This translates as that body's year. The Earth's sidereal period is 365.256 days. In a broader sense, a sidereal period is the orbital, or rotational, period of any object with respect to the fixed stars, or as seen by a distant observer.

Star: An object that is luminous owing to nuclear fusion reactions in its core. Stars range in mass from about 0.08 to 30 times the Sun's mass. Stars spend most of their lifetimes fusing hydrogen nuclei (protons) into helium nuclei (alpha particles).

Supernova, Type I: An exploding white dwarf star whose close companion has transferred enough mass to the white dwarf so that its mass exceeds 1.4 solar masses. No remnant is left behind.

Supernova, Type II: An exploding single star more massive than about eight times the Sun's mass, and as bright as 100 million times the luminosity of the Sun. This type of supernova leaves a very compact remnant, either a neutron star or black hole.

Synodic Period: The orbital, or rotational, period of any object as seen by an observer on the Earth. For the Moon or a planet, the synodic period is the interval between the repetitions of the same phase or configuration.

Tholus: Antoniadi nomenclature for an isolated hill or mountain.

Valles/Vallis: Antoniadi nomenclature for a valley.

Vastitas: Antoniadi nomenclature for a particularly vast planitia or planum.

White Dwarf Star: The end state of the evolution of a star less than about eight times the mass of the Sun. The Sun will become a white dwarf star in five to six billion years, at which time it will amount to only about two percent of its present diameter. The maximum mass of a white dwarf star (the Chandrasekhar limit) is 1.4 solar masses. Most white dwarfs have masses of 0.6 times that of the Sun.

Zodiac: The band of 12 constellations through which the Sun, Moon and planets appear to move. They are: Aquarius, Pisces, Aries, Taurus, Gemini, Cancer, Leo, Virgo, Libra, Scorpio, Sagittarius and Capricorn.

INDEX

Overleaf: **The Pleiades, named for the seven daughters of Atlas, in Greek mythology. It was said that the daughters were transformed into this open cluster of stars. Mankind's hopes and dreams are contained in such myths, and our continued striving for that which lies beyond is symbolized by the brillant and mysterious reaches of the universe in which we live. (Photo by Lee Combs)**

191